M000238211

"This is a remarkable book about the very important issue of ch: faithful…. The author makes copious use of Holy Scripture and beauty of chastity. It is clear that her writing flows from both her research and prayerful heart.'

- Father John F. Harvey, OSFS, Founding Director of Courage Apostolate (from the *Forward*)

"*Clean of Heart: Overcoming Habitual Sins Against Purity*, is an excellent practical and inspiring spiritual guide for those tormented by such sins. I highly recommend it for late teens, young adults, and anyone else struggling with such sins. Confessors will find in it a gold mine for good advice to their penitents."

- Ronda Chervin, Ph.D., Professor of Ethics and author of numerous books about Catholic living.

"*Clean of Heart* is a Spirit-filled work of love and Christian charity that provides a solid program of daily spiritual and practical exercises designed to help addicts to overcome their addiction to the vice of pornography. By incorporating the tried and true meditative and contemplative aspects inherent to Catholic spirituality, and by making consistent use of rigorous prayer, self examination and deepening spirituality, the addict is able to grow measurably closer to His Merciful and Loving God and thus, lift himself or herself further away from the mire of self love that impede true union with God. I cannot endorse this truly inspired work strongly enough."

- Paul Rasavage, Founder, The Serenellians Apostolate (http://www.pornnomore.com/)

"This book is a MUST for anyone who wishes to break free from pornography addiction or any sexual addiction. It is full of authentic Catholic teaching and utilizes the Scriptures, teachings of the saints and Catechism of the Catholic Church in a very powerful and life changing way. I have personally used this book, and I have everyone who participates in my True Knights: Combat Training and True Knights: Purity Corps use it as part of our program for purity."

- Ken Henderson, Founder, True Knights Apostolate (http://www.trueknights.org/)

"In an immodest and unchaste world, the sacred faculty of procreation, which may only be exercised licitly within the bonds of valid marriage, suffers constant onslaught in persons of nearly every age group and in all states of life. With evincing skill, Mrs. Scott lays out comprehensively the weapons which the Catholic Church affords Her children that they be able to recognize sexual addiction for what it is and to set their hearts upon the practice of chastity for the sake of Christ, and for one's salvation.

"This text is an invaluable resource for those serving youth apostolates and sacramental preparation programs, as well as for confessors and spiritual directors."

- F.P.F., member, *Courage* Philadelphia

"Yvonne finds the meditations good. They are strong and refreshing; she also appreciates Mrs. Scott's use of Holy Scripture and spiritual writers who are very inspiring. Yvonne is impressed by her tremendous research. She concludes that the book is well thought out, researched, and written for a heart of Holiness."

- Yvonne (a long time Courage member, last name withheld by request)

O my Good Shepherd, I have strayed far from You and become entangled in sin.
Have mercy on me and deliver me by Your grace, O Jesus!

CLEAN OF HEART

Overcoming Habitual Sins against Purity

Revised and Expanded Edition

By Rosemarie Scott

"Blessed are the clean of heart, for they shall see God" - St. Matthew 5:8

Nihil Obstat: **Reverend John Cush, S.T.L.**
                             Diocesan Censor

Imprimatur: **Most Reverend Nicholas DiMarzio, Ph.D., D.D.**
                             Bishop of Brooklyn

Brooklyn, New York   **December 14, 2006**

Royalties for this book helps a single-income Catholic family with special-needs children. Thank you for your purchase!

Fonts used: Front cover in *BlackChancery*. Text in *Garamond* © Monotype Typography Ltd. 1991-1995.

Cover image and frontspiece courtesy of *ChantArt* (www.catholicdigitalimages.com).

Illustrations on pp. 13, 57, 77, 112 and 114 are public domain images from *KarensWhimsy.com;* pp. 51 and 53 courtesy of *TwoHeartsDesign.com;* pp. 39 and 81 courtesy of *ChantArt* and p. 69 from *BreadSite.org*.

Scripture quotations come from the *Confraternity Douay Version* unless otherwise noted. *Confraternity Douay Version* ©1941, 1952, 1955, 1961 Confraternity of Christian Doctrine (CCD) Washington, DC. It is currently in the public domain. *Jerusalem Bible* © 1966, 1967 Doubleday and Co. *Revised Standard Version: Second Catholic Edition* (Ignatius Edition) © 2006 by Division of Christian Education of the National Council of the Churches of Christ in the United States of America. All rights reserved.

Note: Some of the Psalms are numbered differently in various translations. If a Psalm quotation lists two numbers (i.e. Ps. 50[51]), the lower number pertains to older Catholic translations, the higher number to newer ones like the JB. The CV and RSV-SCE provide both numberings for each psalm, but the CV puts the lower number first and the higher in brackets, while the RSV-SCE does the reverse.

ISBN: 0-9772234-5-0

Printed in the United States of America.

Published by R.A.G.E. Media, Mt. Laurel, NJ http://www.DyingLight.com

TABLE OF CONTENTS:

Dedicated to our Redeemer Jesus Christ,

Who set us free from sin by His grace.

May He deign to use this little book

to help many gain victory over sin.

Also, to our Holy Mother

The Church,

His Virgin Bride,

Who is without spot or wrinkle

though she clasps sinners to her bosom.

FORWARD

By Father John F. Harvey, OSFS.

This is a remarkable book about the very important issue of chastity in the life of the Christian faithful. The subtitle is *Overcoming Habitual Sins Against Purity*. The author makes copious use of Holy Scripture and Divine Tradition in presenting the beauty of chastity. It is clear that her writing flows from both her research and prayerful heart. She empathizes with the struggles of those who are addictive to various sexual sins, including masturbation, and pornography. She is aware that pornography on the Internet is rampant.

Rosemarie gives good advice on handling the near occasions of sin. She warns us about the ways in which we deceive ourselves concerning obstacles to the practice of purity. She wants everyone to spend as much time as possible in prayer before the Blessed Sacrament. She meditates on the Passion and Death of Christ as a motive for purity.

- Fr. John F. Harvey, OSFS, Founding Director of Courage Apostolate.

ACKNOWLEDGMENTS

-- My family for their patience and understanding over the months it took to write - and then revise - this book, particularly my dear husband.

-- Paul Rasavage of the Serenellians, for his advice.

-- Father John F. Harvey and the members of Courage and Encourage, for their helpful suggestions, encouragement and tireless work promoting the first edition of *Clean of Heart*.

-- Kenneth Henderson of TrueKnights.org, for his use and promotion of this book.

-- The various Catholic authors whose books on purity of heart and the "Theology of the Body" have helped me in the past.

-- Our Evangelical separated brethren who have produced similar materials in the past, which partially inspired this book. Keep fighting the good fight against the torrent of impurity that threatens to engulf our society.

Thank you all, and thanks be to God for all of you

+J.M.J+

INTRODUCTION: BEFORE YOU BEGIN

This book is for practicing Catholics who accept all the Church's teachings, yet still struggle with habitual sins against purity. If this describes you, you are not alone. Our sex-saturated society makes the virtue of purity difficult to attain, and the Internet provides millions with a hidden, convenient way to sin. **But take heart; there is hope!** Through our Holy Mother the Church, God provides every grace you need to overcome these sins. No matter how long you have indulged in sins of the flesh, Our Lord loves you and can set you free!

Though this program focuses particularly on the solitary sins of pornography and masturbation, the principles it teaches, drawn from the timeless wisdom of the Church, can help one combat other sins of the flesh as well. After all, how many sexual compulsions began with the occasional viewing of indecent images, only to escalate over time to include other types of immorality? So this book strikes at what is often the root of sins against purity.

If you are truly fed up with how vice is affecting your life, and are determined to stop, then this book is for you. These meditations will challenge you; they tell the unpleasant truth of what impurity does to your soul. Yet they will also show you the way out, if you choose to take it. *There is no magic formula for overcoming this sin,* only the grace of Our Lord Jesus Christ. These meditations will teach you a type of self-mastery based on Catholic principles, but it will only work if you ask for His grace to help you to apply them in your life. Apart from Him you can do nothing, but you can do all things in Him Who strengthens you (Philippians 4:13).

Ask God for the grace to persevere, since victory won't come quickly or easily. It requires a firm resolve and daily battle. If the thought of giving up these sins for the rest of your life seems overwhelming, try to take it "one day at a time," as many addiction recovery programs recommend. Just concentrate on the present, on today, and leave the future in the hands of God: *"Therefore do not be anxious about tomorrow; for tomorrow will have anxieties of its own. Sufficient for the day is its own trouble"* (Mt. 6:34).

One way to do this is, every morning when you say your prayers, say to yourself, 'I choose this day to be pure and to avoid sins of the flesh." Don't even give tomorrow a thought, just resolve to be pure today, and ask for the grace to avoid sin for one day. You should reinforce this with daily prayer, such as, *'O Mary, my good Mother, keep me from sin this day (or night). Amen"* This book is arranged like a daily devotional, so it will fit in well with that daily resolve.

Commit yourself to finish the whole book, reading one meditation per day. Don't rush ahead; each meditation will have plenty for you to ponder and put into practice for one day. Consider keeping a journal for writing down thoughts and prayers.

For some of those who struggle with this vice, certain words can be an occasion for sin. To minimize temptation, this book uses euphemisms as much as possible. If you come across an unfamiliar term, check the Glossary in back.

It is best that you use this book while under the direction of a Catholic spiritual director or confessor, who can give you personal counseling and help you to avoid scrupulosity while dealing with these habitual sins. It might also be helpful to see a good Christian counselor who is trained in this area. It is preferable that the counselor be Catholic; if not then he or she should be respectful of the Catholic Faith and in agreement with Catholic moral teaching (for instance, some non-Catholic counselors don't even consider masturbation a sin - so be aware of that). Psychological counseling may help you to discover what events in your life or personality traits may be exacerbating your problem. Many people find this very helpful in overcoming sins against purity.

It is *very important* to avoid committing impure acts while reading this book. This will help you to break old habits and build new ones. It may prove difficult at first, but ask God for the grace to resist. Of course, if you are married you may engage in conjugal relations; this can even serve as a remedy for concupiscence. If you are single, you must remain celibate, as the Church requires. Despite what the world may tell you, you *can* do this with God's help!

The chart at the end of each meditation will help you keep track of your progress. If your answers for a) through c) on that chart are ever more than zero, read Meditation 19 immediately. It is recommended that you then *start the book all over again* the next day with the first Meditation. The aim of this book is to help you learn how to stay pure, so while reading it you must observe chastity with the help of God's grace. Though you will not have to start over again for having impure thoughts, resist them also as much as possible through prayer and by reading and memorizing Scripture. They should diminish over time as you apply the principles in this book. Also, don't forget to give thanks to God for every day in which you did not engage in sins of the flesh!

Here are three very important things that you *must* do if you are serious about overcoming this vice:

1. *Get rid of all pornography from your home and cut off all access to it.* Any indecent materials in your home or easily accessible to you are near occasions of sin. You will not overcome habitual sin in your life unless you avoid near occasions of sin. So if you are truly serious about this struggle, then you *must* do all you can to cut off all access to indecent pictures, movies, stories and conversations.

If you have any erotica or pornography around the house – pictures, books, magazines, videos, DVDs, etc. - destroy it all *today.* Cut off any access to pay-per-view and X-rated web sites. Cut up your adult video store membership card. Cancel your cable or satellite TV, or at least block out all the adult channels. Avoid other questionable television programs; in fact, you may wish to watch less TV while reading this book and spend extra time praying and reading Scripture instead. Stay away from chat rooms and newsgroups; erase bookmarks to adult web sites. Install filtering software or sign up for a filtered ISP or accountability program. Erase any images stored on your computer, purge the cache, clean the hard drive, erase any disks and smash any CD-ROMs containing indecent pictures. Don't keep any of it around at all! Also, stay away from red light districts; find another route home from work every day in necessary.

If this seems too difficult, ask Our Lord for the grace to do it. It may take some sacrifice, which is not easy, but it is necessary for the sake of your immortal soul. We will discuss this further in Meditation Eight.

2. *Repent of sin and resolve to go to Confession as soon as possible.* Sins of the flesh are mortal if there is sufficient reflection and full consent of the will. If you have not yet confessed to a priest, you will have to do so before you can receive Holy Communion again.

If you cannot go to Confession right away, resolve to go as soon as possible and make an *Act of Perfect Contrition* in the meantime. Gaze at a crucifix and consider Who is suffering and why. Make an act of will to turn away from your sins and to love God. Then say the following prayer sincerely:

> O my God, I am heartily sorry and beg pardon for all my sins, not so much because these sins bring suffering and Hell to me, but because they have crucified my loving Savior Jesus Christ and offended Thy infinite Goodness. I firmly resolve, with the help of Thy grace to confess my sins, to do penance and to amend my life.[i]

Memorize this prayer and pray it as soon as possible after committing a mortal sin. Of course, you will still have to go to Confession before receiving Communion.

3. *Find an accountability partner who can pray for you and ask you daily how you are doing in your struggle against impurity.* This could be a priest, religious, spiritual director or Christian counselor - as long as you can report to him or her *every single day* while reading this book. If not, then you must find someone else, even if you go to regular Confession and counseling as recommended. You need *daily* accountability to overcome these sins!

If you are married, it could be your spouse if he or she knows about your habitual sin. Or it could be a trusted, devout friend of the same sex as you. The True Knights Apostolate has a program called *True Knights Combat Training*, which provides accountability partners for men struggling against habitual sins of the flesh. See the *Resources* section in back for contact information.

As long as you have at least one other person to encourage you, to hold you responsible daily for your actions and to pray for your success in conquering your bad habits. Knowing that you have to answer personally to someone every single day can be a powerful deterrent to sin. Remember: you have to talk to this person *every day*, be *completely honest*, admitting when you've fallen, and be willing to be asked personal questions about how your struggle for purity is going.

If you get rid of near occasions of sin and have an accountability partner, that will go a long way to help you to avoid sins against purity. As you read and apply the spiritual truths and disciplines taught herein, you will gain more strength against temptation and sin. So achieving chastity and purity is not as impossible as it may seem, you *can* gain victory over sins of the flesh by the grace of God!

May Our Lord bless you and grant you victory over habitual sins of the flesh.

Our Lady of Victory, pray for us.

How to Read these Meditations:

1. Make the Sign of the Cross and place yourself in the Presence of God.

2. Read both the Scripture passage and opening prayer slowly and prayerfully.

3. Then read the day's Meditation in a spirit of prayer and resolve to carry out the Resolution at the end.

4. Converse with Jesus for a while afterward in your own words.

5. This would be a good time to read the "list of truths" you will compile after the third Meditation.

6. Say the following traditional *Prayer for Purity* as a closing prayer each day:

> O my God, thou who hast given me a body to keep pure and clean and healthy for thy service and my eternal happiness, forgive me for all my unfaithfulness in this great responsibility. Forgive me for every mean use which I have made of thy gifts in thought, word or deed since my rebirth as thine own adopted child in Baptism and my registration as a soldier of Jesus on the day of my Confirmation.
>
> Create in me a clean heart, O God, and give me a steadfast will that I may be a strength to others around me. Teach me to reverence my body and the bodies of my fellow creatures. Help me to see the glory of perfect manhood in Jesus Christ and of perfect womanhood in Mary Immaculate. Inspire me with such love for the ideals for which our Savior lived and died, that all my passions and energies will be caught up into the enthusiasm of His service and evil things will lose their power. May my body be the servant of my soul, and may both body and soul be Thy servants, through Christ, our Lord. Amen."
>
> *(Note: On some days, an alternate closing prayer will be proposed at the end of the Meditation. Use that one instead for that day, but return to this one on subsequent days when no alternative is proposed.)*

It is also recommended that all who use this program obtain a copy of the book <u>Sex and the Mysteries,</u> by John M. Haffert (AMI Press, 1970). This excellent book discusses how devotion to Mary, and particularly praying the Holy Rosary, aids us in attaining purity of heart. It can be read either alongside or after completing the Clean of Heart program.

MEDITATION 1: RESTLESS HEARTS

I am the bread of life. He who comes to Me shall not hunger, he who believes in Me shall never thirst. - St. John 6:35

Prayer: *You have made us for Yourself, and our hearts are restless until they rest in You.* - St. Augustine

Why do we sin against purity? After all, we know it is wrong; Mother Church has told us that the procreative act is reserved for the married state, and that *any* other use of it is a sin and a distortion of God's plan. Yet we choose to commit sins of the flesh anyway. One reason is because we feel an inner emptiness; our souls are hungering and thirsting for something. At some point, we came to believe that sins such as pornography and masturbation could satisfy our spiritual cravings. So we immersed ourselves in these vices, hoping that they would make us happy, console our loneliness or bring fulfillment.

Though viewing indecent images may cause a brief rush, and self-abuse may feel good and relieve some tension for a short time, sins against purity can never truly satisfy us. After a temporary physical sensation, they leave us feeling empty, ashamed, unhappy and alienated from God. Yet we keep committing these same sins again and again, hoping in vain that maybe *this time* they will fulfill me, maybe *this time* they will do the exact opposite of what they have always done before.

Someone once defined insanity as, "Doing the same thing over and over and expecting different results." What does this say about the futile pursuit of fulfillment through pleasure?

No, sins of the flesh *will never* fill the emptiness inside. Our spiritual hunger and thirst, which we seek in vain to satisfy with sin, is really our need for God. As St. Augustine of Hippo said centuries ago: God made us for Himself, so our hearts will always be restless until they rest in Him. Augustine was himself an unchaste man for many years before his conversion, and his sins never satisfied him either. Take it from him; your heart will *never* find rest in vice - nor even in licit earthly pleasures - but in your Creator alone.

Our loving Savior is the Bread of Life. To our famished souls He says, *"He who comes to Me shall not hunger, he who believes in Me shall never thirst."* Jesus promises to fill the inner emptiness we try in vain to fill with stolen pleasure. Only He can truly comfort and satisfy us, and we must look to Him alone for love, joy and consolation.

Do you hate the guilt and spiritual darkness you experience after a fall? Do you wish you didn't have to confess the same sins *over* and *over* again? Are you tired of living a "double life" and feeling like a hypocrite? Are you sick of fearing you'll be caught and your secret sin exposed? Do you hate being enslaved to sin? Our Savior can set you free: *"Amen, amen, I say to you, everyone who commits sin is a slave of sin. But the slave does not abide in the house forever: the son abides there forever. If therefore the Son makes you free, you will be free indeed"* (Jn. 8:34-36).

Make no mistake; your sins have defiled you; they make you an enemy of God. But Our Lord died for all your sins, including your habitual sins against purity. If you return to Him with your whole heart He will forgive you. No matter how long or how severely you have sinned, Jesus promises that He will not reject you if you repent: *"him who comes to me I will not cast out"* (Jn. 6:37). Yet He wants to do even more than that. By His Holy Cross and Resurrection He has set us free from our enslavement to sin; ask Him to make His victory real in your life.

If you want true love, joy, acceptance and consolation in your life, seek to dwell always in the Most Sacred Heart of Jesus. Receive Him often in the Blessed Sacrament, as long as you are in a state of grace. Daily Mass attendance is highly recommended, if possible. When you cannot receive Him, you may visit Him in a church or adoration chapel, or make an *Act of Spiritual Communion* frequently during the day:

O My Jesus, I believe that You are present in the Blessed Sacrament. I love You above all things, and I desire to receive You into my soul. Since I cannot now receive You sacramentally, come at least spiritually into my heart. I embrace You as if You were already there and unite myself wholly to You. Never permit me to be separated from You. Amen. - St. Alphonsus de Liguori

Read Sacred Scripture daily to encounter Jesus there. This is another course in the feast He lays before us; it helps satisfy our spiritual hunger as well: *"Not by bread alone does man live, but by every word that comes forth from the mouth of God"* (Mt. 4:4). God's word is also a very powerful weapon against sins of the flesh; it even has the power to purify your mind, removing impure thoughts and memories!

Praying with icons is an excellent means to draw close to Him, as is the Jesus Prayer: *Lord Jesus Christ, Son of the Living God, have mercy on me a sinner.* You may also display a Divine Mercy picture, crucifix, statue or other holy image of Christ in your home, or carry one with you, to remind you of His loving Presence. There are many other approved devotions to Our Lord's Sacred Heart, Precious Blood, Holy Wounds, Sacred Head, Holy Face, Divine Mercy, Stations of the Cross, etc. Any or all of these can help you draw close to your loving Savior, so you can find true joy in Him.

If you wish to successfully overcome sins of the flesh and regain purity, *prayer and devotion* must play a central role in your struggle. In his *Introduction to the Devout Life*, Saint Francis de Sales writes:

"While fruits are undamaged, you can store them securely in straw, sand or in their own leaves; but once bruised there is no means of preserving them except in sugar or honey. Similarly, purity which has never been violated may well be preserved to the end, but when once it has been violated nothing can preserve it but genuine devotion, which, as I have often said, is the very honey and sugar of the mind."[iii]

Tomorrow we will see how devotion to the Blessed Virgin Mary helped two men ensnared in vices to change their ways. Later we will discuss how the angels and saints aid us in our struggle. But let us begin by first and foremost cultivating a deep, loving devotion to Jesus Christ Our Lord, and to the Blessed Trinity in general - our Creator, our First Beginning and Last End.

So cease trying in vain to satiate your spiritual hunger with sin, which only sickens your soul. Look instead to *God the Father,* Who sent His Son as the living Bread from Heaven; to *God the Son,* Who offers the living Water of the Spirit; and to *God the Holy Ghost,* Who fills your soul with sanctifying grace. *"For He satisfied the longing soul, and filled the hungry soul with good things"* - (Psalm 106 [107]:9)

Resolution: Ask Jesus for the grace to turn away from sin and to delight in His presence instead. Determine to do so from now on with His help. Make an *Act of Spiritual Communion* often, especially when alone or feeling down, and read Scripture daily to remain close to Him. Look to Him alone for happiness and consolation.

O Heart of Love, I put my trust in You. Though I fear all things from my weakness, I hope all things from Your goodness!

TRACK YOUR PROGRESS: *Since reading the Introduction, how many times have I:*

a) deliberately touched myself impurely while awake?   ___0 ___1 ___2 ___3 or more times
b) deliberately viewed indecent pictures or movies?   ___0 ___1 ___2 ___3 or more times
c) committed unchaste acts with others?   ___0 ___1 ___2 ___3 or more times
d) deliberately entertained/enjoyed impure thoughts?   ___0 ___1 ___2 ___3 or more times

e) When was the last time I went to Confession?_____ to Mass?_____

MEDITATION 2: VIRGIN MOST PURE, MOTHER MOST CHASTE

Now in the sixth month the angel Gabriel was sent from God to a town of Galilee called Nazareth, to a virgin betrothed to a man named Joseph, of the house of David, and the virgin's name was Mary. And when the angel had come to her, he said, "Hail, full of grace, the Lord is with thee. Blessed art thou among women." - St. Luke 1:26-28

Prayer: *To you, O Virgin Mother, who was never touched by any spot of original or actual sin, I commend and entrust the purity of my heart.*

The Church has long recommended devotion to Blessed Mother for the preservation or restoration of purity. The Litany of Loreto invokes her as the *Holy Virgin of virgins... Mother most pure... Mother most chaste... Mother inviolate... Mother undefiled...* and *Queen of virgins.* As an epitome of purity, she has a special role in helping her spiritual sons and daughters remain pure and chaste. If all good earthly mothers want to keep their children clean and healthy, then surely our Heavenly Mother wants our souls to remain spotless before Our Father in Heaven!

As you look to Jesus, your Creator and Savior, to satisfy you, look to Mary your Mother as well to pray for your needs before the throne of God. Devotion to her will also help you draw near to Our Lord. *To Jesus through Mary:* the Holy Virgin always leads us to her Divine Son, for she is close to Him and the surest way to Him.

So entrust yourself, and particularly this aspect of your life, to your heavenly Mother in a special way. Make her the special guardian of your chastity. Ask for her intercession, that she may acquire for you the grace to abandon sin and regain purity. As a sign and reminder of your devotion to her, it is highly commendable to wear a Miraculous Medal and/or Brown Scapular. You may wish to get enrolled in these two sacramentals in order to participate in their spiritual benefits. The Rosary is also a very powerful prayer in her honor.

In his writings, St. Alphonsus de Liguori relates the true story[iv] of a young man who lived in Rome, who was ensnared in gross sins against purity. One day he went to Father Nicholas Zucchi S.J. for confession. The priest had compassion on the poor man, and with Christian charity assured him that devotion to the Holy Virgin could deliver him from his vices. For his penance, the priest told him that every morning when he woke up, and again before going to sleep at night, he was to commend himself to Our Lady as follows: Say three *Ave's* (Hail Marys), consecrate to her in a special way his eyes, ears, mouth, heart and whole body, and then kiss the ground three times.

When the young man returned for his next confession, he reported that he had performed his penance faithfully each day, but it had only curbed his habitual sins a little bit. The priest encouraged him to continue the same devotional practice for the rest of his life and to have confidence in Blessed Mother's patronage.

Soon afterward the man went on a long trip, visiting various countries with some of his friends. When he returned to Rome many years later, he sought out Fr. Zucchi for confession. The priest was delighted to find that all the penitent's former vices were gone - he had changed completely! Fr. Zucchi asked him, "My son, how did you obtain such a wonderful change from God?" The man replied, "Father, Our Blessed Lady obtained this grace for me as a result of that little devotion which you taught me."

Father Zucchi was so impressed that he asked the penitent's permission to mention this during his homily. The young man agreed, and the priest did so the next Sunday. There was a soldier present at Mass that day who had been carrying on an immoral relationship with a certain woman for many years. Inspired by the homily, he also began to say three *Ave's* every morning and evening, with the intention of being delivered from his sin. As a result, God soon gave him the grace to cut off the relationship.

Six months later, he foolishly went to the woman's house one day, hoping to convert her as well. But before he could enter the door he felt himself being pushed back from it, as if by an invisible force. Next thing he knew, he had moved quite a distance away from her dwelling. He decided that Mary must have prevented him from speaking to that woman, since it would have been an occasion of sin for him in which he would most certainly have fallen again!

This anecdote illustrates the efficacy of devotion to Blessed Mother in conquering impurity. We also see the importance of perseverance in prayer, since it took a long time for the young man to change his ways. Though the devotion only helped a little at first, he stayed with it and overcame his vices in the long run. Take a lesson from him and don't give up your pursuit of purity. No matter how difficult it is, ask God for the grace of perseverance.

Finally, this story teaches us to avoid near occasions of sin, even after we have been chaste for a while. We should never presume upon our own strength to avoid sin; we must continue to avoid people, places or things that caused us to fall in the past.

Resolution: Have confidence in Our Lady's intercession and entrust yourself to her powerful help and protection. Every morning and evening, for the duration of these meditations, pray a modified form of Fr. Zucchi's advice to the young penitent. Salute her with three *Ave's*, adding after each one the aspiration (short prayer) that St. Alphonsus de Liguori recommended: *"By thy holy and Immaculate Conception, O Mary, purify my body and sanctify my soul."* Afterward, pray the *O Domina Mea*, composed by Fr. Zucchi himself, to entrust yourself to Mary:

> My Queen, my Mother, I give myself entirely to you, and to show my devotion to you I consecrate to you this day/night my eyes, my ears, my mouth, my heart, my whole body without reserve. Wherefore, good Mother, as I am your own, keep me and guard me as your property and possession. Amen.

Note: You will not be required to kiss the ground, both for sanitary reasons and in case a physical disability prevents you. No one knew about germs in Fr. Zucchi's day, and that young man was physically capable. Of course, you may kiss the ground if you wish. Or you could bless yourself (and your bed at night) with holy water instead. Keep holy water in your house always; it is a powerful weapon against sin and the Devil, as we shall see.

Also, whenever you are tempted to impurity, pray to Our Lady immediately, saying: *"My Queen and my Mother, remember that I belong to you, preserve and defend me as your property and possession."*

Holy Virgin of Virgins, pray for us.

TRACK YOUR PROGRESS: *Since reading the last meditation, how many times have I:*

a) deliberately touched myself impurely while awake? ___0 ___1 ___2 ___3 or more times
b) deliberately viewed indecent pictures or movies? ___0 ___1 ___2 ___3 or more times
c) committed unchaste acts with others? ___0 ___1 ___2 ___3 or more times
d) deliberately entertained/enjoyed impure thoughts? ___0 ___1 ___2 ___3 or more times

e) When was the last time I went to Confession?_____ to Mass?_____

AVE MARIA

MEDITATION 3: LIES AND EMPTY PROMISES

If you abide in my word, you shall be my disciples indeed, and you shall know the truth, and the truth shall make you free. - St. John 8:32

Prayer: *Come, Holy Spirit, come dispel the darkness of impurity with the Light of Purity.*

Satan is a liar and the father of lies (Jn. 8:44). He will tell us any lie in order to convince us to violate God's moral law. Sometimes we internalize these lies, using them over and over again throughout our lives to justify our abuse of God's gift of sex. Our thinking becomes twisted and our minds darkened; we develop an attachment to sin that feeds compulsive behaviors, which we find difficult to control. We then are enslaved to sin: *"Do you not know that if you yield yourselves to any one as obedient slaves, you are slaves of the one whom you obey, either of sin, which leads to death, or of obedience, which leads to righteousness?"* (Romans 6:16 RSV).

We can only escape this spiritual slavery by allowing Christ the Truth to dispel these dark lies. We must renew our minds (Rom. 12:2), and changing our beliefs and attitudes toward sins of the flesh is a good place to start. So what are some of the lies the devil has used to develop an attachment to sins against purity within you? Here are a few possible justifications; you may just find some of them familiar:

Maybe Satan has told you that viewing indecent images is okay because "nudity is natural." Yet pornography itself is not natural. Its fantasies are unrealistic, its bodies are often airbrushed or even cosmetically or surgically enhanced, and it often portrays unnatural acts. It also gives the viewer a distorted view of sexuality, and of humanity, which is contrary to God's will and design. The *Catechism of the Catholic Church* says:

> Pornography consists in removing real or simulated sexual acts from the intimacy of the partners, in order to display them deliberately to third parties. It offends against chastity because it perverts the conjugal act, the intimate giving of spouses to each other. It does grave injury to the dignity of its participants (actors, vendors, the public), since each one becomes an object of base pleasure and illicit profit for others. It immerses all who are involved in the illusion of a fantasy world. It is a grave offense. (CCC 2354)

Pope John Paul II, of happy memory, once said that the problem with indecent images is not just that they reveal too much, but that they reveal too *little*. They display the body but cannot reveal the soul. Pornography takes a human being, who by God's design is both a soul and a body, and reduces him or her to a mere picture of a body, an object to be used for ones selfish gratification, and ultimately a commodity to be bought and sold. In effect, it tries to have the body without the soul, and that is anything but natural! Nor did Our Creator intend that the procreative act be viewed as entertainment or sold as a commercial commodity. So, from God's point-of-view, pornography is quite *unnatural*.

Or perhaps you are alone, and Satan has convinced you that sins of the flesh will help you deal with your loneliness. Though it may temporarily numb the pain, you are just as alone while viewing indecent images as you were before. You cannot have a relationship with a photograph, and self-abuse is a sad, lonely act. After it is all over the loneliness returns, along with remorse, self-loathing and alienation from God. You're even worse off *after* than you were *before!*

Maybe the Tempter has told you, "You deserve a little pleasure!" The truth is, we do not "deserve" anything sinful. A Christian has no right to commit sin or to experience illicit pleasure. Only married people have a right to intercourse, and only with their own spouse. Your body is a member of Christ and a temple of the Holy Spirit; it belongs to God, is not your own, and you just cannot do whatever you want with it.

Then the Deceiver might whisper, "God is unfair to *deny* you this pleasure!" Now he's trying to make you think that God wants to deprive you of something. The truth is, your Maker wants what is best for you and He knows that impurity is just not the best thing for you. It is actually *Satan* who wants to *deny* you freedom by enslaving you to sin, *deny* you peace of mind by filling you with self-loathing, and ultimately to *deny* you eternal happiness by depriving you of Heaven!

Then there's the old chestnut: "It's okay, God will forgive you. You can always go to Confession afterward." Consider that there may be people in Hell today because they believed this excuse and died before they could repent! You don't know how long you will live, so why put your soul in danger for even a short time?

Another favorite lie of the Tempter is: "You can't possibly resist this temptation; you've failed so many times in the past it must be force-of-habit by now!" This is supposed to cause you to *despair,* to make you think, "It's no use, I can't resist; I might as well just give in to the temptation." The truth is, you *can* resist by the grace of God, no matter how many times you've failed before. Our Lord promises that He will *always* provide a way of escape (see 1 Corinthians 10:13). To thwart this lie you must pray for the *virtue of hope* to counteract despair, believe that you can resist with God's help and look for the way of escape He has made for you.

Or perhaps you think, "I'll do it just this one last time, then I'll never need to do it again." This is a lie to get you to sin yet again! It never really is the last time, though, is it? The Tempter tells you that same lie over and over again; you've probably thought, "This will be the last time," literally hundreds of times before!

Maybe none of the above sound familiar, and you're thinking, "I just do it because it feels good." In that case, the lie may be the belief that physical gratification is a good to be pursued at all costs, even if it endangers your immortal soul. Yet no pleasure, no matter how strong, is worth the loss of your salvation. The joy and peace of a soul in a state of grace, and the eternal bliss of the Beatific Vision, are much greater than a few seconds of physical sensation.

There are many more possible lies the Tempter uses; these are by no means the only ones. Appendix I contains a few more of them, so read it after competing this meditation. Pornography itself is nothing but a big lie, a sham, full of empty promises that it cannot deliver. Sins against purity won't make you happy or fulfilled or comfort you, and they ultimately won't satisfy you. If you are lonely, porn has nothing to do with love and acceptance; those pictures don't love you at all, but Jesus does. He is the Truth, and His Body the Church is the pillar and ground of the truth. Turn to Jesus for love and consolation, for He alone can satisfy you.

You don't need indecent pictures or self-abuse to make you happy. In fact they only make you miserable in the end. God alone gives true happiness and fulfillment; HE loves you and will ease your loneliness. If you never see indecent pictures again or touch yourself impurely again, you will not be "deprived" at all. God still loves you infinitely; He wants to save you, not to condemn you. Allow Him to set you free from your slavery to sin and walk in His light.

Resolution: Read Appendix I. Ask God to show you which lies you have embraced and to free you from them. If you go to counseling, draw on any insights into yourself gained from that. *Write down* all the truths that refute those lies, phrasing them in the first person (for instance: "I don't need pornography to be happy," etc.). Read your list of truths out loud to yourself *every day,* preferably right after the daily meditation. Do this for the full duration of these meditations, asking Our Lord to help you to internalize these truths. This will change your though processes and renew your mind by conforming it to His truth. Continue to draw close to Jesus and ask Mary's intercession.

Saint John the Evangelist, pray for us.

TRACK YOUR PROGRESS: *Since reading the last meditation, how many times have I:*

a) deliberately touched myself impurely while awake? ✓0 ___1 ___2 ___3 or more times
b) deliberately viewed indecent pictures or movies? ✓0 ___1 ___2 ___3 or more times
c) committed unchaste acts with others? ✓0 ___1 ___2 ___3 or more times
d) deliberately entertained/enjoyed impure thoughts? ___0 ___1 ___2 ✓3 or more times

e) When was the last time I went to Confession?_____ to Mass?_____

MEDITATION 4: WHAT IS GOD'S WILL FOR YOU?

For this is the will of God, your sanctification; that you should abstain from immorality, that every one of you learn how to possess his vessel in holiness and honor, not in the passion of lust like the Gentiles that do not know God....For God has not called us unto uncleanness, but unto holiness.
- I Thessalonians 4:3-7

Prayer: *O most sweet Jesus, let me renounce all uncleanness; let me be always a stranger to carnal desires and earthly lusts, which war against the soul; and with Thy help let me preserve chastity without stain.*[ii]

God wills for His children to be holy and abstain from immorality. This is what He wants for us, and He offers us the grace to realize it in our lives. Whether you've indulged in impurity for a few days or a few decades, and no matter how deep you have sunk into the mire of vice, Our Lord still loves you and wants you to be pure and can help you to attain holiness in your life. Nothing is impossible for Him!

Perhaps you still harbor the secret hope that self-abuse isn't really a sin, so that you might continue indulging in it. The Tempter may even ask you, "Where does Scripture condemn it?" Well, the Book of Sirach actually condemns solitary sins of impurity: *"Two types of men multiply sins, a third draws down wrath; For burning passion is a blazing fire, not to be quenched till it burns itself out: A man given to sins of the flesh, who never stops until the fire breaks forth"* (Sirach 23:16).[†] Also, the *Catechism* says:

> "Both the Magisterium of the Church, in the course of a constant tradition, and the moral sense of the faithful have been in no doubt and have firmly maintained that masturbation is an intrinsically and gravely disordered action." "The deliberate use of the sexual faculty, for whatever reason, outside of marriage is essentially contrary to its purpose." For here sexual pleasure is sought outside of "the sexual relationship which is demanded by the moral order and in which the total meaning of mutual self-giving and human procreation in the context of true love is achieved" (CCC 2352).

God created the procreative act, not for our selfish gratification, but to be used within the bond of matrimony for the procreation of children and the one-flesh union of husband and wife. Its accompanying pleasure is but a means to those ends, not an end in itself. Touching yourself impurely and viewing indecent images are distorted, selfish uses of God's gift, which make pleasure itself an end while ignoring the true ends.

St. Paul leaves no room for us to justify our sin by saying "It's not so bad," or "Maybe it's really not a sin," or "Just this one last time and then I'll give it up completely." Elsewhere, he writes:

> Do you not know that your bodies are members of Christ? Shall I then take the members of Christ and make them members of a harlot? By no means! Or do you not know that he who cleaves to a harlot, becomes one body with her? "For the two," it says, "shall be one flesh." But he who cleaves to the Lord is one spirit with him. Flee immorality. Every sin that a man commits is outside the body, but the immoral man sins against his own body. Or do you not know that your members are the temple of the Holy Spirit, who is in you, whom you have from God, and that you are not your own? For you have been bought with a price. Glorify God and bear him in your body. - 1 Corinthians 6:15-20

This is why we must possess our bodies in holiness and honor; they are not our own! They belong to our Creator; they are members of Christ and temples of the Holy Spirit. Sins against purity actually defile God's temple, and are thus a form of sacrilege.

Paul also tells us that we have *died to sin* in Baptism, and so should not continue to habitually commit it:

---

† The footnote in the *Confraternity Version* and *NAB* indicates that this passage condemns "solitary sins" of impurity. The corresponding passage in the *Douay Rheims* and some other older Catholic Bibles is Ecclesiasticus 23:21-23.

Baptism, by which we die to sin and are made one body with Christ, obliges us to mortify in ourselves all sensual pleasure…. This is St. Paul's teaching: "We that are dead to sin, how shall we live any longer therein? Know you not that all we who are baptized in Christ Jesus are baptized in His death? For we are buried together with Him by baptism into death: that as Christ is risen from the dead by the glory of the Father, so we also may walk in the newness of life" (Rom. 6:2-4). Thus, the baptismal immersion represents death to sin and to the concupiscence which leads to sin. The coming out of the baptismal waters typifies that newness of life through which we are made sharers in the risen life of the Savior. Hence, our baptism obliges us to mortify the concupiscence that remains in us and to imitate our Lord who by the crucifixion of His flesh merited for us the grace of crucifying our own. The nails wherewith we crucify it are the various acts of mortification we perform.[vii]

Take heart, for God wills that all His baptized children be holy and pure before Him; not just in the future in Heaven after a stay in Purgatory, but *right now.* If He wills it, He also gives sufficient grace to achieve it. Even if you are ensnared in impurity, your sanctification is still God's will and is still possible if you submit to His will and mortify your passions. You *can* become pure by the grace of God!

So what is a Christian to do about sins against purity? Start by considering your baptismal vows - the promises you made (or your Godparents made in your name) when you died to sin at Baptism. Their traditional form begins: *"Do you renounce Satan? And all his works? And all his pomps?"* (Today "pomps" is sometimes rendered "empty promises"). A newer alternate version of the vows similarly asks:

> Do you reject sin so as to live in the freedom of God's children?
> Do you reject the glamour of evil and refuse to be mastered by sin?
> Do you reject Satan, father of sin and prince of darkness?

Each question must be answered in the affirmative. This is the only attitude a Christian can take toward sin – *Reject it!* Pornography is the work of Satan - *Renounce it!* Its "glamour" is the glamour of evil – *Reject it!* Sins against purity are his pomps, his empty promises – *Reject them in the Name of Our Lord!* Refuse to be mastered by sin, choose to live instead in freedom as God's children, by His grace.

The Church wants her children to renew their baptismal promises every Easter, and on certain other occasions as well. You will renew them again *today,* specifically rejecting all sins against purity. It is recommended that you bless yourself with holy water after the renewal of your vows, in remembrance of your Baptism. If that is not possible, renew them now anyway and use the holy water later – *don't delay this, lest you forget!*

Resolution: Turn to Appendix II in back and renew your baptismal promises. Ask God to sever any attachments to sin in your heart and for the grace to remain faithful to those vows from now on. Memorize 1 Corinthians 6:15-20 (cited above) and recite it to yourself whenever tempted by impurity. Continue in your resolutions from the past three days; stay close to Jesus, pray with childlike trust to Mary twice daily, and reject the lies that keep you enslaved to sin.

Saint Paul the Apostle, pray for us.

TRACK YOUR PROGRESS: *Since reading the last meditation, how many times have I:*

a) deliberately touched myself impurely while awake?   ___0 ___1 ___2 ___3 or more times
b) deliberately viewed indecent pictures or movies?   ___0 ___1 ___2 ___3 or more times
c) committed unchaste acts with others?   ___0 ___1 ___2 ___3 or more times
d) deliberately entertained/enjoyed impure thoughts?   ___0 ___1 ___2 ___3 or more times

e) When was the last time I went to Confession?_____ to Mass?_____

MEDITATION 5: THE SACRAMENT OF PENANCE

For you were once darkness, but now you are light in the Lord. Walk, then, as children of light (for the fruit of the light is in all goodness and justice and truth), testing what is well pleasing to God; and have no fellowship with the unfruitful works of darkness: but rather expose them. For of the things that are done by them in secret it is shameful even to speak; but all the things that are exposed are made manifest by the light: for all that is made manifest is light. Thus it says, "Awake, sleeper, and arise from among the dead: and Christ will enlighten thee." - Ephesians 5:8-14

Prayer: *O my God, I am sorry for having offended You, because I love You.*

Sins against purity are often committed in secret, especially since devout Catholics may not want others to know about their struggles in this area. They are sometimes even quite literally committed in the dark. Of course, darkness and secrecy can never hide our sins from God: *"No created thing can hide from him; everything is uncovered and open to the eyes of the one to whom we must give account of ourselves"* (Heb. 4:13 JB). Yet sins of the flesh are still often hidden from other people's sight (Jn. 3:19-20). So the above passage from St. Paul's Epistle to the Ephesians very aptly speaks of these sins as "works of darkness" which are done "in secret." And the remedy for such sins, according to St. Paul, is to expose them to the Light.

So how do we expose our secret sins in the Light of Our Lord? By confessing them, especially in the Sacrament of Penance:

God is light and in him is no darkness at all. If we say we have fellowship with him while we walk in darkness, we lie and do not live according to the truth; but if we walk in the light, as he is in the light, we have fellowship with one another, and the blood of Jesus his Son cleanses us from all sin. If we say we have no sin, we deceive ourselves, and the truth is not in us. **If we confess our sins,** he is faithful and just, and will forgive our sins and cleanse us from all unrighteousness. - I St. John 1:5-10 RSV

The mere act of telling someone else about your sins helps break their power over you. Hopefully you have found a friend to hold you daily accountable while you are reading these meditations, as prescribed in the Introduction. A spiritual director or psychological counselor can serve this purpose as well, if you go to one. Yet the Sacrament of Reconciliation also provides absolution and powerful graces from God, which help strengthen your soul against sin. So the Confessional combines both the admission of secret sin to another person and the graces of the Sacrament; a "double-punch" to weaken the grip of sin and diminish its influence in our lives. St. Francis de Sales writes:

One great remedy against all manner of temptation, great or small, is to open the heart and lay bare its suggestions, likings, and dislikings, to your director; for, as you may observe, the first condition which the Evil One makes with a soul, when he wants to seduce it, is silence. Even as a bad man, seeking to seduce a woman, enjoins silence concerning himself to her father or husband, whereas God would always have us make known all His inspirations to our superiors and guides.[viii]

So let us begin to break the secrecy and silence of our sinful lives by exposing our dark sins and temptations to the light in the Sacrament of Penance. Let us avail ourselves of what Jesus called the "Tribunal of Mercy" in His apparitions to St. Faustina Kowalska. His merciful Heart is always ready to forgive us there, and to cleanse us with His Most Precious Blood. If our sins are like scarlet, He will make them white as snow.

Steps for Making a Good Confession

1. Examine your conscience, asking God to help you recall all the sins you've committed since your last confession. Be as thorough as possible, covering all sins against purity in thought, word and deed, plus sins of omission in doing good. Use a guide to the Sacrament of Reconciliation or Appendix III in this book, which contains a thorough examination of conscience focused on sins of the flesh.

2. Be truly sorry for all your sins. Gaze at a crucifix or meditate on the Passion of Christ (Stations of the Cross, Sorrowful Mysteries of the Rosary, etc.) and consider what your sins have done to Our Loving Savior.

WOULD I SLAP THE LORD IN THE FACE?

3. Firmly resolve to amend your life and not sin again. If this seems too difficult, ask God for grace. You may perceive that you have a particular "attachment to sin" in your heart; that is, a certain fondness, comfortable feeling or emotional tie to a sin, which makes you want to keep sinning. If so, ask God to help you break that attachment to sin.

4. Go to Confession as soon as possible. Tell the priest *all* of your mortal sins and how often you committed them. Expose them all to the Light of Christ, Who is there acting through the priest. No matter how ashamed you are of your sins against purity, don't be afraid to confess them. The priest has heard it all before, and may even have heard people confess *worse* things in the past. Don't think that he'll be shocked; he may not be, and anyway is there to counsel and forgive you. Never hide embarrassing sins from him; if you leave them in the dark they will continue to grow and haunt you. Bring them *all* out into the Light.

5. Don't forget to do the penance the priest gives you. This will remove temporal punishment from your soul, and so help decrease any future suffering in Purgatory for these sins.

6. Ask God every day for grace to avoid all occasions of sin. Meditations Eight and Eleven will cover this.

7. Continue to go to Confession *as often as possible.* This is very important for those who struggle with habitual sins against purity. Receive the Sacrament of Penance every week if possible, if not then every other week. At the *very least* go once a month, but it is better with this type of sin to confess much more frequently than that. You literally need all the grace you can get! Your accountability to the priest is also a great help, so try to go to the same confessor every week. Don't sink back into the darkness; keep bringing all your sins into the Light. That is the way to weaken and ultimately conquer them.

Even if, by the grace of God, you go for a whole week without committing a mortal sin of the flesh, go to Confession anyway. Even if you only confess venial sins, the graces of the Sacrament will be a great help to you for avoiding sin the next week. Though not spiritually deadly like mortal sins, venial sins can be very insidious. They may weaken the soul to the point where one commits a mortal sin. So confess them as well.

Resolution: Make an *Act of Perfect Contrition* now. Examine your conscience, go to Confession as soon as possible and confess regularly afterward. If you don't have an accountability partner yet, find one as soon as possible. Continue with previous resolutions.

Saint Faustina Kowalska, Apostle of Divine Mercy, pray for us.

TRACK YOUR PROGRESS: *Since reading the last meditation, how many times have I:*

a) deliberately touched myself impurely while awake? ✓0 __1 __2 __3 or more times
b) deliberately viewed indecent pictures or movies? ✓0 __1 __2 __3 or more times
c) committed unchaste acts with others? ✓0 __1 __2 __3 or more times
d) deliberately entertained/enjoyed impure thoughts? ✓0 __1 __2 __3 or more times

e) When was the last time I went to Confession? *SAT. — 1 DAY AGO* to Mass? *TUES — 6 DAYS AGO*

MEDITATION 6: BLESSED ARE THE CLEAN OF HEART

Who can ascend the mountain of the Lord? or who may stand in his holy place?
He whose hands are sinless, whose heart is clean, - Psalm 23[24]:3-4

Prayer: *Burn our desires and our hearts with the fire of the Holy Spirit, O Lord, that we may serve you with a chaste body, and with a clean heart be pleasing to you.* - from the <u>Litany of the Saints</u>

Pope St. Gregory the Great wrote about the "seven daughters of lust." By this he meant the seven destructive effects that lust has on our intellect and our will. The very first of these "daughters" is *blindness of mind,* followed by *thoughtlessness, inconstancy, rashness, self love, hatred toward God,* and *love of this world* (with hatred or despair of a future world).[ix] If we are honest with ourselves, we may recognize some of these "daughters" at work in our own lives. This meditation will focus on the first, *blindness of mind.*

Impurity blinds our minds so that we cannot see what is good or think about spiritual things. In particular, it blinds us to the greatest Good of all, Our Creator. St. Alphonsus de Liguori once wrote: *"When a raven finds a dead body its first act is to pluck out the eyes; and the first injury that incontinency inflicts on the soul is to take away the light of the things of God".* Over time, habitual sins of the flesh will blind us spiritually, deaden our souls to heavenly matters and alienate us from Our Lord.

Perhaps you have been experiencing a spiritual "dryness" in your own interior life lately. Have you wondered why? It could have many causes, and indulgence in sins of the flesh is one possible culprit! Jesus meant it when He said, *"Blessed are the clean of heart, for they shall see God"* (Mt. 5:8), for impurity actually prevents one from seeing His Face. If you desire a deep interior life, you cannot wallow in sins of the flesh. For without purity of heart you cannot hope to "see God" - have a close relationship with Him on earth and be happy with Him forever in Heaven.

In order to stand before Our Lord, we must have sinless hands and a clean heart. Thus St. James admonishes Christians in his Epistle to: *"Cleanse your hands, you sinners, and purify your hearts, you double minded"* (St. James 4:8). "Hands" refers to ones outward actions, while "hearts" refers to inner thoughts and intentions. Both must be clean before Our Lord; if we cleanse ourselves within, our actions will also become pure (Mt. 23:25-26).

A clean heart not only enables us to draw close to God, it has other wonderful benefits as well. For instance, it can actually restore to you the joy of life, which impurity tends to destroy:

"Freedom" which hippies advocate for happiness is really found only in cleanness of heart. The clean of heart are FREE. They really live in three dimensions.

Pleasure is one dimensional...on the plane of the physical. The clean of heart are able to live intensely on all planes--with a full awareness of all the world, of the music, of the flowers, of the children, friends, and above all of the supernatural. Those of unclean heart become increasingly blind to these other dimension of love and beauty....

A clean heart frees us from the problems of sex as though by a pair of giant wings--invisible to those around us--which enables us to soar, and to rise and plunge with the freedom of a great eagle in flight, landing as we will, choosing the air we want to breathe, the scenery we want to see, a place we want to nest. Together with all its other attributes, a clean heart is God's key to freedom.

Does this imply that, having achieved cleanness of heart, one is free from danger...free to fly anywhere, at will, into the zone of sexual intemperance whether that zone lies in an illicit rendezvous...a questionable book...a record...a theater...even in the turning of a radio or of a TV dial? Hardly! Our Lord, who cautioned the apostles to "watch and pray without ceasing, lest you too enter into temptation," would hardly recommend an adventure in imprudence for us lesser souls.

Rather, c leanness of heart acts as a light to our conscience, a strong impellent to goodness, and a straight road to joyful freedom-in-God. It is a cleanness that cautions where caution is needed, encourages where fear would hold us back, yet protects us with a shield of light when, in innocence, we wander in the smog and into immediate dangers of concupiscence.

A clean heart is just the opposite to a substitute for prudence. A clean heart IS prudent. If it were not, how could it be really clean? A clean heart is lightsome. It does not wallow in doubts. It is free. And oddly enough, with this freedom comes an all around happiness which sex in itself promises but does not deliver.[xi]

So how does one become clean of heart? *"Ask, and it shall be given you: seek, and you shall find: knock, and it shall be opened to you"* (Mt. 7:7). After he committed adultery with Bathsheba, King David prayed for purity of heart: *"Create in me a clean heart, O God, and put a new and right spirit within me"* (Ps. 51[50]:10 RSV). Make his prayer your own, and use it especially when tempted with impure thoughts. Pray fervently and perseveringly for the grace of chastity and purity of heart, and your Heavenly Father will help you to achieve it.

It may take some time, but you can regain a clean heart by His grace. No matter how filthy your heart has become, no matter how long it has been soiled, Our Lord can create in you a clean heart. Following the resolutions after each of these meditations will also enable you to achieve purity of heart.

Cleanse your heart of evil, O Jerusalem, that you may be saved. How long must your pernicious thoughts lodge within you? - Jeremiah 4:14

But flee the cravings of youth and pursue justice, faith, charity and peace with those who call on the Lord with a pure heart. - 2 Timothy 2:22

By removing the distortions of lust, a clean heart will help you to make peace with and appreciate your sexuality. You will ultimately begin to see it as a friend rather than an enemy, as a blessing, not a curse. Pray for the grace to appreciate the virtue of chastity, to want to be chaste according to your state in life, and to desire to do God's will in this matter. Thank God for your sexuality and realize it is a blessing that God gives us to be used only in marriage. Ask Him daily to help you to want to only use it according to His will.

Resolution: Memorize King David's prayer for a clean heart and pray it sincerely to Our Lord every time you are tempted to sin against purity. Make this aspiration a plea from the depths of your soul. Memorize as well the short Scripture passage at the beginning of this meditation (Psalm 23:3-4) and Matthew 5:8. Use all of these verses as part of your prayer and meditation, to draw close to Jesus. Such devout use of Sacred Scripture helps to cleanse the heart and mind of impurity. Continue with previous resolutions.

Pope St. Gregory the Great, pray for us.

TRACK YOUR PROGRESS: *Since reading the last meditation, how many times have I:*

a) deliberately touched myself impurely while awake? ✓0 ___1 ___2 ___3 or more times
b) deliberately viewed indecent pictures or movies? ✓0 ___1 ___2 ___3 or more times
c) committed unchaste acts with others? ✓0 ___1 ___2 ___3 or more times
d) deliberately entertained/enjoyed impure thoughts? ✓0 ___1 ___2 ___3 or more times

e) When was the last time I went to Confession?_____ to Mass?_____

MEDITATION 7: DIVINIZATION

(God) has granted us the very great and precious promises, so that through them you may become partakers of the divine nature, having escaped from the corruption of that lust which is in the world
- 2 St. Peter 1:4

Prayer: *May we come to share in the divinity of Christ who humbled himself to share in our humanity.*

The priest's words at the Offertory during Mass express the awesome truth that God actually makes His children in Christ *partakers of the divine nature* by grace. The Church Fathers called this wonderful gift *divinization.*

Consider the immense goodness of God. He loves us infinitely, and created us out of nothing in order to give us a share in His own life. Though our created human nature is infinitely inferior to His Divinity, the Eternal Word assumed it to make us partakers of His own Nature. As St. Athanasius wrote, *"God became man that man might become God"* (*On the Incarnation* I:108).

We are not, and never can become, God by very nature. Yet we can participate in His life by grace and so in a sense "become God" by participation. Our Lord wants to exalt us by grace, fill us with His Light, Life, Glory and Love, and grant us the Beatific Vision, the immediate perception of the Divine Nature.

The Church Fathers often compared divinization to what happens to metal when it is cast into a blacksmith's furnace. As the heat permeates it, the metal actually takes on the color and heat of the fire. After a while it even looks like fire. Yet it still remains metal by nature; it never actually *becomes* fire. Even so, the divinized creature is permeated by God and radiates His Glory, resembling Him as closely as a creature possibly can. Yet he still remains a creature, essentially distinct from the Creator in both nature and person.[†]

"Behold what manner of love the Father has bestowed upon us" (1 Jn. 3:1). What an incredible gift! What eternal joy and bliss await us in the World to come, far beyond our ability to imagine. *"Eye has not seen nor ear heard, nor has it entered into the heart of man, what things God has prepared for those who love him"* (1 Cor. 2:9).

Beauties like the beauties of paradise, eye hath never seen; harmonies like unto the harmonies of paradise, ear hath never heard; nor hath ever human heart gained the comprehension of the joys which God hath prepared for those who love Him. Beautiful is the sight of a landscape adorned with hills, plains, woods, and views of the sea. Beautiful is the sight of a garden abounding with fruit, flowers and fountains. Oh, how much more beautiful is paradise![xii]

Yet St. Peter writes that we can only partake in the divine nature after *"having escaped from the corruption of that lust which is in the world."* The sin of lust can rob us of our share in the intimate life of the Godhead, of eternal bliss - of our very salvation! Our Lady of Fatima said that more souls go to Hell for sins of the flesh than for any other kind of sin. Considering the allure and prevalence of such sins, that seems quite probable.

The pinnacle of divinization is to see God face-to-face in the Beatific Vision. Yet, as we have seen, only the clean of heart can see God, only the innocent in hands shall stand in His holy place. Scripture assures us that those who indulge in unchaste acts will be excluded from the New Jerusalem (Apocalypse 22:15).

Or do you not know that the unjust will not possess the kingdom of God? Do not err; neither fornicators, nor idolaters, nor adulterers, nor the effeminate, nor sodomites, nor thieves, nor the covetous, nor drunkards, nor the evil-tongued, nor the greedy will possess the kingdom of God.
- 1 Corinthians 6:9-10

---

† I drew some of the text of this meditation from an article I wrote entitled, "Grace and the Divinization of Humanity." It can be found on my now-inactive web site, the Mystical Rose Catholic Page.

Consider the horror of unchastity, which takes a creature capable of becoming a partaker in the divine nature and reduces him to a lost soul, eternally cut off from Our Lord in Hell! When we commit sins against purity we impede God's plan to divinize us and jeopardize our very souls. Lust is an ugly, hateful thing! May God grant us the grace to despise this vice with all our heart and soul.

Anyone ensnared in sins of the flesh desperately needs the grace of Christ to overcome them and become holy, as He is holy. Jesus truly loves you; no matter how badly you have soiled your heart, mind and soul with sin, He *still* loves you infinitely. Do not despair of His Divine Love and Mercy. He wants to free you from the chains of this vice, and He can do so if you ask Him and allow Him to help you.

Abandoning habitual sin will be a change; you may have to give up certain things that have been a part of your life for a very long time. This may seem daunting at first. Yet whatever you may have to give up cannot compare with the benefits of purity of heart: a clean conscience, a closer walk with God and ultimately divinization. So do not focus on what you must leave behind. Rather, think about all you will gain when you exchange the deceptive and fleeting pleasures of sin for the true joy of the presence of God in your soul, and for the eternal bliss of the Beatific Vision in Heaven. These are the true spiritual delights for a Christian: "*You will show me the path to life, fullness of joys in your presence, the delights at your right hand forever*" (Ps. 15[16]:11).

Resolution: Thank God for His great gift of divinization, and think about it often. Ask for His grace to truly appreciate it and to desire to never forfeit it by sin. Resolve to overcome your habitual sins against purity with the help of His grace, and to find your enjoyment in Jesus Christ rather than in sin. Continue drawing close to Jesus and Mary, and with previous resolutions.

Saint Athanasius of Alexandria, pray for us.

TRACK YOUR PROGRESS: *Since reading the last meditation, how many times have I:*

a) deliberately touched myself impurely while awake?   __0 ___1 ___2 ___3 or more times
b) deliberately viewed indecent pictures or movies?   __0 ___1 ___2 ___3 or more times
c) committed unchaste acts with others?   __0 ___1 ___2 ___3 or more times
d) deliberately entertained/enjoyed impure thoughts?   __0 ___1 ___2 ___3 or more times

e) When was the last time I went to Confession?_____ to Mass?_____

MEDITATION 8: CUT OFF OCCASIONS OF SIN

If your right eye is an occasion of sin to thee, pluck it out and cast it from thee; for it is better for thee that one of thy members should perish than that thy whole body should be thrown into hell. And if thy right hand is an occasion of sin to thee, cut it off and cast it from thee; for it is better for thee that one of thy members should be lost than that thy whole body should go into hell. - St. Matthew 5:29-30

Prayer: *I firmly resolve, with the help of Thy grace, to sin no more and to avoid the near occasions of sin.*

This is one of the most difficult sayings of Our Divine Master, yet we must obey it as much as any other of His commands. He is not advocating physical mutilation, as St. John Chrysostom explains:

"(Christ) has given these commands not as a discussion about our limbs - far from it! For He nowhere says that our body is to be blamed for such things, but He always accuses the evil mind. For it is not the eye that sees, but the mind and thought…. Also, were Christ speaking of members of the body, He would not have said this of just one eye, nor of the right eye only, but of both. For he who is caused to sin by his right eye, will obviously incur the same evil by his left also" (Homily XVII on the Gospel of Matthew)

The saint makes an excellent point here. If we were to pluck out our right eye, we could just continue to view indecent pictures with the left one. If we cut off our right hand, the left hand could be trained for self-abuse as well. What Jesus is really saying that sometimes the only way to gain victory over habitual sin is to go to *extreme measures* to remove from our lives all near occasions of sin. *"Whatever is an immediate occasion of sin, however near or dear it may be, must be abandoned . . . though it prove as dear to us, or as necessary as a hand, or an eye, and without delay or demur."*[xiii]

This is definitely the case with sins against purity. In the Introduction you were instructed to destroy all your pornography and cut off all sources of it. If you have not yet done so, do it *today*. If you find it more difficult to get rid of certain magazines or videos than others you may have a particular attachment to those items. Ask God to help you sever that attachment to them.

This housecleaning may prove difficult and inconvenient for you. It may even be as difficult and inconvenient as chopping off your hand or plucking out your eye. This is why Jesus used that metaphor to describe it. Yet if you are serious about overcoming sins of the flesh, you will make an effort to rid yourself of all access to pornography. Experience shows that people who don't do so are bound to keep sinning again and again.

Why must you take this seemingly extreme measure? Why can't you just leave all the dirty magazines in a box in the closet and never look at them again? Because sins against purity are a form of idolatry, as St. Alphonsus writes:

By offending God for the sake of his pleasure, the sinner makes that pleasure his god, by making it his last end. St. Jerome says: "What a person desires, if he worships it, it is to him a god. A vice in the heart is an idol on the altar." Hence St. Thomas says; "If you love delights, delights are your god." And according to St. Cyprian, "Whatever man prefers to God, that he makes a god to himself."[xiv]

When man prefers a vile pleasure to divine grace, he makes his pleasure his last end, he makes it his God. What a dishonor it must be to God, who is infinitely good, to see himself exchanged for something so vile and wretched![xv]

Scripture closely associates impurity with idolatry (Rom. 1:22-26, Colossians 3:5). The Old Testament records how often the Israelites disobeyed the commandment *Thou shalt not have strange gods before me*, and it is interesting to note that their idolatry often involved some form of unchaste behavior. For instance, worship the golden calf turned into an orgy (Exodus 32:6). Some of the men of Israel both committed unchaste acts with Moabite women and worshipped their gods (Numbers 25:1-3). After entering the Promised Land, many Israelites began to worship the Canaanite fertility gods Asherah and Baal, which were represented by lewd idols and whose rites involved ritual fornication (Num. 25:1-9) and religious prostitution (1 Kings 14:23:24).

Sacred Scripture records these things to warn and instruct us (1 Cor. 10:6-11). The sins against purity in which we indulge are our false gods. They are idols we set up before Our Lord, no less than those of the children of Israel. As God demanded that His chosen people purge all lewd, immoral idols from the land, so He now commands us to get rid of ours as well. Never did He say it was okay for them to just hide their idols in a closet and never worship them again; He *repeatedly* commanded them to *utterly destroy* them all:

> The graven images of their gods you shall burn with fire; you shall not covet the silver or the gold that is on them, or take it for yourselves, lest you be ensnared by it; for it is an abomination to the LORD your God. And you shall not bring an abominable thing into your house, and become accursed like it; you shall utterly detest and abhor it; for it is an accursed thing. - Deuteronomy 7:25-26 RSV

> Destroy without fail every place on the high mountains, on the hills, and under every leafy tree where the nations you are to dispossess worship their gods. Tear down their altars, smash their sacred pillars, destroy by fire their sacred poles, and shatter the idols of their gods, that you may stamp out the remembrance of them in any such place. - Deuteronomy 12:2-3

Destroy… Tear down… Smash… Shatter… Burn…. As He once commanded the Israelites, so God now commands us do these things to the idols in our own lives!

Christ our Lord once said, "No man can serve two masters; for either he will hate the one and love the other, or else he will stand by the one and despise the other. You cannot serve God and mammon" (Mt. 6:24). Similarly, you cannot serve God and Asherah, or Venus, or Dionysus. You will either hate the false gods of impurity and love Our Lord, or you will love impurity and despise God! You read that right. Remember: *hatred toward God* is one of the seven daughters of lust. You may not have experienced that yet, but if you continue worshipping the idols of impurity and unchastity you will end up hating Our Blessed Lord. Lust does that to the soul.

So let us obey God; let us remove all these "abominable things" from our houses. Let us smash all our idols of impurity and purge this foul idolatry from our lives. Christ is our King, let us bow the knee before Him alone. Let us look to Him alone for consolation. Let us fill our souls from now on with the Bread of Life rather than poison of vice.

Resolution: If you have not already done so, destroy all your impure idols. Ask God to show you any other near occasions of sin in your life, and to inspire you with ideas for cutting them off. If you have already removed all near occasions of sin, continue with previous resolutions.

Saint John Chrysostom, pray for us.

TRACK YOUR PROGRESS: *Since reading the last meditation, how many times have I:*

a) deliberately touched myself impurely while awake?   ✓0 ___1 ___2 ___3 or more times
b) deliberately viewed indecent pictures or movies?   ✓0 ___1 ___2 ___3 or more times
c) committed unchaste acts with others?   ✓0 ___1 ___2 ___3 or more times
d) deliberately entertained/enjoyed impure thoughts?   ✓0 ___1 ___2 ___3 or more times

e) When was the last time I went to Confession?_____ to Mass?_____

MEDITATION 9: HUMBLE YOURSELF

Be subject therefore to God, but resist the devil, and he will flee from you. Draw near to God: and he will draw near to you. Cleanse your hands, you sinners, and purify your hearts, you double minded. Be sorrowful, and mourn, and weep; let your laughter be turned into mourning and your joy into sadness. Humble yourselves in the sight of the Lord, and he will exalt you. - St. James 4:6-10

Prayer: *O Jesus, Model of humility, divest me of all pride and arrogance. Let me acknowledge my weakness and sinfulness, so that I may bear mockery and contempt for your sake and esteem myself as lowly in your sight.*[xvi]

You may wish to memorize the above quote. It is a concise description of how to overcome habitual sin:

* **Be subject therefore to God.** Acknowledge Him alone as your King, abandon the pagan altar of impurity.

* **Resist the devil, and he will flee from you.** Reject the devil's lies and renounce him along with all his works and pomps.   Resist his temptations and avoid occasions of sin as well.

* **Draw near to God: and he will draw near to you.** Hopefully you are drawing near to Jesus daily in prayer and worship, looking to Him for love and consolation.

* **Cleanse your hands, you sinners, and purify your hearts, you double minded.** As we saw in the sixth meditation, only the innocent of hands and clean of heart will see God.

* **Be sorrowful, and mourn, and weep**… Tomorrow we will discuss penitence and the "gift of tears."

* **Humble yourselves in the sight of the Lord, and he will exalt you.** The theme of today's ~~mediation.~~ MEDITATION

One of the seven daughters of lust is "self-love," so those who struggle with sins of the flesh also tend to have a problem with the cardinal sin of pride. Some of the lies discussed in the third meditation appeal to pride, such as "You deserve a little pleasure." St. Alphonsus explains that, in order to conquer sins against purity,

> It is necessary to practise humility. Cassian says that he who is not humble cannot be chaste. It happens, not unfrequently, that God chastises the proud by permitting them to fall into some sin against purity. This, as David himself confessed, was the cause of his fall *Before I was humbled I offended* (Ps. 118:67). It is by humility that we obtain chastity, says St. Bernard…. St. John Climacus used to say, that he who expects to conquer the flesh by continence alone is like a man in the midst of the ocean who wishes to save his life by swimming with a single hand. Therefore it is necessary to unite humility to continence.[xvii]

As *Pride* plays a role in sins against purity, so *Humility* is essential for repentance. The Gospels provide many examples of humble repentance. In the Parable of the Pharisee and Publican, for instance, the tax collector stands far off, his eyes downcast and beats his breast, saying, *"O God, be merciful to me a sinner!"* (Lk. 18:13) The prodigal son does not even ask his father to reinstate him into the family: *"Father, I have sinned against heaven and before thee; I am no longer worthy to be called thy son; make me as one of thy hired men"* (Lk. 15:18-19). St. Dismas, the Good Thief on the cross, doesn't ask to be admitted to Christ's kingdom, but simply says, *"Lord, remember me when thou comest into thy kingdom"* (Lk. 23:42).

Each of these people displayed such profound humility that they did not even presume that God would restore them to His good graces. Yet each received more than he expected and much more than he deserved. *"For every one who exalts himself will be humbled, but he who humbles himself will be exalted"* (Lk. 18:14).

We must similarly approach God with humility, acknowledging our sinfulness and inability to make ourselves righteousness. We cannot say *No* to temptation and lust without His grace. In fact, thinking that we can conquer habitual sin by our own strength is just another manifestation of Pride! It is also a sure sign that we will fail, for *"Pride goes before disaster, and a haughty spirit before a fall"* (Proverbs 16:18).

The heretical belief that we can save ourselves apart from God's grace is called Pelagianism. Perhaps you have tried in the past to overcome your habitual sins by "will-power," but just kept failing again and again. That didn't work because, though you meant well, you were unwittingly acting more like a Pelagian than a Christian. It is impossible to overcome sin, especially habitual sin, by ones own strength apart from the grace of Our Lord.

This is why these meditations keep emphasizing that we must ask for the grace of God; because we can do nothing by ourselves. We cannot save ourselves, we cannot free ourselves from habitual sin, we cannot sanctify ourselves and we cannot divinize ourselves. Grace does all of these things in us. Yet we must cooperate with that grace, and ask for it often, as St. Alphonsus writes:

> But above all, to acquire the virtue of chastity prayer is necessary: it is necessary to pray, and to pray continually. It has been already said that chastity can neither be acquired nor preserved unless God grant his aid to preserve it; but this aid he gives only to those who ask it. Hence the holy Fathers teach that, according to the words of Scripture: *We aught always to pray, and not to faint. Ask, and it shall be given you....* It is impossible, says Cassian, for man, by his own strength, without aid from God, to keep himself chaste; and therefore, in our struggle with the flesh, we must ask the Lord, with all the affection of our soul, for the gift of chastity.[xviii]

Humility will help you to recognize your total dependence upon His grace. Don't think that conquering impurity is "all up to you"; it is not. You can't gain any merit in the Christian life without God's aid. We are not saved by our own efforts, but by the grace of God working in and through us, enabling us to do good and resist evil (Eph. 2:8-10). That is how we overcome sin as well. Here is an anecdote from the Desert Fathers:

> It was related of Amma Sara that for thirteen years she was severely attacked by a demon of unchastity. Yet she never prayed to be released from this warfare; she just kept saying, "Lord give me strength." Then she was attacked by an even more hostile and threatening demon of unchastity, who tempted her severely by filling her mind with worldly deceptions. Yet, standing firm in her fear of God and profession of chastity, she went to pray in her inner chamber. There the demon appeared to her in bodily form and said, "You have conquered me, Sara." But she replied, "Not I, but Christ my Lord."[xix]

It is not you who will conquer your habitual sin, but Christ your Lord. Ask Him to give you strength.

Resolution: Humble yourself profoundly before God, ask Him to help you root out pride from your life, and for His grace to keep you from falling. Continue with previous resolutions, always in a spirit of humility.

Saint Dismas the Good Thief, pray for us.

TRACK YOUR PROGRESS: *Since reading the last meditation, how many times have I:*

a) deliberately touched myself impurely while awake? ___0 ✓1 ___2 ___3 or more times
b) deliberately viewed indecent pictures or movies? ✓0 ___1 ___2 ___3 or more times
c) committed unchaste acts with others? ✓0 ___1 ___2 ___3 or more times
d) deliberately entertained/enjoyed impure thoughts? ✓0 ___1 ___2 ___3 or more times

e) When was the last time I went to Confession?_____ to Mass?_____

MEDITATION 10: COMPUNCTION OF HEART

Yet even now, says the Lord, return to me with your whole heart, with fasting, and weeping, and mourning; rend your hearts, not your garments, and return to the Lord, your God. For gracious and merciful is he, slow to anger, rich in kindness, and relenting in punishment. - Joel 2:12-13

Prayer: *Feed me, O Lord, with the bread of tears and give me to drink of tears in measure*[xx]

Another necessary part of true repentance is *compunction of heart;* that is, a deep sorrow for one's sins, perhaps even to the point of shedding tears over them. Read carefully the *Catechism's* description of repentance:

Interior repentance is a radical reorientation of our whole life, a return, a conversion to God with all our heart, an end of sin, a turning away from evil, with repugnance toward the evil actions we have committed. At the same time it entails the desire and resolution to change one's life, with hope in God's mercy and trust in the help of his grace. This conversion of heart is accompanied by a salutary pain and sadness which the Fathers called *animi cruciatus* (affliction of spirit) and *compunctio cordis* (repentance of heart). (CCC 1431)

Such deep penitence is essential to overcoming habitual sins against purity and breaking ones attachment to sin. This is not just a matter of saying "I'm sorry" and then moving on, with no change occurring in ones life. You've probably done that many times before yet remain trapped in habitual sin. Rather, we must *radically reorient* our whole lives toward God, turn away from evil deeds, *hate our sins passionately,* desire to change with all our hearts, trust in God's mercy, and feel deep pain and sorrow over our wicked ways.

These meditations have often recommended making an *Act of Perfect Contrition,* yet until now we have not discussed what "perfect contrition" is. The *Catechism* tells us:

Among the penitent's acts contrition occupies first place. Contrition is "sorrow of the soul and detestation for the sin committed, together with the resolution not to sin again." When it arises from a love by which God is loved above all else, contrition is called "perfect" (contrition of charity). Such contrition remits venial sins; it also obtains forgiveness of mortal sins if it includes the firm resolution to have recourse to sacramental confession as soon as possible.

The contrition called "imperfect" (or "attrition") is also a gift of God, a prompting of the Holy Spirit. It is born of the consideration of sin's ugliness or the fear of eternal damnation and the other penalties threatening the sinner (contrition of fear). Such a stirring of conscience can initiate an interior process which, under the prompting of grace, will be brought to completion by sacramental absolution. By itself however, imperfect contrition cannot obtain the forgiveness of grave sins, but it disposes one to obtain forgiveness in the sacrament of Penance. (CCC 1451-1453)

Perfect contrition is superior to imperfect contrition, since in an extreme emergency it can even obtain for us forgiveness of mortal sins. So if you do not already have perfect contrition for your sins, ask God for that wonderful grace. Here is a helpful tip from Father Joseph Stedman: *"Perfect Contrition becomes easy by meditation on a Crucifix:* **"Who"** *is suffering?* **"What"** *is He suffering?* **"Why?"** *To* **feel** *sorry is not necessary. It is sufficient if the will turns from sin to the love of God."*[xxi]

"Affliction of spirit" may not sound pleasant, but it is necessary for us to change our ways. As we saw in the last meditation, St. James told his readers: *"Be sorrowful, and mourn, and weep; let your laughter be turned into mourning and your joy into sadness"* (4:8-9). Though our modern culture wants to laugh and be entertained all the time, Jesus taught that weeping can actually be spiritually beneficial: *"Blessed are they who mourn, for they shall be comforted"* (Mt. 5:5). Consider the sinful woman, traditionally identified with Saint Mary Magdalen, who wept at His feet and received full pardon for her many sins (Lk. 7:36-50). Her example shows us that compunction of heart will ultimately lead to the true joy and consolation of a clean heart: *"Blessed are you who weep now, for you shall laugh"* (Lk. 6:21).

Yet we sinners must weep before we can laugh, for Jesus also warns: *"Woe to you who laugh now! for you shall mourn and weep"* (Lk. 6:25). Sorrow for our sins must come first, and only afterward can we know joy in Our Lord. *"Weeping may last for the night, but joy comes with the morning"* (Ps. 30[29]:5 RSV).

Ponder the words of *The Imitation of Christ* on "Compunction of Heart":

If you wish to make any progress, keep yourself in the fear of God, be not too free, but restrain all your senses by discipline, and do not give yourself up to foolish joy. Give yourself to compunction of heart and you will find devotion. Compunction opens the way to much good, which dissipation is usually quick to lose. It is a wonder that any man can heartily rejoice in this life when he weighs and considers his banishment and the many dangers of his soul.

Through levity of heart and neglect of our defects we feel not the sorrows of soul, but we often vainly laugh when in all reason we ought to weep. There is no true liberty, nor real joy, but in the fear of God with a good conscience.

Happy is he who can throw aside all impediments of distractions and recollect himself in the union of holy compunction. Happy is the man who separates himself from all that may burden or stain his conscience. Strive manfully; habit is overcome by habit.... (I)f we do not have divine consolations, or seldom experience them, it is our own fault, because we do not seek compunction of heart, nor wholly cast off vain and outward satisfactions.

Acknowledge yourself unworthy of divine consolation, and more worthy of much suffering. When a man has perfect compunction, the whole world is burdensome and distasteful to him. A good man always finds enough reason for mourning and weeping. For whether he considers himself, or thinks of his neighbour, he knows that no man lives here below without suffering; and the more thoroughly he considers himself, the greater his sorrow. The subjects for just grief and interior compunction are our vices and sins, in which lie entangled in such a manner as seldom to be able to fix our mind on heavenly things.[xxii]

Do you have deep compunction of heart? Do you weep over your past sins? As with all things, such holy sorrow is a gift from God. If you do not feel it now, ask Him for the "gift of tears," the grace to truly weep over your sins.

Resolution: Ask God for the gift of tears, or at least a deep, heartfelt repentance for your sins. Sacrifice some enjoyable activity or entertainment as an act of reparation for your sins. For instance, refrain from watching a funny movie or television show you would otherwise watch, as an expression of sorrow for your sins.

Saint Mary Magdalen, patroness of penitent sinners, pray for us.

TRACK YOUR PROGRESS: *Since reading the last meditation, how many times have I:*

a) deliberately touched myself impurely while awake? ✓0 ___1 ___2 ___3 or more times
b) deliberately viewed indecent pictures or movies? ✓0 ___1 ___2 ___3 or more times
c) committed unchaste acts with others? ✓0 ___1 ___2 ___3 or more times
d) deliberately entertained/enjoyed impure thoughts? ✓0 ___1 ___2 ___3 or more times

e) When was the last time I went to Confession?_____ to Mass?_____

MEDITATION 11: CUSTODY OF THE SENSES

He who practices virtue and speaks honestly,… stopping his ears lest he hear of bloodshed, closing his eyes lest he look on evil - he shall dwell on the heights, his stronghold shall be the rocky fastness; his food and drink in steady supply. - Isaias 3:15-16

Prayer: *Turn away my eyes from seeing what is vain; by your way give me life.* - Psalm 118[119]:37

An *occasion of sin* is any person, object or situation that might cause us to fall. There are four different types:

1. Near occasions - through which we always tend to fall
2. Remote occasions - through which we may sometimes fall
3. Voluntary occasions - meaning ones we are able to avoid
4. Involuntary occasions – which we are unable to avoid

Mother Church warns us to avoid all near and voluntary occasion of sin, and if we are truly serious about overcoming sins against purity we will take her warning very seriously. In Meditation Eight we heard Christ tell us to cut off anything that causes us to sin. Hopefully, you will have done that by now; if you have not then know that your Divine Master and His Virgin Bride, Holy Mother Church, command you to do so now.

If you have cut yourself off from all near and voluntary occasions of sin, you will still have to deal with remote and involuntary occasions of sin throughout your life. One example is the unexpected sight of an immodestly dressed person on the street. *"You have heard that it was said to the ancients, `Thou shalt not commit adultery.' But I say to you that anyone who so much as looks with lust at a woman has already committed adultery with her in his heart"* (Mt. 5:27-28). This is why we need to exercise *Custody of the senses.*

Our five senses are the doors to our mind and heart. Whatever we see, hear, feel, etc. can create thoughts, which may stir up desire and lead us astray into sin. *Custody of the senses* involves controlling our five senses, particularly our sight, in order to maintain the virtue of purity. Here is what the Venerable Louis of Granada has to say about custody of the senses in *The Sinners Guide.*

(W)e must carefully guard our senses, particularly the eyes, that they may not rest upon anything capable of exciting sinful desires. A man may inflict a deep wound upon his soul by inconsiderately turning his eyes upon a dangerous object. Prudently guard your eyes in your (dealings) with the other sex, for such glances weaken virtue.

Hence we are told by the Holy Ghost: "Look not round about thee in the ways of the city. Turn away thy face from a woman dressed up, and gaze not upon another's beauty" (Eccl. 9:7-8). Think of Job, that great servant of God, of such tried virtue, who kept so vigilant a guard over his senses that, in the expressive language of Scripture, he made a covenant with his eyes not so much as to think upon a virgin (cf. Job 31:1). Behold also the example of David, who, though declared by God to have been a man after His own Heart, yet fell into three grievous crimes by inconsiderately looking upon a woman.[xxiii]

Some modern guides to purity recommend a practice they call "bouncing the eyes." Since taking that second look at an attractive person is a bad habit developed since puberty, one can actually break that habit. One does so by retraining ones eyes to immediately look away at the first site of such a person or picture, and to focus instead on something else. The guides also recommend quoting a brief Scripture verse, such as: *"I made a covenant with my eyes, that I would not so much as think upon a virgin"* (Job 31:1).

Proponents of bouncing the eyes say it takes about four to six weeks for the average man to change his habit. They don't say how long it may take for a woman - even though some women have the same problem.

Many men report success with bouncing the eyes, while others say that it helps a little but not quite enough for them to achieve purity. Since custody of the senses is but one strategy in our battle against this vice, bouncing the eyes would probably work better as part of an overall program like this one than it would all by itself.[†]

So definitely practice this method as a way of taking custody of your eyes; this will help starve your mind of impure images and thoughts. Yet don't rely on it alone; follow the other recommendations in this book as well, and remember that God's grace is the ultimate key to victory over sin.

Next, there is custody of the ears. Louis of Granada continues:

> Be no less watchful in protecting your ears from impure discourses. If unbecoming words are uttered in your presence, testify your displeasure by at least a grave and serious countenance; for what we hear with pleasure we learn to do with complacency. Guard with equal care your tongue. Let no immodest words escape you; for "evil communications," says the Apostle, "corrupt good morals" (1 Cor. 15:33). A man's conversation discovers his inclination, for, to quote the words of the Gospel, from the abundance of the heart the mouth speaketh.[xxiv]

Custody of the ears may involve avoiding certain popular songs, radio programs or other sources of immoral conversation. This could prove difficult for you, especially if your roommates or coworkers often engage in indecent discussions. Do the best you can and ask God for wisdom and help. It may also prove helpful to ask the Guardian Angels of your roommates or coworkers to work out the situation for the best.

You will also have to gain custody of your tongue by exercising modesty of speech. Begin to curb your cussing; this may prove a difficult habit to break, so give yourself time and ask for God's help. Here's a tip: a lot of cussing arises from anger, so try to adopt an attitude of forgiveness toward others and thankfulness toward God. This may help curb your anger. A later meditation will further discuss modesty in speech.

After taking custody of your senses, do not neglect to fill them with holy sights, sounds and conversations in place of impure ones. Keep some icons, holy pictures and statues around your house; listen to Scripture on tape, sacred music or uplifting religious teaching tapes, discuss spiritual matters with devout friends, use your tongue to praise God often. These holy inspirations will soon replace impure images and thoughts and help renew your mind (Rom. 12:2).

Resolution: Make a "covenant" with your eyes as Job did. Start retraining yourself to look away at the first sight of something indecent. Focus on something else and pray a memorized Scripture verse about purity. Avoid both hearing and participating in impure conversations as much as possible as well. Surround yourself with holy images and sounds instead. Stay close to the Sacred Heart of Jesus always.

LORD JESUS, SON of GOD, GIVE HER EVERYTHING SHE NEEDS HERE oN

Holy Job, pray for us   EARTH & IN HEAVEN.

TRACK YOUR PROGRESS: *Since reading the last meditation, how many times have I:*

a) deliberately touched myself impurely while awake? ___0 ___1 ✓2 ___3 or more times
b) deliberately viewed indecent pictures or movies? ✓0 ___1 ___2 ___3 or more times
c) committed unchaste acts with others? ✓0 ___1 ___2 ___3 or more times
d) deliberately entertained/enjoyed impure thoughts? ✓0 ___1 ___2 ___3 or more times

e) When was the last time I went to Confession?_____ to Mass?_____

[†] Information about bouncing the eyes is drawn from the article "Every Young Man's Battle: How to Beat Lust," Breakaway Magazine, 13 July 2005 <http://www.family.org/teenguys/breakmag/features/a0023847.html>.

MEDITATION 12: YOU WILL BE TEMPTED

Blessed is the man who endures temptation; for when he has been tried, he will receive the crown of life which God has promised to those who love him. - St. James 1:12

Prayer: *Our Lady of Fatima ... help us to resist temptation.*[xxv] *Virgin most Pure, help me!*

Make no mistake: you will be tempted to impurity. Your spiritual Enemy is not at all pleased that you now want to abandon the habitual sins he has so carefully cultivated in you for so long. The last thing he wants is for a Christian soul that he has enslaved to the evils of pornography and masturbation to become clean of heart. You may have already begun experiencing strong temptations; this is a sure sign the Devil is alarmed as he sees you slipping from his grasp. If you have not been severely tempted recently, he will surely try to attack you at the next opportunity. Fear not, for God can help you resist, but *be vigilant and be prepared!*

Even after you break your bad habits with the help of God's grace, you will still experience occasional temptations. In this life you will never be completely free from all enticement to sin. God allows this because temptations show us how weak we are, and how much we need His aid to live a truly Christian life. They also help detach our affections from the things of this world and to seek first the kingdom of God.

Perhaps the most encouraging reason God permits the Evil One to tempt us is because *the struggle against temptation can actually benefit us spiritually!* If you were never tempted you would never have to resist temptation, and resisting temptation makes you stronger. By allowing the evil one to tempt you, God is giving you an opportunity to gain more merit and grow in His grace. St. Francis de Sales tells us that:

> GOD never permits such grievous temptations and assaults to try any, save those souls whom He designs to lead on to His own living, highest love, but nevertheless it does not follow as a natural consequence that they are certain to attain thereto. Indeed, it has often happened that those who had been steadfast under violent assaults, failing to correspond faithfully to Divine Grace, have yielded under the pressure of very trifling temptations. I would warn you of this, my child, so that, should you ever be tried by great temptations, you may know that God is showing special favour to you, thereby proving that He means to exalt you in His Sight; but that at the same time you may ever be humble and full of holy fear, not overconfident in your power to resist lesser temptations because you have overcome those that were greater, unless by means of a most steadfast faithfulness to God.[xxvi]

Of course, you cannot resist temptation or gain merit on your own. This is why God gives you sufficient grace to resist any temptation that He lets you endure. *"God is faithful and will not permit you to be tempted beyond your strength, but with the temptation will also give you a way out that you may be able to bear it"* (1 Cor. 10:13).

If God offers us sufficient grace to resist temptation, then why have we so often given in? Because we often fail to seek His help to avoid sin. The grace is there all the time, but we fix our eyes instead on the pleasure of sin and ignore the way of escape He has made for us. So let us earnestly beg Our Lord right now, before the next temptation comes along, to give us the grace to look for the way of escape when the next temptation strikes.

Even though resisting temptation can cause us to grow in virtue, this does not mean we should seek out temptation ourselves. We must *never* do that, as St. Alphonsus explains:

> This must not, however, lead us to seek after temptations; on the contrary, we must pray to God to deliver us from temptations, and from those more especially by which God foresees we should be overcome; and this is precisely the object of that petition of the Our Father. *Lead us not into temptation;* but when, by God's permission, we are beset with temptations, we must then, without either being alarmed or discouraged by those foul thoughts, rely wholly on Jesus Christ, and beseech him to help us; and he, on his part, will not fail to give us the strength to resist. St. Augustine says: "Throw thyself on him, and fear not; he will not withdraw to let thee fall."[xxvii]

Also remember that though temptation is an invitation or enticement to sin, it is *not* a sin on your part. St. Francis de Sales speaks of the three steps of *"temptation, delectation,* and *consent."*[xxviii] Only if you willingly take pleasure in the thought of sinning (*delectation*) do you actually begin to sin. As long as you resist the Tempter's suggestions, you commit no sin.

Francis de Sales relates the following story from the life of St. Catherine of Siena:

The Evil One having obtained permission from God to assault that pious virgin with all his strength, so long as he laid no hand upon her, filled her heart with impure suggestions, and surrounded her with every conceivable temptation of sight and sound, which, penetrating into the Saint's heart, so filled it, that, as she herself has said, nothing remained free save her most acute superior will.

This struggle endured long, until at length Our Lord appeared to her, and she exclaimed, "Where were You, O most Dear Lord, when my heart was so overwhelmed with darkness and foulness?" Whereupon He answered, "I was within your heart, My child." "How could that be, Lord," she asked, "when it was so full of evil? Can You abide in a place so foul?"

Then our Lord replied, "Tell Me, did these evil thoughts and imaginations give you pain or pleasure? did you take delight, or did you grieve over them?" To which S. Catherine made answer, "They grieved me exceedingly." Then the Lord said, "Who do you think was it that caused you to be thus grieved, save I Myself, hidden within your soul? Believe Me, My child, had I not been there, these evil thoughts which swarmed around your soul, and which you could not banish, would speedily have overpowered it, and entering in, your free will would have accepted them, and so death had struck that soul; but inasmuch as I was there, I filled your heart with reluctance and resistance, so that it set itself steadfastly against the temptation, and finding itself unable to contend as vigorously as it desired, it did but experience a yet more vehement abhorrence of sin and of itself. Thus these very troubles became a great merit again to you, and a great accession of virtue and strength to your soul"[xxix]

So even if you experience a severe temptation, take heart. As long as you do not consent to it you have committed no sin, and resisting it with God's help makes you stronger in virtue and richer in merit. Just stay close to Jesus and Mary, continue to reject sin and its lies, to humble yourself before God, weep over your sins, seek a clean heart, avoid all occasions of sin, and trust that God will give you the victory by His grace.

Resolution: From now on, whenever you are tempted, see it as an *opportunity* to gain merit and draw closer to our loving God. Yet never seek temptation, nor rely on your own strength, but always ask for grace.

Saint Catherine of Siena, pray for us.

TRACK YOUR PROGRESS: *Since reading the last meditation, how many times have I:*

a) deliberately touched myself impurely while awake? ✓0 ___1 ___2 ___3 or more times
b) deliberately viewed indecent pictures or movies? ✓0 ___1 ___2 ___3 or more times
c) committed unchaste acts with others? ✓0 ___1 ___2 ___3 or more times
d) deliberately entertained/enjoyed impure thoughts? ✓0 ___1 ___2 ___3 or more times

e) When was the last time I went to Confession? *8 DAYS AGO* to Mass? *YESTERDAY*

MEDITATION 13: RESISTING TEMPTATION

Be sober, be watchful! For your adversary the devil, as a roaring lion, goes about seeking someone to devour. Resist him, steadfast in the faith, knowing that the same suffering befalls your brethren all over the world. - 1 St. Peter 5:8-9

Prayer: *Come, Holy Spirit, come dispel the darkness of lust with the Light of Hope. Come, Holy Spirit, come by means of the powerful Intercession of the Immaculate Heart of Mary, your well beloved spouse.*[xxx]

How do you resist temptation? In a word, *flee!* Don't try to stand and fight it on your own strength; you are just not strong enough. Scripture counsels us to *"Flee immorality;"* (1 Cor. 6:18) and to *"flee the cravings of youth and pursue justice, faith, charity and peace with those who call on the Lord with a pure heart"* (2 Tim. 2:22). This is the way to victory over temptation and habitual sin. St. Philip of Neri used to say that it is the "cowards" who win the battle against sins of the flesh; that is, those who flee are those who win!

The beginning of a temptation against purity is the most important time, for it is easiest to turn away from it at the very start. If you entertain it, the temptation becomes stronger and more difficult to resist. So when you are tempted by impurity, immediately turn your eyes and thoughts away from it:

> Vigorously…resist the first attacks of this vice. If we do not resist it in the beginning, it rapidly acquires strength and gains an entrance to our souls. "When a taste for sinful pleasures," says St. Gregory, "takes possession of a heart, it thinks of nothing but how to gratify its inordinate desires" (Moral. 21,7). We must, then, struggle against it from the beginning by repelling every bad thought, for by such fuel is the flame of impurity fed. As wood nourishes fire, so our thoughts nourish our desires; and, consequently, if the former be good, charity will burn in our breast – but if they are bad, the fire of lust will certainly be kindled.[xxxi]

If the temptation arises from a situation, you may have to physically walk away, turn off the TV or computer, etc. Get out of that situation as soon as possible! If you experience any difficulty, ask God for help.

As you turn away from the temptation, turn your heart and mind toward Jesus Christ. Remember that He is with you always, and ask Him to help you resist. Prayer is *absolutely essential* in this spiritual battle. If St. Peter had taken Our Lord's advice to *"Watch and pray that you enter not into temptation"* (Mt. 26:41), he would not have denied Christ later that night. St. Alphonsus writes:

> Spiritual masters prescribe a variety of means (to vanquish temptations); but the most necessary, and the safest… is to have immediate recourse to God with all humility and confidence, saying: *Incline unto my aid, O God; O Lord, make haste to help me!* (Ps. 69:2) This short prayer will enable us to overcome the assaults of all the devils of hell; for God is infinitely more powerful than all of them. Almighty God knows well that of ourselves we are unable to resist the temptations of the infernal powers; and on this account the most learned Cardinal Gotti remarks, "that whenever we are assailed, and in danger of being overcome, God is obliged to give us strength enough to resist as often as we call upon him for it."[xxxii]

Humble yourself before Our Lord and earnestly beg Him for the grace to avoid sin. Tell Him that you know you cannot resist this sin without the help of His Holy Spirit, and ask humbly for His help. You may wish pray the inspired words of Sacred Scripture, such as *"Create in me a clean heart, O God, and put a new and right spirit within me"* or First Corinthians 6:15-20 (cited in the fourth meditation), or other such passages on the virtue of purity. Scripture is a very powerful help in resisting temptation; Jesus Himself used it when Satan tempted Him (Mt. 4:3-11) in order to set an example for us. Though we should not directly address the Devil as Our Lord did, we can still recite, meditate on and pray with the word of God when tempted.

St. Alphonsus continues:

If the impure temptation has already forced its way into the mind, and plainly pictures its object to the imagination, so as to stir the passions, then, according to the advice of St. Jerome, we must burst forth into these words: "O Lord, Thou art my helper." As soon, says the saint, as we feel the sting of concupiscence, we must have recourse to God, and say: "O Lord, do Thou assist me;" we must invoke the most holy names of Jesus and Mary, which possess a wonderful efficacy in the suppression of temptations of this nature. St. Francis de Sales says, that no sooner do children espy a wolf than they instantly seek refuge in the arms of their father and mother; and there they remain out of all danger. Our conduct must be the same: we must flee without delay for succor to Jesus and Mary, by earnestly calling upon them. I repeat that we must instantly have recourse to them, without giving a moment's audience to the temptation, or disputing with it.[xxxiii]

Other recommended aspirations are: *"Lord Jesus Christ, have mercy on me!"* or *"Jesus, Mary, help me!"* or *"Mary, protect me from this sin!"* Of course, any earnest, sincere prayer from the heart will do. Whether the temptation lasts for a long or short time, it won't last forever; so ask for the grace to persevere till the end.

And as long as the temptation lasts, let us never cease calling on Jesus and Mary. It is also very profitable, in the like importunity of temptations, to renew our firm purpose to God of suffering every torment, and a thousand deaths, rather than offend him; and at the same time we must invoke his divine assistance. And even should the temptation be of such violence as to put us in imminent risk of consenting to it, we must then redouble our prayers, hasten into the presence of the Blessed Sacrament, cast ourselves at the feet of the crucifix, or of some image of our Blessed Lady, and there pray with increased fervor, and cry out for help with groans and tears. God is certainly ready to hear all who pray to him; and it is from him alone, and not from our own exertions, that we must look for strength to resist; but sometimes Almighty God wills these struggles of us, and then he makes up for our weakness, and grants us the victory. It is an excellent practice also, in the moment of temptation, to make the sign of the cross on the forehead and breast. It is also of great service to discover the temptation to our spiritual director. St. Philip of Neri used to say, that a temptation disclosed is half overcome.[xxxiv]

When the temptation does end, don't forget to thank God for helping you to avoid committing sin. Your resistance proves that He has helped you; you don't have to just "give in" to temptation! This can give you more hope and confidence in His grace for the next time temptation strikes.

Resolution: Put the above suggestions into practice the next time that you are tempted. Stay close to Our Lord and Our Lady always, and continue with previous resolutions.

Saint Alphonsus de Liguori, pray for us.

TRACK YOUR PROGRESS: *Since reading the last meditation, how many times have I:*

a) deliberately touched myself impurely while awake?   ✓0   __1   __2   __3 or more times
b) deliberately viewed indecent pictures or movies?   ✓0   __1   __2   __3 or more times
c) committed unchaste acts with others?   ✓0   __1   __2   __3 or more times
d) deliberately entertained/enjoyed impure thoughts?   ✓0   __1   __2   __3 or more times

e) When was the last time I went to Confession?_____ to Mass? TODAY_____

MEDITATION 14: BE PREPARED FOR TEMPTATIONS

My son, if you come forward to serve the Lord… prepare yourself for temptation. Set your heart right and be steadfast…and do not be hasty in time of calamity. Await God's patience, cling to him and do not depart, that you may be wise in all your ways. Accept whatever is brought upon you, and endure it in sorrow; in changes that humble you be patient. For gold and silver are tested in the fire, and acceptable men in the furnace of humiliation. Trust in God, and he will help you; hope in him and he will make your ways straight. Stay in fear of him, and grow old in him. You who fear the Lord, wait for his mercy; and turn not aside, lest you fall. – Sirach 2:1-7 RSV

Prayer: *O Eternal God and King of all creation, Who hast granted me to reach this hour, forgive the sins I have committed this day in deed, word, and thought; and cleanse, O Lord, my humble soul of all impurity of flesh and spirit. Grant me, O Lord, to pass the sleep of this night in peace; that, rising from my lowly bed, I may please Thy most holy name all the days of my life, and thwart the enemies, fleshly and bodiless, that war against me. Deliver me, O Lord, from vain thoughts and evil desires which defile me. For Thine is the kingdom, and the power, and the glory: of the Father, and of the Son, and of the Holy Spirit, now and ever, and unto the ages of ages. Amen.* St. Macarius of Egypt.

You may have noticed that temptation is more likely to attack you at certain times than at others. For instance, it often strikes after a deep spiritual experience, like Mass, a prayer meeting, retreat, etc. Another time may be shortly before one receives Communion: on Saturday night, Sunday morning or on a Holy Day of Obligation. This temptation is timed to put you in a state of mortal sin and so prevent you from receiving Jesus in the Blessed Sacrament - or perhaps the Tempter hopes you will receive Him anyway, which is a sacrilege.

Temptation also often attacks when you are alone, particularly at night or upon awakening in the morning. Or when you are angry with a spouse or other loved one, since anger often leads to selfish behavior. Or it may strike when you feel sick, exhausted or hungry and so have less strength to resist. If you experience physical pain or discomfort, the devil may even suggest self-abuse as a temporary escape from your suffering. Women may notice that they are more susceptible to sins against purity at certain times during their cycle, due to normal hormonal fluctuations in the body. The Tempter knows this and will surely take advantage of it.

Knowing when a temptation will likely occur can help you prepare for it. Then you can perhaps work out a strategy for next Saturday night, or at the end of a retreat, or during your next illness, or after an argument.

Example: you may find that temptations often come at night, in the form of fantasies before falling asleep or impure dreams while sleeping. While the former most likely are voluntary and therefore sinful, the latter come from your subconscious mind, not your will, so they are not sinful acts on your part. However, they are often the unhappy result of many years of entertaining impure thoughts, and can create a strong desire to sin after you wake up.

So what strategy could you devise? Regular bedtime prayers (such as the three Ave's and *O Domina Mea* you should be saying every night since the second meditation) may prove helpful in this matter. Some people pray the Holy Rosary in bed before falling asleep, so you might try that. Others find that reading Sacred Scripture and meditating on it before going to sleep helps to fill ones mind with holy thoughts rather than impure ones. You could try reading a psalm or two, or a short passage from one of the Gospels, after your bedtime prayer.

Blessed Pope John XXIII employed a number of strategies for keeping his heart pure, one of which involved sleeping every night with a rosary around his neck and his hands crossed over his chest[xxxv]. You may wish to try to accustom yourself to that sleep posture - but don't be too discouraged if you simply can't sleep comfortably that way. Other strategies mentioned in this book may work better for you.

If you wake up in the middle of the night, instead of fantasizing recall the Scripture passage you read earlier, and meditate on it some more before falling asleep again. Or pick up your rosary and resume praying (if you have fallen asleep while praying it, as sometimes happens). If you experience a very strong temptation, you can pray something like the following: *"O Jesus, O Mary, let me die rather than offend you by though, word or deed. In the name of the Father, and of the Son, and of the Holy Ghost. Amen."*[xxxvi]

This is a very strong sentiment, one which many saints made their life's motto: "Death before sin!" we might be tempted to consider that a bit extreme, until we consider that mortal sin is actually worse than physical death. The latter only kills the body, leaving the soul untouched, while mortal sin kills your very soul, cutting you off from God Who is your greatest Good. So sin is a greater evil than even death itself!

Hopefully, you will never find yourself in a situation where you must choose between committing a mortal sin and dying. Such situations are, thankfully, rare. What this prayer means is that you must learn to hate and avoid mortal sin even more than you fear and try to avoid death itself! That doesn't mean you must love death; just loathe sin more. (We will discuss *hatred of sin* further in Meditation 27)

If you find you are having difficulty working out strategies for your particular situation, try talking it over with your priest, spouse or accountability friend. Perhaps they will have some ideas that you would have never considered.

A word of caution here: if you ever go for a period of time without falling into sins against purity, you might be tempted to think that you have finally beaten your dirty habit for good and will never fall into it again. *Beware!* This seemingly innocuous thought is actually the voice of *Pride*. What it is really saying is, "You're strong enough now to be righteous all by yourself, without the help of grace" (remember the Pelagian heresy!). Once you begin to seriously entertain such thoughts, you can be almost certain that a temptation and fall is immanent. Remember: *"Pride goes before disaster, and a haughty spirit before a fall"* (Prov. 16:18).

"Therefore let any one who thinks that he stands take heed lest he fall" (1 Cor. 10:12)! Remember that we can only resist sin by God's grace, not by our own efforts (the Pelagian heresy). So if the thought that you've overcome your habit ever crosses your mind, contradict it; tell yourself that it is by the grace of God that you haven't fallen, and that left to yourself you would succumb again in a second!

Resolution: Figure out the Tempter's usual "schedule" for temptation in your life. Write down any patterns you discern and be prepared to resist temptation at those times. Don't forget that giving in is not inevitable, and ask Jesus and Mary for the grace to not succumb. Continue to pray and humble yourself, to reject sin and its near occasions, to mourn your sinful past and seek purity with all your heart.

For more valuable information on temptation and how to fight it, read <u>How to Resist Temptation</u> by Fr. Francis J. Remler, C.M. (reprinted by Sophia Institute Press).

Our Father Who art in Heaven, lead us not into temptation, but deliver us from evil.

TRACK YOUR PROGRESS: *Since reading the last meditation, how many times have I:*

a) deliberately touched myself impurely while awake?   ✓0 ___1 ___2 ___3 or more times
b) deliberately viewed indecent pictures or movies?   ✓0 ___1 ___2 ___3 or more times
c) committed unchaste acts with others?   ✓0 ___1 ___2 ___3 or more times
d) deliberately entertained/enjoyed impure thoughts?   ✓0 ___1 ___2 ___3 or more times

e) When was the last time I went to Confession? 3-4-17   to Mass? YESTERDAY

MEDITATION 15: THE PASSION AND DEATH OF OUR LORD

But as for me, God forbid that I should glory save in the cross of our Lord Jesus Christ, through whom the world is crucified to me, and I to the world. – Galatians 6:14

Prayer: *Hail, O Most Precious and Life Giving Cross of Our Lord, for thou drivest away the demons by the power of Our Lord Jesus Christ crucified on thee, Who descended into hell and trampled on the power of the devil, giving us thee, His Precious Cross, to drive away every adversary. O Most Precious and Life Giving Cross of Our Lord, assist me together with Our Holy Lady, the Virgin Mother of God, and with all the saints, now and forever. Amen. Guard me, O Lord, with the power of Thy Holy and Life Giving Cross, and preserve me from all evil.* – Eastern Christian Prayer to the Precious Cross.

You have good reason to glory in the Cross of Our Lord, for the Cross is your hope of victory over your sins. It was there that Jesus Christ died for your transgressions. Were it not for the Holy Cross we would all be dead in our sins, with no hope of ever attaining a clean heart or becoming partakers of the divine nature.

Perhaps this is why demons hate the Sign of the Cross. Many saints tell us that this simple gesture - which most of us probably learned as children - if made devoutly with faith in God, actually repels demons and might even put an end to a temptation. The Sign of our Redemption is a symbol of their defeat; how the evil spirits hate that! So remember to cross yourself during your next temptation; use holy water too, if available.

Meditation on the Passion and Death of Christ will help you immensely in your struggle for purity. As discussed earlier, recalling the suffering that Jesus willingly endured for love of you can help deepen your love for Him and develop in you Perfect Contrition for your past transgressions. The magnitude of His suffering also reveals how terrible sin really is, which will help you learn to hate sin (Meditation 27 will discuss this topic further).

Dom Lorenzo Scupoli argues that, in times of temptation, we should think about Christ's Passion:

Your prayer should be conducted in the following manner. When you see these thoughts present themselves and attempt to make an impression, recollect yourself and speak to Christ crucified saying: "Sweet Jesus, come to my rescue, that I may not fall a victim to my enemies." On certain occasions you may embrace a Crucifix representing your dying Savior, kiss the marks of the Sacred Wounds on His feet and say with great confidence and affection: "O adorable, thrice holy Wounds! Imprint your figure on my heart which is filled with evil, and preserve me from consenting to sin."

In your meditations I am not of the opinion (as several authors are) that, when the temptation is most violent, you should consider the degrading and insatiable nature of these sins in order to establish a hatred for impurity, that you should consider how they are followed by disgust, remorse and anxiety, even by the loss of one's fortune, health, life, honor, etc. These considerations are not appropriate to the situation and, instead of freeing us from the danger, they frequently only increase it. If the understanding drives away evil thoughts, these reflections naturally call them back.

The best way to become free of these is to remove not only the thoughts themselves, but also the reflections directly contrary to them. In attempting to dissipate them by their contraries, we merely renew the impure ideas and unconsciously imprint them still deeper. Be satisfied with meditation on the life and death of our Savior.[xxxvii]

The Church offers us many different ways to ponder the saving Death of Jesus. For instance, one can cultivate a devotion to His Precious Blood or Holy Wounds. Then there are the Stations of the Cross and Sorrowful Mysteries of the Rosary. Those who struggle with habitual sins against purity will find elements in these devotions which apply specifically to them. For instance, the Tenth Station, *Jesus Is Stripped of His*

Garments, is often prayed for the intention of "purity in body and mind." The fruit of the Second Sorrowful Mystery, *The Scourging of Jesus at the Pillar*, is listed as either "the virtue of purity" or "overcoming the flesh" or "mortification of the senses" (the same as *custody of the senses*, discussed earlier). Many saints have said that Jesus endured the horrific Scourging to atone for sins of the flesh.

Finally, meditation on the Passion and Death of Christ should remind us of our own duty to take up our cross and follow Him. Indulgence in solitary sins such as fantasies, viewing indecent images and self-abuse indicate that one is self-centered, focused on ones own gratification and pursuing it at any cost. This is opposed to Our Creator's intention that we use our procreative organs only during an act of *communion* between two persons, not for solitary pleasure. So impurity is often a symptom of a deeper problem with selfishness. Unless one deals with this root cause, one will have little hope for a lasting victory over this vice, or for a fruitful Christian life.

We Christians must be Christ-centered, not self-centered. We must deny ourselves rather than indulge ourselves. Remember our Lord's words: *"If anyone wishes to come after me, let him deny himself, and take up his cross, and follow me. For he who would save his life will lose it; but he who loses his life for my sake will find it. For what does it profit a man, if he gain the whole world, but suffer the loss of his own soul? Or what will a man give in exchange for his soul?"* (Mt.16:24-26)

What would it profit you, dear Christian, if you experienced all the pleasure in the world yet forfeited your immortal soul? "Wretched indeed is that hour of gratification which is purchased at the expense of endless suffering."[xxxviii]

In order to follow Christ, we must deny ourselves, even die to ourselves. We must mortify our desires, ask for the grace to say "No!" to temptation and to our lust, to do God's will rather than our will. If you have been carrying out the Resolutions at the end of each meditation, you have already begun to deny yourself. Keep it up. We will also revisit this topic in later meditations.

As stated in the verse at the beginning of this meditation, through Christ and His Holy Cross, the world has been crucified to you, and you to the world. Live as though you have died to the world.

Resolution: If you don't have a crucifix on your wall, put one there or at least carry a small one with you to remind you of the great price Jesus paid for your sins. Meditate often on the Passion of Christ, especially in times of temptation. Humbly ask God for the grace to embrace your cross, deny yourself the pleasures of the flesh and learn the self-discipline that is part of the Christian life.

The next time the Tempter whispers "You deserve a little pleasure," tell yourself "I must deny myself this pleasure, take up my cross and follow Christ. I will offer up this act of self-denial in union with His death on the Cross." Then ask for God's grace to accomplish that.

We adore Thee, O Christ, and we bless Thee, because by Thy Holy Cross Thou hast redeemed the world.

TRACK YOUR PROGRESS: *Since reading the last meditation, how many times have I:*

a) deliberately touched myself impurely while awake? ___0 ✓1 ___2 ___3 or more times
b) deliberately viewed indecent pictures or movies? ___0 ✓1 ___2 ___3 or more times
c) committed unchaste acts with others? ✓0 ___1 ___2 ___3 or more times
d) deliberately entertained/enjoyed impure thoughts? ✓0 ___1 ___2 ___3 or more times

e) When was the last time I went to Confession? 3-4-17 to Mass? YESTERDAY
TODAY IS: 3-15-17

MEDITATION 16: THE BLESSED SACRAMENT

For Christ, our passover, has been sacrificed. Therefore let us keep the festival, not with the old leaven, nor with the leaven of malice and wickedness, but with the unleavened bread of sincerity and truth. -1 Corinthians 5:7-8

Prayer: *O Holy Bread, Living Bread, Pure Bread, You who descended from heaven and give life to the world, come into my heart and cleanse me from every defilement of flesh and spirit. Enter into my soul: heal and cleanse me both within and without; be the safeguard and constant health of my soul and body.*[xxxix]

In the first meditation we learned that Jesus is the true Bread from Heaven, which satisfies our spiritual hunger. As physical food nourishes our bodies and strengthens us against illness, so our Eucharistic Lord strengthens our souls and preserves our spiritual health. The Blessed Sacrament is also a holy Medicine for our sin-sickened souls, which cleanses us of past venial sins and strengthens us against committing mortal sins in the future. Many great saints recognized that the Eucharist actually subdues our disordered passions (concupiscence), and so recommended frequent reception of Holy Communion as a powerful remedy against sins of the flesh:

If you feel the itch of intemperance, nourish yourself with the Flesh and Blood of Christ, Who practiced heroic self-control during His earthly life; and you will become temperate… if you feel scorched by the fever of impurity, go to the banquet of the Angels; and the spotless Flesh of Christ will make you pure and chaste. - St. Cyril of Alexandria[xl]

Devotion to the Blessed Sacrament and devotion to the Blessed Virgin are not simply the best way, but in fact the only way to keep purity. At the age of twenty nothing but Communion can keep ones heart pure… Chastity is not possible without the Eucharist – St. Philip of Neri[xli]

We read in the Gospel that when Jesus Christ went into St. Peter's house, he asked Him to cure his mother-in-law who was sick of a violent fever. Jesus Christ commanded the fever to leave her, and instantly she was so completely cured that she was able to serve them at table. The fever, says St. Ambrose, is our avarice, our anger, our sensuality. These passions boil up in our flesh, and agitate the soul, the spirit and the senses. They have their remedy in the Blessed Eucharist, the food and strength of the Christian soul. Let us thank Our Lord for this healing and sanctifying gift….

The precious Blood of Jesus Christ which flows in our veins, and His adorable Body which is blended with ours, can it do less than destroy, or at least greatly diminish the attraction towards forbidden pleasures that the sin of Adam has left in us…. A heart that is about to receive a God who is so pure, who is holiness itself, will it not feel born in it an invincible horror of all sins of impurity, and would it not rather let itself be cut in pieces rather than consent, I do not say to a bad action, but even to a bad thought? A tongue which a short time ago has been so happy as to bear its Creator and Saviour, could it dare to lend itself to lascivious words, to sensual kisses? No, without doubt, it would never dare to act thus. Eyes which just now desired so earnestly to contemplate their Creator, who is more pure than the sun's rays, could they after such happiness, look on indecent objects? That would seem to be impossible. – St. John Vianney, the Curé of Ars[xlii]

As the above Scripture verse states, Christ is our Passover Lamb. Recall that the Israelites passed from enslavement in Egypt to freedom after roasting and eating a lamb, and spreading its blood on the lintel and door posts of their houses. Even so, we pass out of enslavement to sin and into the freedom of God's children by eating the Flesh and drinking the Blood of the Lamb of God in the Blessed Sacrament, our Passover meal.[†]

[†] This insight appears in the Evangelical Pure Freedom course (pp. 49-50), though it identifies eating His Flesh with meditating on the Bible. The Catholic Church has always taught that we eat Our Lord's Flesh and drink His Blood in the Eucharist.

You may be thinking, "But I've received Communion hundreds, even thousands, of times before, yet I still keep committing sins against purity!" Dear friend, the grace to overcome sin has always been there. Yet as with all the graces of the Eucharist, one either doesn't know to ask for it or doesn't have the right dispositions to receive it. Ask God now for the grace of a proper disposition, for He wants to free you from captivity to sin.

It is a pious belief that our prayers at Mass are strongest at the Consecration, particularly at the moment the priest raises the Host and Chalice. For this is when Christ, in the person of the priest, offers Himself to the Father. If we unite our petitions with His most holy Offering, they become particularly efficacious.

Many saints tell us that the time we spend in prayer after receiving Our Lord is also very valuable. Saint Alphonsus writes:

> To reap also more abundant fruit from Communion, we should make a fervent thanksgiving. Father John of Avila said that the time after Communion is "a time to gain treasures of graces." St. Mary Magdalene of Pazzi used to say that no time can be more calculated to inflame us with Divine love than the time immediately after our Communion. And St. Teresa says: "After Communion let us be careful not to lose so good an opportunity of negotiating with God. His Divine majesty is not accustomed to pay badly for His lodging, if He meets with a good reception."[xliii]

So at the Consecration and again after receiving Communion, ask Our Eucharistic Lord for the grace of a clean heart, strength against temptation, and for anything else you need. The *Thanksgiving Prayer after Mass* composed by St. Thomas Aquinas may prove helpful:

> I give thanks to You, Holy Lord, Father Almighty, Eternal God, who has deigned to feast me, a sinful and unworthy servant, with the precious Body and Blood of Your Son, Jesus Christ our Lord, not through any merit of my own, but only because of Your merciful goodness. I pray that this Holy Communion will not condemn me to punishment but will bring about my pardon and salvation, encompassing me with the armor of faith and the shield of a good will. By it let my vices be done away, all lustful desires extinguished. May it advance me in charity, patience, humility, obedience, and every other virtue. Let it be strong defense against the wiles of all my enemies, visible and invisible, perfectly allaying my passions, physical and spiritual, binding me firmly to You, the one true God, and bringing my last hour to a happy close. I pray, too, that it may be Your pleasure to one day call me, a sinner, to that ineffable Banquet where You, with Your Son and the Holy Spirit, feast Your saints on the vision of Yourself: Who are True Light, Complete Fulfillment, Eternal Joy, Consummate Delight, and Perfect Bliss. Through the same Christ our Lord. Amen.

Resolution: The next time you receive Our Lord, ask Him to let *this* Communion be *your* personal Passover, from enslavement to impurity into holy freedom. Take time after Communion to ask your Divine Guest for all the graces you need to overcome sin and draw closer to Him. Continue with previous resolutions

Saint John Baptist Mary Vianney, the Curé d'Ars, pray for us.

TRACK YOUR PROGRESS: *Since reading the last meditation, how many times have I:*

a) deliberately touched myself impurely while awake?   ✓0 ___1 ___2 ___3 or more times
b) deliberately viewed indecent pictures or movies?   ✓0 ___1 ___2 ___3 or more times
c) committed unchaste acts with others?   ✓0 ___1 ___2 ___3 or more times
d) deliberately entertained/enjoyed impure thoughts?   ✓0 ___1 ___2 ___3 or more times

e) When was the last time I went to Confession?_____ to Mass? YESTERDAY

MEDITATION 17: LIVING SACRIFICE

I beseech you therefore, brethren, by the mercy of God, that you present your bodies a living sacrifice, holy, pleasing unto God, your reasonable service. - Romans 12:1

Prayer: *Mary, loving Spouse of the Holy Spirit, I give my body to your care. Let me always remember that my body is a home for the Holy Spirit who dwells in me. Let me never sin against Him by any impure actions alone or with others, against the virtue of purity.*[xlii]

St. Paul urges us to present our bodies to God as living sacrifices. Now a sacrifice is both an offering to Our Lord and an act of self-denial. When one of the children of Israel brought a lamb to the Temple in ancient times, he was denying himself the benefits of owning it: that was one less animal from which he might get milk or wool, or could kill for its meat and skin. Even so, when one presents ones body as a living sacrifice, one both consecrates it to Our Lord for His service and denies oneself the illicit gratification that comes from sins against purity. Such self-denial may not be easy, but Christians do it for a purpose - to draw closer to God.

If you have been turning to sins against purity out of emptiness and loneliness, trying to use pleasure as a substitute for love, you may fear that if you deny yourself you will feel lonely and empty again. But if you deny yourself in order to cultivate cleanness of heart, it will bring you closer to Jesus' Sacred Heart. You will not be left empty, but will be filled with God's love and grace.

So how do you offer your body as a living sacrifice? As St. Paul writes elsewhere in that Epistle: *"Let not sin therefore reign in your mortal bodies, to make you obey their passions. Do not yield your members to sin as instruments of wickedness, but yield yourselves to God as men who have been brought from death to life, and your members to God as instruments of righteousness"* (Rom. 6:12-13 RSV).

In the past, you used your body shamefully as a servant of sin. Now consecrate it to be used in the service of Our Lord alone, for His greater glory. St. John Chrysostom gives some practical advice here:

Let the eye look upon no evil thing, and it has become a sacrifice; let your tongue speak nothing filthy, and it has become an offering; let your hand do no lawless deed, and it has become a whole burnt offering. Or rather this is not enough, but we must have good works also: let the hand give alms, the mouth bless those who annoy you, and the hearing find enjoyment evermore in Scripture readings. For sacrifice allows of no unclean thing: sacrifice is a first-fruit of the other actions. Let us then from our hands, and feet, and mouth, and all other members, yield first-fruits to God.[xlv]

Note that self-denial is but the first way to offer your body as a living sacrifice; you must follow it up with acts such as almsgiving, blessing others and listening to Sacred Scripture. These also consecrate the body to God's service.

The greatest "living sacrifice" we can make of our bodies is to unite ourselves to the Sacrifice of Christ Himself in the Holy Mass. Pope Pius XII writes:

"In order that the oblation by which the faithful offer the divine Victim in this sacrifice to the heavenly Father may have its full effect, it is necessary that the people add something else, namely, the offering of themselves as a victim. This offering in fact is not confined merely to the liturgical sacrifice. For the Prince of the Apostles wishes us, as living stones built upon Christ, the cornerstone, to be able as "a holy priesthood, to offer up spiritual sacrifices, acceptable to God by Jesus Christ" (1 St. Peter 2:5). St. Paul the Apostle addresses the following words of exhortation to Christians, without distinction of time, "I beseech you therefore, that you present your bodies, a living sacrifice, holy, pleasing unto God, your reasonable service."

But at that time especially when the faithful take part in the liturgical service with such piety and recollection that it can truly be said of them: "whose faith and devotion is known to Thee," it is then, with the High Priest and through Him they offer themselves as a spiritual sacrifice, that each one's faith ought to become more ready to work through charity, his piety more real and fervent, and each one should consecrate himself to the furthering of the divine glory, desiring to become as like as possible to Christ in His most grievous sufferings....

While we stand before the altar, then, it is our duty so to transform our hearts, that every trace of sin may be completely blotted out, while whatever promotes supernatural life through Christ may be zealously fostered and strengthened even to the extent that, in union with the immaculate Victim, we become a victim acceptable to the eternal Father."[xlvi]

The quote at the beginning of this meditation says that presenting your body as a living sacrifice is "your reasonable service." In the original Greek, the word "service" is *latria*, the term for the highest form of worship offered to God alone. If offering your body as a living sacrifice is a form of *worship*, then it should certainly be united to the Holy Sacrifice of the Mass, which is the worship most pleasing to God.

As your soul has died with Christ to sin in baptism, so now "crucify" your physical urges with Christ at the Holy Sacrifice of the Mass. It is time to begin denying yourself, to take up your cross and follow Him to Calvary.

Almighty and Eternal Father, I am sorry for offending you in the past by my sins against purity. In the most Holy Name of Our Lord Jesus Christ, I reject all these sins and any sinful use I have ever made of my body. If I have not yet confessed any of them in the Sacrament of Penance, I now resolve to do so as soon as possible. I renounce Satan, all his works and pomps; may Our Lord Jesus rebuke him, I humbly pray. May Mary, the Immaculate Queen of Angels and Terror of demons crush him underfoot; may St. Michael the Archangel cast him into Hell, along with any evil spirits who seek to ruin my soul.

By Your grace, I refuse to be mastered by sin from now on. I offer You my body as a living sacrifice, and present my members to You as instruments for righteousness, not for sin. I beg you to create a clean heart and a right spirit in me; may I live and die for You alone, my God and my All! I ask all this in the Name of Our Lord Jesus Christ, Your Son, Who lives and reigns with You in the unity of the Holy Spirit, God forever and ever. Amen.

Resolution: After you entrust yourself to Mary every morning in the *O Domina Mea*, consecrate your body to God as well. Live this sacrifice daily through self-denial, taking custody of your senses and doing good. Every time you go to Mass, place yourself, so to speak, on the paten with the Host during the Offertory, and when the priest offers the Host and Chalice to our Heavenly Father, offer your body, your self-denial and good deeds to God as a living sacrifice in union with the Sacrifice of Christ on Calvary.

Saint Philip of Neri, pray for us.

TRACK YOUR PROGRESS: *Since reading the last meditation, how many times have I:*

a) deliberately touched myself impurely while awake? ___0 ✓1 ___2 ___3 or more times
b) deliberately viewed indecent pictures or movies? ✓0 ___1 ___2 ___3 or more times
c) committed unchaste acts with others? ✓0 ___1 ___2 ___3 or more times
d) deliberately entertained/enjoyed impure thoughts? ✓0 ___1 ___2 ___3 or more times

e) When was the last time I went to Confession?_____ to Mass? YESTERDAY

MEDITATION 18: RENEWING THE MIND

Do not be conformed to this world but be transformed by the renewal of your mind, that you may prove what is the will of God, what is good and acceptable and perfect. - Romans 12:2 RSV

Prayer: *Come, O Spirit of Love; O Fire of Love, Purify my heart, mind, and soul; Sanctify all I think, say, and do; And bestow on me in plenitude thy holy gifts. May I always and only give thanks, and praise, and glory to you, my Lord and my God.*[xlvii]

Having told us to offer up our bodies to God, St. Paul now advises us what to do with our minds. In order for us to be transformed, our minds, which are so used to dwelling on and condoning sin, must be renewed: *"Take care, lest you imitate the practices of worldlings. Let your heart, your ambition, carry you to heaven: ever despise those things which the world admires, that every one may see my your actions that you are not of the society of worldlings, and have neither regard nor friendship for them."*[xlviii]

To "renew ones mind" essentially means to stop thinking like a sinner and start thinking like a saint. Don't let that though intimidate you, for many saints start out as sinners. Yet by the grace of God they eventually learn to think according to the mind of Christ. Saints love what Our Lord loves and hate what He hates. They strive to do what He commands and to avoid what he forbids. They set their minds above, on the things of the Spirit, rather than on matters of the flesh:

"For those who live according to the flesh set their minds on the things of the flesh, but those who live according to the Spirit set their minds on the things of the Spirit. To set the mind on the flesh is death, but to set the mind on the Spirit is life and peace. For the mind that is set on the flesh is hostile to God; it does not submit to God's law, indeed it cannot; and those who are in the flesh cannot please God." - Romans 8:5-8 RSV

If you have been following these meditations and their resolutions, you have already begun to renew your mind. When you started to turn to Christ for joy and fulfillment in life rather than to vice, that was a change of mind. When you rejected the lies that kept you captive to sin and began to embrace the Truth, you began to change the way you thought about sin. Every time you have meditated on, memorized or prayed a passage of Sacred Scripture, it has helped renew your mind little by little.

Continue doing these things. If you don't already do so, start reading Scripture every day. The daily Mass readings are excellent for this. Don't just read it as any book, but as nourishment for your soul. Learn a method of meditation, such as lectio divina or one of the three methods of prayer found in the Spiritual Exercises of St. Ignatius of Loyola. Use it while reading Scripture. God's holy Word really has the power to cleanse your mind of impure thoughts.

How can a young man keep his way pure? By guarding it according to your word...
I have laid up your word in my heart, that I might not sin against you. - Psalm 119 [118]:9, 11 RSV

You might also listen to recordings of Sacred Scripture while driving in your car or working around your house or office. Or write Bible quotes on index cards and memorize them during your spare time. The Family Life Center sells two sets of Scripture memory cards for this purpose called *Pure Mind Scriptural Memory Kits: Key Verses for a Pure Mind,* which you may find helpful. (See the *Resources* section in back for contact information)

Other devotional practices, such as the Jesus Prayer or praying with icons, will also help cleanse and renew your mind. Edifying spiritual reading and stories from the lives of the saints are an excellent source of holy thoughts and inspiration. Louis of Granada writes: *'Endeavor to keep your mind occupied with good thoughts and your body employed in some profitable exercise, "for the devil," says St. Bernard, "fills idle souls with bad thoughts, so that they may be thinking of evil if they do not actually commit it."*[xlix]

If you have not already done so, you will have to begin avoiding impure thoughts and fantasies as much as possible. If you are married, start focusing your thoughts on your spouse alone. If you are unmarried, you must stop entertaining impure thoughts. If a thought or image pops into your head, do not take pleasure in it, but turn away and pray for God's help to avoid temptation. Ask Him for the grace to hate the sins you once enjoyed, even as He hates them. Ask Him to help you think the way He does about sin. Don't forget to replace sinful thoughts with holy ones; give your mind something else to think about!

> God of my heart!--But can I dare
> To give this heart to Thee,
> With thoughts and wishes lurking there
> I blush myself to see.
> A heart, O God, clean, undefiled,
> Create in me I pray.
> Then shall I be indeed Thy child,
> And childlike duty pay.
>
> Would that the purest thoughts alone
> Found shelter in this breast,
> So oft Thy Eucharistic throne,
> The Dove's beloved nest.
> O God! Thou knowest, knowest well
> Thy feeble creature's heart.
> Yet here Thou dost delight to dwell,
> Come, Lord, and never part.[1]

In general, we should not allow our minds to dwell on anything base or evil, taking instead Paul's advice to the Philippians: *Whatever things are true, whatever honorable, whatever just, whatever holy, whatever lovable, whatever of good repute, if there be any virtue, if anything worthy of praise, think upon these things.... And the God of peace will be with you.* (Phil. 4:8-9)

O Almighty and most Merciful God, graciously hear my prayer and free my heart from the temptation of evil thoughts, that I may become a worthy dwelling place for Thy Holy Spirit. Amen.[li]

Resolution: Memorize the above verse from Philippians, and put it into practice. Do the other things this meditation recommends. Continue drawing close to Jesus, humbling yourself before Him, entrusting yourself to Mary, regretting your past sins, turning away from temptation and avoiding occasions of sin.

Saint Ignatius of Loyola, pray for us.

TRACK YOUR PROGRESS: *Since reading the last meditation, how many times have I:*

a) deliberately touched myself impurely while awake? ___0 ___1 ___2 ✓3 or more times
b) deliberately viewed indecent pictures or movies? ✓0 ___1 ___2 ___3 or more times
c) committed unchaste acts with others? ✓0 ___1 ___2 ___3 or more times
d) deliberately entertained/enjoyed impure thoughts? ✓0 ___1 ___2 ___3 or more times

e) When was the last time I went to Confession?_____ to Mass? *YESTERDAY*

MEDITATION 19: WHAT IF I FALL AGAIN?

Have mercy on me, O God, in your goodness; in the greatness of your compassion wipe out my offense. Thoroughly wash me from my guilt and of my sin cleanse me. For I acknowledge my offense, and my sin is before me always. Against you only have I sinned, and done what is evil in your sight. – Psalm 50 (51):3-6

Prayer: *O my God, I am heartily sorry and beg pardon for all my sins, not so much because these sins bring suffering and Hell to me, but because they have crucified my loving Savior Jesus Christ and offended Thy infinite Goodness. I firmly resolve, with the help of Thy grace to confess my sins, to do penance and to amend my life.*[lii]

Though we hope it won't happen, it is possible that you may fall during this series of meditations. If so, don't despair. Instead, follow the excellent advice of Dom Lorenzo Scupoli, in the twenty-sixth chapter of *The Spiritual Combat*.

When you realize that you have been wounded by sin, whether through weakness or malice, do not lose your courage or become panic-stricken. Turn to God with a great and humble confidence saying: "See, O Master, what I am able to do. When I rely on my own strength, I commit nothing but sins."

Meditating on this, recognize the extent of your humiliation and express to our Lord your sorrow for the offense committed. With an unperturbed heart, indict your vicious passions, especially the one that has occasioned your fall, and confess: "O Lord, I would not have stopped at this had not Your goodness restrained me."

Give thanks to God, and more than ever give to Him the complete love of your heart. What generosity on His part! You have offended Him and, despite this, He extends His hand to prevent another fall.

With your heart full of confidence in His infinite mercy, say to Him: "O Master, show forth Thy Divinity and pardon me! Never permit me to be separated from Thee, deprived of Thy help; never permit me to offend Thee again!"

After you have done this, do not upset yourself by examining whether God has forgiven you or not. This is a complete loss of time, an outcropping of pride, a spiritual sickness, an illusion of the devil who seeks to harm you under cover of an apparently good act. Place yourself in the merciful arms of God, and plunge into your usual duties, as though nothing had happened.

The number of times during the day that you fall cannot shake the basis of a true confidence in Him. Return after your second, your third, your last defeat, with the same confidence. Each lapse will teach you greater contempt for your own strength, greater hatred for sin, and, at the same time, will give you greater prudence.

This will dismay your enemy because it is pleasing to God. The devil will be thrown into confusion, baffled by one he has so often overcome. As a result, he will bend every effort to induce you to change your tactics. He frequently succeeds when a strict watch is not kept over the tendencies of the heart.

The efforts expended in conquering yourself must correspond to the difficulties encountered. A single performance of this exercise is not sufficient. It should be frequently repeated though but one fault has been committed.

Consequently, if you have fallen, if you are greatly perturbed and your confidence is shaken, you must first recover your peace of mind and confidence in God. Raise your heart to Heaven. Be convinced that the trouble that sometimes follows the commission of a fault is not so much a sorrow for having offended God, but is a fear of punishment.

The way to recover this peace is to forget, for the moment, your fault and to concentrate on the ineffable goodness of God and His burning desire to pardon the gravest sinners. He uses every possible means to call the sinners back, to unite them entirely to Himself, to sanctify them in this life, and make them eternally happy in the next.

This consideration, or others of its kind, will bring peace back to your soul. Then you may reconsider the malice of your error in the light of what has been said above.

Finally, when you approach the Sacrament of Penance - I advise you to do this frequently - recall all of your sins and sincerely confess them. Reawaken your sorrow for having committed them, and renew your resolutions to amend your life in the future.[liii]

Now, the Devil may try to take advantage of your fall by telling you: "Since you must go to Confession anyway, you might as well sin some more before then!" *This is yet another lie don't fall for it!* You don't know when you will die, so you can't be sure you will even live to confess to a priest. This is why you must repent and get right with God *right now* instead of compounding your sin. You can say an Act of Perfect Contrition *at any time* and resolve to go to Confession as soon as possible. In the event that you die before receiving the Sacrament of Penance, that Act of Perfect Contrition will actually remove those sins. Since even conditional forgiveness is possible *right now*, you have no excuse whatsoever to keep sinning.

Finally, don't give up! Don't despair of the Divine Mercy. Don't feel so ashamed that you stay away from Confession. In fact, sometimes our extreme disappointment with ourselves when we sin is itself a sign of Pride. Perhaps you expected too much of yourself. But Our Lord has no such illusions; He knows exactly how frail you are spiritually, and is tremendously merciful. *"As a father has compassion on his children, so the Lord has compassion on those who fear him, For he knows how we are formed; he remembers that we are dust"* (Ps. 102[103]:13-14). If nothing else, a fall shows you that you really are weak and desperately need His forgiveness and grace. This may be why God allows us to fall occasionally; to teach us not to trust in ourselves but in Him.

And if we are ever worsted in the struggle, we must not forget that the Immaculate Heart of Mary is also the sure refuge of sinners, that through the invocation of Her Name we shall find the grace of repentance, followed by the grace of absolution. Who could better ensure our perseverance than the Virgin most Faithful?[liv]

Resolution: If you are reading this meditation because you have fallen, start over tomorrow with the first meditation. If not, continue with your previous resolutions. If you do fall in the future, return to this meditation. Never stop drawing close to Jesus and Mary.

All you holy penitent saints, pray for us.

TRACK YOUR PROGRESS: *Since reading the last meditation, how many times have I:*

a) deliberately touched myself impurely while awake? ___0 ___1 ___2 ___3 or more times
b) deliberately viewed indecent pictures or movies? ___0 ___1 ___2 ___3 or more times
c) committed unchaste acts with others? ___0 ___1 ___2 ___3 or more times
d) deliberately entertained/enjoyed impure thoughts? ___0 ___1 ___2 ___3 or more times

e) When was the last time I went to Confession?_____ to Mass?_____

MEDITATION 20: THE CHURCH MILITANT

Let us consider how to stir up one another to love and good works, not neglecting to meet together, as is the habit of some, but encouraging one another, and all the more as you see the Day drawing near. - Hebrews 10:24-25

Prayer: *Come Spirit of Chastity and fill the hearts of your faithful. Come, Holy Spirit, come by means of the powerful Intercession of the Immaculate Heart of Mary, your well beloved spouse.*[lv]

The Catholic Church is a community, a family; a Mystical Body made up of many members. None of us need try to live a Christian life all by ourselves, for we have many brothers and sisters, many members of the Mystical Body of Christ to help us all along the way.

In the Introduction you were counseled to find a partner who can pray for you and hold you responsible daily for your actions. Hopefully you have done so. Though your priest-confessor, spiritual director or psychological counselor could certainly fulfill that role for you, he might be too busy to talk to you every single day. If that is the case, then a religious brother or sister, a spiritual director, your spouse (if he or she knows about your struggles), or a spiritual friend of the same gender as yourself can be just as effective for this particular purpose.

In the fifth meditation we saw how the Sacrament of Penance brings our deeds of darkness out into the Light of Christ. Though telling our sins to a fellow lay person does not give us the benefit of the sacramental graces of Reconciliation (and is certainly no substitute for that Sacrament), it still helps expose our secret sins and so robs them of some of their power over us. So even if you *are* accountable daily to a priest-confessor, having an extra friend or two to talk to wouldn't hurt. In fact, they may come in handy if your confessor is suddenly unavailable for a day or so; after all, nowadays priests are awfully busy.

You really do need someone to talk to, to encourage you when you succeed, to strengthen your resolve and pray for you when you are tempted, to hold you accountable for your activities. If you don't have such a person, you cannot expect to overcome this sin. You can't do this on your own; nor does God expect you to struggle against the Enemy all by yourself. That is why He gave you a family, both in Heaven and on earth!

Here is another instructive anecdote from the Desert Fathers:

Another brother goaded by sexual thoughts got up in the middle of the night and ran to an old man to confess and receive counsel. Helped and strengthened he returned to his cell. And behold the devil tempted him again, so that again he ran to the old man. This happened several times. The old man by no means discouraged him, but gave him appropriate advice, "Don't give in to the devil, don't relax your mind, but as often as the devil is troublesome, come to me so that he may be rebuked and put to flight, for nothing wearies the devil so much as having his attacks brought out into the open, and nothing rejoices him so much as thoughts being concealed."[lvi]

The Scripture quote above tells Christians to "stir up one another to love and good works" and encourage one another. We need each other. Like coals in a fire, if one gets separated from the other coals it will go out, but if it stays together with the rest it will continue to glow, for the coals preserve each other's heat. Even so, if we separate ourselves from other Christians our zeal will grow cold, but if we help and encourage one another our fervor will increase.

Also, you may have given up some of your old acquaintances because they were an occasion of sin for you. If so, do not neglect to make new acquaintances of people who seek to live upright lives. The company we keep is very important; as bad company can corrupt ones morals, so good company can aid ones journey to Heaven.

So perhaps you can join an apostolate, Scripture study or prayer group in your parish, or even start one yourself. Or if your parish has a food pantry or soup kitchen, get involved in that. Fellowship with others and helping those in need can actually curb ones selfish tendencies, which, as we have seen, is another trait associated with habitual sins of the flesh. It will also leave one with less idle time in which to sin. Do not underestimate the value of this!

Most of all, you need prayer. Consider having a Mass said for your intentions; you don't necessarily have to specify what those intentions are. Steve Wood of the Family Life Center suggests that those who struggle with habitual sin get in touch with a contemplative religious order and ask them to pray for their intentions. This is very excellent advice. By their lives of constant prayer, contemplative religious orders generate a tremendous amount of spiritual benefit for the Church. Why not take advantage of that?

Resolution: If you have not yet done so, find a partner to hold you responsible daily for your actions. Consider doing some of the other suggestions in this meditation, and continue as always with previous resolutions.

Jesus, Mary, Joseph, I offer you my heart and my soul

TRACK YOUR PROGRESS: *Since reading the last meditation, how many times have I:*

a) deliberately touched myself impurely while awake? ✓0 ___1 ___2 ___3 or more times
b) deliberately viewed indecent pictures or movies? ✓0 ___1 ___2 ___3 or more times
c) committed unchaste acts with others? ✓0 ___1 ___2 ___3 or more times
d) deliberately entertained/enjoyed impure thoughts? ✓0 ___1 ___2 ___3 or more times

e) When was the last time I went to Confession? _TODAY_ to Mass? _YESTERDAY_

The great weapon of the Church Militant.

MEDITATION 21: MOST PURE HEART OF MARY

Say to Wisdom, "You are my sister!" and call Understanding, "Friend!" That she may keep you from another's wife, and from the adulteress with her smooth words. - Proverbs 7:4-5

Prayer: *O Heart most pure of the Blessed Virgin Mary, obtain for me from Jesus a pure and humble heart.* - Raccolta #387

Toward the beginning of the twentieth century, a century that would be marked by a tremendous increase in impurity, Our Lady appeared at Fatima, Portugal. Lucia, Jacinta and Francisco, the children who saw her there, reported that Blessed Mother showed them a terrifying vision of Hell and sinners in torment there. She would later tell Jacinta that more souls go to Hell for sins of the flesh than for any other kind of sin. Yet Our Lady of Fatima also revealed that God had a plan to save souls from the coming torrent of impurity:

> "You have seen hell where the souls of poor sinners go. To save them, God wishes to establish in the world devotion to my Immaculate Heart. If what I say to you is done, many souls will be saved and there will be peace."

What could devotion to the Immaculate Heart of Mary have to do with combating sins against purity? When the Vatican released the Third Secret of Fatima in 2000, the Congregation for the Doctrine of the Faith (CDF) promulgated a document called "The Message of Fatima," which contains the following explanation of this statement of Our Lady:

> In biblical language, the "heart" indicates the centre of human life, the point where reason, will, temperament and sensitivity converge, where the person finds his unity and his interior orientation. According to Matthew 5:8, the "immaculate heart" is a heart which, with God's grace, has come to perfect interior unity and therefore "sees God." To be "devoted" to the Immaculate Heart of Mary means therefore to embrace this attitude of heart, which makes the fiat – "your will be done" - the defining centre of one's whole life.[lvii]

The Heart of the Blessed Virgin Mary is the epitome of the "clean heart" extolled in Sacred Scripture. This is why it is called the "Immaculate Heart," for *immaculate* means "impeccably clean, pure, spotless; free from any stain or blemish." Her Heart is so pure that she doesn't just stand in God's holy place - she *is* His Holy Place, the very Tabernacle that housed Him for nine months. Mary not only saw God, but held Him in her hands, nursed Him and cared for Him during most of His earthly life.

Devotion to the Immaculate Heart doesn't just mean displaying a picture of her Heart and praying to her. Yes, that is part of it, an external manifestation of our love for the Heart of our heavenly Mother. But the very essence of devotion to the Immaculate Heart of Mary is to be "pure of heart" oneself, to imitate Mary's purity and loving obedience to God's will. This is what God wants us to do to overcome lust.

> Most compassionate Heart of Mary, Queen of Virgins, watch over my mind and heart and preserve me from the deluge of impurity which you lamented so sorrowfully at Fatima. I want to be pure like you. I want to atone for the many crimes committed against Jesus and you. I want to call down upon this country and the whole world, the peace of God in Justice and Charity.[lviii]

Those struggling with impurity would do well to cultivate a particular devotion to the Most Pure Heart of Mary, as she requested at Fatima.

O Immaculate Heart of Mary, Virgin Most Pure, mindful of the terrible moral dangers threatening on all sides, and aware of my own human weakness, I voluntarily place myself, body and soul, this day and always, under your loving maternal care and protection.

I consecrate to you my body, with all its members, asking you to help me never to use it as an occasion of sin to others. Help me to remember that my body is "The Temple of the Holy Ghost," and to use it according to God's Holy Will, for my own personal salvation, and the salvation of others.

I consecrate to you my soul, asking you to watch over it and to bring it home safe to you and to Jesus in Heaven for all eternity.

Oh Mary, my Mother, all that I am, all that I have is yours. Keep me and guard me under your mantle of mercy as your personal property and possession. "Jesus, Mary, I love you, save souls!"[xlix]

The Feast of the Immaculate Heart of Mary falls on the day after the Feast of the Sacred Heart of Jesus. There is also a feast day in honor of the Purity of the Blessed Virgin Mary. It is a local commemoration observed on either 16 October or the third Sunday of October. Perhaps you would like to do something special on one of these days, such as go to Mass, renew your baptismal vows or consecration to Mary, etc.

Resolution: If you don't already have one, find a lovely image of the Immaculate Heart. Set it up in your home and look at it often, especially in times of temptation. You may wish to carry a smaller picture in you wallet or purse, or keep one by your computer for when you surf the Internet. Ask Our Lady to acquire from God for you the grace of a clean heart, and to keep you close to her Divine Son.

For more on how devotion to the Immaculate Heart of Mary and praying the Rosary bring about cleanness of heart, read the book Sex and the Mysteries, by John M. Haffert.

Immaculate Heart of Mary, pray for us who have recourse to thee.

TRACK YOUR PROGRESS: *Since reading the last meditation, how many times have I:*

a) deliberately touched myself impurely while awake? ___0 ___1 ___2 ✓3 or more times
b) deliberately viewed indecent pictures or movies? ___0 ___1 ✓2 ___3 or more times
c) committed unchaste acts with others? ✓0 ___1 ___2 ___3 or more times
d) deliberately entertained/enjoyed impure thoughts? ✓0 ___1 ___2 ___3 or more times

e) When was the last time I went to Confession? YESTERDAY to Mass? SUNDAY

As a closing prayer today, instead of the *Prayer for Purity* you may wish to pray the traditional *Prayer to Mary for the Feast of the Immaculate Conception,* found in Appendix IV.

MEDITATION 22: JOSEPH MOST CHASTE

An angel of the Lord appeared to him in a dream, saying, "Do not be afraid, Joseph, son of David, to take to thee Mary thy wife, for that which is begotten in her is of the Holy Spirit. And she shall bring forth a son, and thou shalt call his name Jesus, for he shall save his people from their sins." - St. Matthew 1:20-21

Prayer: *Blessed be Saint Joseph, her most chaste spouse! St. Joseph, guardian of Mary's virginity, guard thou my soul from every sin.*[ix]

Saint Joseph was the earthly protector of Mary most Pure and guardian of Our Lord Jesus Christ, the Lover of Chastity. His official litany invokes him as *Chaste guardian of the Virgin, Joseph most chaste* and *Protector of Virgins*. These titles show why he is especially associated with the preservation of purity and chastity. He is a particularly excellent role model for men in this regard.

A traditional *Novena in Honor of St. Joseph* invokes this wonderful saint on day four as "Saint Joseph, Model of Purity." Here is an excerpt from that novena:

"How beautiful is the chaste generation!" (Wisdom iv), "The whole weight of gold is as nothing in comparison with a pure soul" (Sir. xxv).

Saint Joseph was preeminent in purity because he feared God and faithfully observed His holy law; because he safeguarded his virtue by fear of the Sovereign Good and by prudence; because he sheltered it under the virginity of Mary, and felt the influence of Jesus, the divine Son of all sanctity.

How pure must he have been who was to become the worthy spouse of the Immaculate Virgin! How holy must he have been whose relations with the thrice-holy God were so intimate.

Prayer: O Joseph, help me to understand the excellence of thy purity and how dear it is to the heart of God. Teach me to preserve carefully this delicate virtue under the shadow of the fear of God; to safeguard it by prayer, by vigilance, by shunning the world, by careful watch over my heart and my senses. Grant that I may henceforward close my heart to all disorderly affections; that I may deserve to enjoy like thee upon earth the friendship and intimacy of Jesus, and that it may be given to me one day to sing in Heaven the canticle reserved for Virgins.

Cincture or Cord of St. Joseph

The Cincture or Cord of St. Joseph is another sacramental that might aid you in your struggle against impurity. It was invented in 1637 by an Augustinian nun in Belgium named Sister Elizabeth. She was very sick and in a lot of pain. The doctors had declared her condition terminal and given up, but Sr. Elizabeth asked St. Joseph to intercede for her healing. She made a white cincture with seven knots on one end, in honor of the seven joys and seven sorrows of St. Joseph, had it blessed and wore it around her waist. Shortly afterward, while wearing it and praying intensely before his statue, the pain stopped and she was cured.

Though this sacramental originated with a physical healing, its use eventually became associated with the virtue of purity, so Cords of St. Joseph have sometimes been called "chastity cords."[†] This happened in part because of St. Joseph's renowned purity and in part because the cincture in general is a symbol of chastity. In the past, when a priest tied a cincture around his waist while vesting for Mass, he said the prayer, "Gird me, O Lord, with the cincture of purity and extinguish in my heart the fire of concupiscence so that, the virtue of continence and chastity always abiding in my heart, I may better serve Thee."

---

† Some of the information here about St. Joseph's cords is taken from <http://www.osjoseph.org/stjoseph/liturgy/partB.php>

As with all sacramentals, the Cord of St. Joseph is not magical; it is a sign of the wearer's trust in God and dependence upon the intercession of the foster father of Our Lord. Its efficacy depends on the faith and prayers of the wearer. Devout and prayerful use of the Cord of St. Joseph is said to provide the following graces: *The special protection of Saint Joseph, Purity of soul, Preservation or recovery of chastity, Final perseverance,* and *Particular assistance at the hour of death* (since he is also Patron of the Dying).

This cincture is associated with the Archconfraternity of St. Joseph, and one must join that Archconfraternity in order to gain the indulgences associated with wearing it. However, non-members can also wear the cord simply as an act of devotion to St. Joseph and to gain the virtue of purity.

Some religious article suppliers sell Cords of St. Joseph, or you can make one yourself. Tie and braid together three long strands of white 100% cotton twine or yarn. Tie seven knots, spaced slightly apart, at the other end when done. After all the braiding and knotting the cord should be long enough to fit around your waist with the seven knots hanging down, so make sure the original three strands are long enough for that. Have the finished cincture blessed by a priest and wear it around your waist.

Pray the *Gloria patri* (Glory Be) seven times every day in honor of St. Joseph. Use the seven knots on the cincture to count the prayers, as you would on rosary beads. After the seventh *Glory Be*, say the following *Prayer for Purity*:

O Guardian of Virgins and holy Father St. Joseph, into whose faithful keeping were entrusted Christ Jesus, Innocence itself, and Mary, Virgin of virgins, I pray and beseech thee by these dear pledges, Jesus and Mary, that, being preserved from all uncleanness, I may with spotless mind, pure heart and chaste body ever serve Jesus and Mary most chastely all the days of my life. Amen.

It is traditional to meditate on the *Seven Sorrows and Joys of St. Joseph* while praying the seven *Gloria Patri's*: They are:

1. St. Joseph's doubt (Mt. 1:19) and the Angel's Message (Mt. 1:20)
2. The poverty of Christ's birthplace (Lk. 2:7) and the Nativity of our Savior (Lk. 2:7)
3. Our Lord's Circumcision (Lk. 2:21) and the Most Holy Name of Jesus (Mt. 1:25)
4. The prophecy of Simeon that many would fall (Lk. 2:34) and that many would rise (Lk. 2:34)
5. The Flight into Egypt (Mt. 2:14) and the Overthrow of the Egyptian idols (Isa. 19:1)
6. The Return from Egypt (Mt. 2:22) and Life with Jesus and Mary (Lk. 2:39)
7. The loss of the Child Jesus (Lk. 2:45) and the Finding of Jesus in the Temple (Lk. 2:46)

Resolution: Cultivate a devotion to Joseph most Chaste, and consider wearing the Cord of St. Joseph. Continue with past resolutions.

Joseph most chaste, pray for us.

TRACK YOUR PROGRESS: *Since reading the last meditation, how many times have I:*

a) deliberately touched myself impurely while awake? ✓0 ___1 ___2 ___3 or more times
b) deliberately viewed indecent pictures or movies? ✓0 ___1 ___2 ___3 or more times
c) committed unchaste acts with others? ✓0 ___1 ___2 ___3 or more times
d) deliberately entertained/enjoyed impure thoughts? ✓0 ___1 ___2 ___3 or more times

e) When was the last time I went to Confession? _YESTERDAY_ to Mass?_2 DAYS AGO_

As a closing prayer today, instead of the *Prayer for Purity* you may wish to pray the *Prayer to Our Lady and St. Joseph for Purity,* found in Appendix IV.

MEDITATION 23: YOUR GUARDIAN ANGEL

For to his angels he has given command about you, that they guard you in all your ways. Upon their hands they shall bear you up, lest you dash your foot against a stone. You shall tread upon the asp and the viper; you shall trample down the lion and the dragon. - Psalm 90[91]:11-13

Prayer: *O angel of Christ, holy guardian and protector of my soul and body, forgive me everything wherein I have offended you every day of my life, and protect me from all influence and temptation of the Evil One. May I never again anger God by my sins. Pray for me to the Lord, that He may make me worthy of the grace of the All Holy Trinity, and of the blessed Mother of God, and of all the saints. Amen.*[lxi]

God has graciously given each of us a heavenly companion who, though unseen, remains with us throughout our lives. We know that our Guardian Angel may help us avoid physical injury, yet he also protects us from numerous spiritual dangers, of which we are often unaware. He removes many occasions of sin, helps us resist temptation and avoid sin, inspires holy thoughts and desires, prays for us, and teaches us how to grow in holiness that we may attain Heaven. So this often-ignored friend is actually a powerful ally in your struggle for purity!

Perhaps just remembering that your Holy Angel is with you, watching everything you do, may help you avoid committing sin. Louis of Granada writes:

In all temptations, but particularly in temptations against purity, remember the presence of your guardian angel and of the devil, your accuser, for they both witness all your actions, and will render an account of them to Him who sees and judges all things. If you follow this counsel, how can you, before your accuser, your defender, and your Judge, commit a base sin, for which you would blush before the lowest of men?[lxii]

Yet more than that, your Guardian Angel offers actual assistance by his prayers and inspirations. He is very powerful, though he does have a few limitations:

Although they cannot penetrate the inner sanctuary of human hearts which God has reserved for Himself, they do all they can to help us. However, it is in our power by an act of our free will to expose our intimate thoughts to our angelic companion. And it is to our advantage for such confidence in his enlightened guidance is of great benefit to our soul. After God and our Blessed Mother, he is surely our best friend, and if we really love him, we will have no secrets to hide from him.[lxiii]

So consider disclosing your innermost thoughts to your Angel Guardian by an act of will. It may actually help him offer better prayers and guidance for you. Here is another suggestion from a spiritual writer:

Choose, therefore, sometimes a quarter of an hour, half an hour, an hour or more and, retiring apart, converse at leisure with your good Angel. Place yourself on your knees before him, prostrate yourself on the ground--for it is well to adopt this practice occasionally when alone; ask his pardon for your ingratitude; beg his holy benediction; say all that a good heart would prompt one to say to a faithful and loving friend. Speak to him at one time of your needs, of your miserable failings, of your temptations, of your weaknesses; at another of Divine love--and of the holy ways which lead to God. Converse with him sometimes concerning the offenses which men commit against their Sovereign Lord Jesus and His most blessed Mother; at other times, consider in detail the obligations you are under to him, his goodness to you, his beauty, his perfections, his admirable qualities. Deal with him as with a kind father, as with a loving mother, a true brother, an incomparable friend, a zealous lover, a vigilant pastor, a charitable guide, the witness of your most important secrets, a learned physician to heal all your ailments, an advocate, a powerful protector and a compassionate judge; invoke him in all these characters, and in others which your love will suggest to you. They will serve you as so many considerations which will make you pass your time much more agreeably than with the creatures of earth.[lxiv]

Your Guardian Angel is not your only heavenly ally. All the holy angels of God are present and willing to help His children to resist temptation, as this story from the Desert Fathers illustrates:

It happened that Abba Moses was struggling with temptations against chastity. Unable to remain any longer in his cell, he went and told Abba Isidore. The old man took Moses out onto the terrace and said to him, "Look towards the west." He looked and saw hordes of demons flying about and making a noise before launching an attack. Then Abba Isidore said to him, "Look towards the east." He turned and saw an innumerable multitude of holy angels shining with glory. Abba Isidore said, "See, these are sent by the Lord to the saints to bring them help, while those in the West fight against them. Those who are with us are more in number than they are". Then Abba Moses gave thanks to God, plucked up courage and returned to his cell.[lxv]

So you would do well to also ask the help and prayers of other holy angels in times of temptation.

Resolution: Thank your holy Guardian Angel for his constant help and prayers. If you are not already devoted to him, befriend your heavenly companion. Ask him to help you overcome habitual sins against purity. Remember his presence when you are tempted and ask for his aid.

My holy Guardian Angel, pray for me.

TRACK YOUR PROGRESS: *Since reading the last meditation, how many times have I:*

a) deliberately touched myself impurely while awake? ___0 ___1 ___2 ✓3 or more times
b) deliberately viewed indecent pictures or movies? ___0 ___1 ___2 ✓3 or more times
c) committed unchaste acts with others? ✓0 ___1 ___2 ___3 or more times
d) deliberately entertained/enjoyed impure thoughts? ___0 ___1 ___2 ✓3 or more times

e) When was the last time I went to Confession? _2 DAYS AGO_ to Mass? _YESTERDAY_

As a closing prayer today, instead of the *Prayer for Purity* you may wish to pray the *Prayer to Ones Guardian Angel,* found in Appendix IV.

MEDITATION 24: CLOUD OF WITNESSES

Therefore let us also, having such a cloud of witnesses over us, put away every encumbrance and the sin entangling us, and run with perseverance to the fight set before us. – Hebrews 12:1

Prayer: *All ye holy virgins, who follow the divine Lamb whithersoever He goeth, be ever watchful over me a sinner, lest I should fail in thought, in word, or in deed, and lest at any time I should depart from the most chaste Heart of Jesus.*[lxvi]

Never forget that you are not fighting this battle all alone. The saints and angels in Heaven are always ready to help us. Consider these words from *The Spiritual Combat:*

THE FIRST THING to do when you awake is to open the windows of your soul. Consider yourself as on the field of battle, facing the enemy and bound by the iron-clad law - either fight or die.

Imagine the enemy before you, that particular vice or disorderly passion that you are trying to conquer - imagine this hideous opponent is about to overwhelm you. At the same time, picture at your right Jesus Christ, your Invincible Leader, accompanied by the Blessed Virgin, St. Joseph, whole companies of Angels and Saints, and particularly by the glorious Archangel Michael. At your left is Lucifer and his troops, ready to support the passion or vice you are fighting and resolved to do anything to cause your defeat.

Imagine your guardian Angel thus spurring you on: "Today you must fight to conquer your enemy and anyone who tries to ruin you. Be courageous. Do not be afraid or cowardly. Christ your Captain is here with all the power of Heaven to protect you from the enemy, and to see that they never conquer you, either by brute power, or by trickery. Hold your ground! Do violence to yourself, no matter how painful it is. Call out for the help of Jesus and Mary and all the Saints. If you do this, you will be victorious."

It does not matter how weak you are - how strong the enemy may seem, either in number or in power. Do not be discouraged. The help you have from Heaven is more powerful than all that Hell can send to destroy the grace of God in your soul. God, the Creator and the Redeemer, is Almighty and more desirous of your salvation than the devil can be of your destruction.[lxvii]

We can benefit greatly from the example and intercession of saints who struggled against and overcame temptations to impurity while on earth. Some patron saints of those who suffer temptations and of reformed sinners are: Blessed Angela of Foligno, Saints Margaret of Cortona, Mary of Egypt and Mary Magdalen. To this list we might add St. Augustine of Hippo, since he repented from a wild youth. We will learn more about some of these saints in later meditations.

In his Autobiography, St. Anthony Mary Claret recounts a severe temptation against purity that he experienced in his youth:

I had the following experience while I was in my second year of philosophy at Vic. That winter I had caught a bad cold and was ordered to bed; so I obeyed. One day as I lay there at about ten-thirty in the morning, I felt a terrible temptation. I turned to Mary, called on my guardian angel, and prayed to all my name-saints as well as to those whom I have a special devotion. I fixed my attention on indifferent objects so as to distract myself and forget about the temptation. I made the sign of the cross on my forehead so that the Lord would free me from evil thoughts, but everything I did was in vain.

Finally I turned over on my other side, to see if the temptation would go away, when suddenly I saw the Blessed Virgin Mary, very beautiful and gracious. Her dress was crimson, her mantle blue, and in her arms I was a huge garland of the most beautiful roses. I had seen lovely artificial and real roses in Barcelona but none as lovely as these. How beautiful it all was! As I lay face up in bed, I saw myself as a beautiful white child kneeling with hands joined. I never lost sight of the Blessed Virgin, on whom I kept my eyes fixed. I remember distinctly thinking to myself, "She is a woman and yet she doesn't give you any evil thoughts; on the contrary, she has taken them all away from you." The Blessed Virgin spoke to me and said, "Anthony, this crown is yours if you overcome." Next I saw the Blessed Virgin place on my head the crown of roses that she held in her right hand (besides the garland, which she held between her arm and her right side). I saw myself crowned with roses in the person of that little child, and I was speechless.

I also saw a band of saints standing at her right hand, in an attitude of prayer. I did not recognise them, except that one seemed to be St. Stephen. I believed then, as I do now, that those were my patron saints praying and interceding for me so that I would not fall into temptation. Then, on my left, I saw a great crowd of demons in battle array, like soldiers who fall back and close ranks again after a battle. I said to myself, "What a host of them there is - and so fearful!" During all of this I remained as if caught by surprise, without quite realising what was happening to me. As soon as it had passed, I felt free of the temptation and filled with a joy so deep that I could not grasp what had been going on within me.

I am quite sure that I was neither asleep nor suffering from dizziness or anything else that could have caused a state of illusion. What made me believe that what had happened was real, and a special grace from Mary, was the fact that from that moment on I was free from temptation against chastity. If later there have been any such temptations, they have been so insignificant that they hardly deserve to be called temptations. Glory to Mary! Victory through Mary![lxviii]

His story is very instructive. It not only illustrates various methods of fighting temptation: Prayer to Mary, ones Guardian Angel and patron saints; distraction, devoutly crossing oneself on the forehead, etc.. It also shows how the saints in Heaven aid us with their prayers when we are tempted. Finally, it shows that God wishes to reward us for resisting temptation.

Let us not be tempted to jealousy when we hear of saints like Anthony Mary Claret, who after experiencing a severe temptation against purity were never tempted again. We all have our crosses to bear. For some of us that cross is a problem with lust, but even those of us who don't struggle in that area must endure other temptations and battles throughout life. No Christian ever has it easy. God, in His wisdom, has a reason for allowing us each to endure certain trials rather than others. Let us trust in Him.

Resolution: Ask all your heavenly patrons - name saint(s), patrons of your occupation, etc. - to pray for your ultimate victory over habitual sin. Pray especially to some of the patron saints of those who suffer temptation to impurity. In time of temptation, remember that you are not alone; the armies of Heaven are with you and will help you fight. Don't forget their concern for you.

Saint Anthony Mary Claret, pray for us.

TRACK YOUR PROGRESS: *Since reading the last meditation, how many times have I:*

a) deliberately touched myself impurely while awake?   ✓0 ___1 ___2 ___3 or more times
b) deliberately viewed indecent pictures or movies?   ✓0 ___1 ___2 ___3 or more times
c) committed unchaste acts with others?   ✓0 ___1 ___2 ___3 or more times
d) deliberately entertained/enjoyed impure thoughts?   ✓0 ___1 ___2 ___3 or more times

e) When was the last time I went to Confession? 3 DAYS AGO to Mass? 2 DAYS AGO

MEDITATION 25: THE WHOLE ARMOR OF GOD

For the rest, brethren, be strengthened in the Lord and in the might of his power. Put on the armour of God, that you may be able to stand against the wiles of the devil. For our wrestling is not against flesh and blood, but against the Principalities and the Powers, against the world-rulers of this darkness, against the spiritual forces of wickedness on high." - Ephesians 6:10-12

Prayer: *August Queen of Heaven! Sovereign Mistress of the angels! You who from the beginning have received from God the power and mission to crush the head of Satan, we humbly beseech you to send your holy Legions, that, under your command and by your power, they may pursue the evil spirits, encounter them on every side, resist their bold attacks and drive them hence into the abyss of eternal woe. Amen.*

Never forget that you are not merely trying to overcome a bad habit. You are waging a spiritual battle for your very soul. If you have already gained some victories in this struggle, you better believe that the Devil is infuriated with you. It is a good thing that you have Mary, the angels and saints as heavenly allies, for were it not for their prayers and protection you would have fallen many more times than you actually have!

You, too, must participate in this spiritual struggle, for you registered as a soldier of Christ at your Confirmation. Even as an earthly soldier would never go into battle without his armor, so you must *"take up the armor of God, that you may be able to resist in the evil day, and stand in all things perfect"* (Eph. 6:13). St. Paul describes this spiritual armor in Ephesians 6:14-18, so let us now study that passage:

Stand, therefore, having girded your loins with truth.... In St. Paul's day, men wore loose garments called tunics. If they wanted to do some difficult or strenuous work, they had to tie the tunic close to the body with a belt; which restrained the garment and enabled them to move more freely. This practice, called "girding ones loins," eventually became a figure of speech that meant "getting ready for action." Here, St. Paul writes that the first thing a soldier of Christ must do is "gird his loins" - get ready for spiritual battle!

St. Thomas Aquinas believes that this spiritual "girding the loins" symbolically relates to chastity: "In spiritual warfare it is first necessary to check carnal desires, just as the nearest enemy must be conquered first. This is done by bridling the loins in which sensuality thrives; such girding is done through temperance which is opposed to gluttony and sensuality."[lxix] It is no coincidence that the cincture, worn by religious and some devout lay people, is symbolic both of this piece of spiritual armor and of the virtue of chastity.

St. Paul further writes that you are to gird your loins with **truth.** In the third meditation we saw how putting our faith in lies leads to sin, while the truth sets us free from enslavement to sin. Every time you prayerfully repeat your list of truths, you "gird your loins with truth" - prepare yourself to counter satanic lies and temptations with the Truth.

And having put on the breastplate of justice.... The Catholic RSV renders this as "breastplate of righteousness," for justice in this context means righteousness. When Christ *justifies* us we become the very *righteousness* of God in Him (2 Cor. 5:21), filled with sanctifying grace. St. Paul likens this to a breastplate, the piece of armor that protects the heart. One must remain in a state of grace in order to wage effective spiritual warfare, otherwise you are going into battle without your breastplate! So be sure to avoid mortal sin and go to Confession regularly. The Brown Scapular is an apt symbol of this piece of armor, since those who wear it must remain in a state of grace in order to gain its spiritual benefits.

And having your feet shod with the readiness of the gospel of peace.... The Gospel of Jesus Christ is the Good News of His life, death and resurrection. St. Paul calls it the *gospel of peace* (Rom. 10:15) for through the Gospel we gain peace with God, within ourselves and with one another. Here he compares it to a soldier's footwear, which enables him to move swiftly and stand his ground in battle. We Christians must live the Gospel, walking in Christ's ways every day, following in Our Lord's steps by our good works, following Him even to Calvary by our penances and self-denial: *"Take up your cross and follow Me."* We must also be ready to proclaim the Good News of Christ to others by both word and action. By daily living and spreading the Gospel of peace, we will be ready and able to stand firm against our infernal enemy on the field of battle.

In all things taking up the shield of faith.... St. Thomas writes, "Just as a shield wards off the arrows, so faith repels what is aimed against it and gains the victory. The saints 'by faith conquered kingdoms' (Heb. 11:33), whereas we conquer the powers of darkness by the moral virtues."[lxx] **...with which you may be able to quench all the fiery darts of the most wicked one....** These "fiery darts" are temptations to sin. As St. Thomas explains:

> Thus he says *wherewith you may be able to extinguish all the fiery darts of the most wicked one,* the devil, whose arrows are certain interferences from evil angels (el. Ps. 77:49). They are fiery since evil desires burn.... These are extinguished through faith; it quenches present and transitory temptations with the eternal and spiritual blessings promised in Holy Scripture. Thus the Lord brought forward authoritative texts of Holy Scripture to oppose the devil's temptations. We ought to do the same; if tempted to gluttony, [counter it with] "Not in bread alone doth man live" (Deut. 8:3), or "The kingdom of God is not meat and drink" (Rom. 14:17). If tempted to sensuality, "Thou shalt not commit adultery" (Ex. 20:14); if to theft, "Thou shalt not steal" (Ex.. 20:15) and so on.[lxxi]

Our faith - our belief in God and in the teachings of His holy Church - enables us to extinguish temptations. If you find that praying and quoting Scripture every time you are tempted has increased your trust in God's grace and strengthened your acceptance of Catholic moral teaching, you have begun to use the shield of faith.

And take unto you the helmet of salvation.... In I Thessalonians 5:8, St. Paul more specifically calls this helmet the *hope of salvation.* Scripture presents salvation as a process: Christ saved us in the past at our Baptism (1 Pet. 3:21), He continually saves us in His Mystical Body the Church through the Sacraments (1 Cor. 15:2), and will finally save us at the hour of death if we remain in His grace (Mt. 24:13). The latter is our blessed hope of salvation: that He who began a good work in us will also perfect it (Phil 1:6). So salvation is not just something we possess now, but something we *hope* to possess in its fullness someday.

As we have seen, the virtue of hope counters despair, which is one of the most effective weapons in the Devil's arsenal. Other temptations may be like flaming arrows, flying toward you seemingly from all directions, but despair is more like a club or mace. When the Tempter says, "You can't resist this temptation, so you might as well give in!" he is attempting a "blow to the head" - a swift, lethal strike. How often we succumb to that weapon! This is why St. Paul compares hope to a helmet - the piece of armor that protects the head. The sure hope that God will not abandon us in the hour of temptation, but is able to preserve us from sin and present us spotless before the presence of His glory (Jude 1:24) protects us from the temptation to despair and to give in to the suggestions of the evil one.

So to "put on the whole armor of God" means to know the truth, strive to practice chastity, remain in a state of grace, live and preach the Gospel of peace, believe firmly in the Church's teachings - using that faith to resist temptations - and to place your hope of salvation in Jesus Christ, especially in the hour of temptation. Tomorrow's meditation will discuss our offensive weapons in the battle.

Resolution: Ask God for the grace to cultivate these virtues and qualities in your spiritual life, so that you will always wear your spiritual armor and be ready at all times for the Enemy's attacks.

Holy Mary, Terror of demons, pray for us.

TRACK YOUR PROGRESS: *Since reading the last meditation, how many times have I:*

a) deliberately touched myself impurely while awake? ✓0 __1 __2 __3 or more times
b) deliberately viewed indecent pictures or movies? ✓0 __1 __2 __3 or more times
c) committed unchaste acts with others? ✓0 __1 __2 __3 or more times
d) deliberately entertained/enjoyed impure thoughts? ✓0 __1 __2 __3 or more times

e) When was the last time I went to Confession? _YESTERDAY_ to Mass? _TODAY_

MEDITATION 26: THE WEAPONS OF OUR WARFARE

For though we walk in the flesh, we do not make war according to the flesh; for the weapons of our warfare are not carnal, but powerful before God to the demolishing of strongholds, the destroying of reasoning - yes, of every thing that exalts itself against the knowledge of God, bringing every mind into captivity to the obedience of Christ - 2 Corinthians 10:3-5

Prayer: *Saint Michael the Archangel, defend us in battle. Be our protection against the wickedness and snares of the devil. May God rebuke him, we humbly pray; and do Thou, O Prince of the heavenly host, by the power of God cast into hell Satan and all the evil spirits who prowl about the world seeking the ruin of souls.*

"Beloved, I beseech you as aliens and exiles to abstain from the passions of the flesh that wage war against your soul" (1 Pet. 2:11). Since the struggle for purity is a spiritual battle against our flesh, the world and the Devil, we obviously cannot fight it using carnal weapons like swords and guns. We must use weapons that God the Holy Spirit renders effective against our spiritual enemies. In the last meditation we considered our spiritual armor, so now let's have a look at our spiritual "arsenal."

The **Most Precious Blood of Jesus,** the Price of our salvation, is a very powerful weapon against evil (Apoc. 12:11). Do not fail to have recourse to It often. When you wake up after having an impure dream, or any time you feel tempted, ask Jesus to cleanse your mind and heart with His Blood and help you forget any impure thoughts. When the priest elevates the chalice at the Consecration, look at it and pray the words of the *Te Deum,* "We beseech Thee, therefore, help Thy servants whom Thou hast redeemed with Thy Precious Blood." Ask God to sprinkle your soul with the Blood of Christ, to cleanse you and keep you free from sin.

The **Most Holy Name of Jesus Christ,** the Name above every Name (Phil. 2:9), is also very effective in driving our spiritual enemies away. Whispered with faith as an aspiration, or as part of the Jesus Prayer, it will cause temptation to flee. The demons also find **the holy name of Mary** very offensive, since she is the Queen of Angels and the New Eve, who has defeated the ancient serpent by the redeeming power of her Divine Son. One of her titles is "Terror of demons."

Sacred Scripture is another mighty weapon. As we saw in the last meditation, St. Paul calls it the "sword of the Spirit" (Eph. 6:17). You have probably used this one a lot over the past few weeks, memorizing various passages and praying them when tempted. If so, then you have experienced the wonderful power of God's written word to drive away temptation and cleanse your mind and heart. *"For the word of God is living and efficient and keener than any two edged sword, and extending even to the division of soul and spirit, of joints also and of marrow, and a discerner of the thoughts and intentions of the heart"* (Heb. 4:12).

A variety of **Sacramentals** also serve as both armor and weaponry in our warfare. The **Brown Scapular** has been called "Mary's uniform." As we saw in the last meditation, it is like a breastplate of righteousness to protect our hearts and souls. The **Cincture of St. Joseph,** mentioned in Meditation 22 above, girds our loins with the virtue of chastity.

The **Holy Rosary** is a very powerful spiritual weapon. Blessed Mother's third promise to those who recite the Rosary is: *"The Rosary shall be a very powerful armor against hell; it will destroy vice, deliver from sin, and defeat heresies."* She then gave this fourth promise: *"It will cause virtue and good works to flourish; it will obtain for souls the abundant mercy of God; it will withdraw the hearts of men from the love of the world and its vanities, and will lift them to the desire of eternal things. Oh, that souls would sanctify themselves by this means."*

The book <u>Sex and the Mysteries,</u> by the late John M. Haffert, has a section of excellent meditations on the traditional fifteen Mysteries of the Rosary with regard to purity of heart. (It was written before the promulgation of the new Luminous Mysteries). It is a custom in Mexico to end each decade of the Rosary with an invocation. One such invocation, which you may wish to add to your rosary prayers, is as follows: *"For the sake of your Immaculate Conception, O Sovereign Princess, I ask you for purity, with all my heart."* The Chaplet of the Immaculate Conception, discussed in Appendix IV in back, is another excellent devotion for those who seek purity.

LORD JESUS, SON OF GOD, HAVE MERCY ON ME A SINNER.

DOMINE JESU FILI DEI, MISERERE MEI PECCATORUS

There is also the **Sign of the Cross,** as we discussed in the fifteen Meditation above. **Holy Water** also repels demons when used with faith and devotion, so make sure you keep some around the house at all times. It can be either sprinkled or used to cross oneself during times of temptation. Saint Teresa of Avila writes: *"From long experience I have learned that there is nothing like holy water to put devils to flight and prevent them from coming back again. They also flee from the cross, but return; so holy water must have great value."*

Holy water has many other spiritual benefits as well. For instance, it removes venial sin from our souls. If you are aware of having committed venial sin, dip your fingers in the holy water and make the Sign of the Cross devoutly while praying, "By this holy water and by Thy Precious Blood, wash away all my sins, O Lord."

Blessed Salt is another sacramental that is becoming more well known. As salt naturally prevents infection and preserves food from spoiling, so salt blessed by the Church preserves us from sin, demonic influences or other evils. Bring some salt to a priest and ask him to bless it, using this official prayer from the Roman Ritual: *"Almighty God, we ask you to bless this salt, as once you blessed the salt scattered over the water by the prophet Elisha. Wherever this salt (and water) is sprinkled, drive away the power of evil, and protect us always by the presence of your Holy Spirit. Grant this through Christ our Lord Amen."*

Then, putting your faith in God, prayerfully sprinkle some in your bedroom, on your bed, near your computer, in your car, etc.; any place where you might be tempted to sin. Place a few grains in your food or drink as well; this is said to give great benefits, both spiritually and physically. Ask God to purify your heart by means of this Blessed Salt, even as He once purified the polluted spring when the Prophet Elisha sprinkled salt on its waters (2 [4] Kings 2:19-22).

Remember that these sacramentals receive their efficacy from the blessing of God and the prayer of Holy Mother Church. They are not magical and we should always use them with faith in Our Lord, not superstitiously. Though they are material objects, the Holy Spirit imbues them with His power, as He once performed miracles through St. Peter's shadow (Acts 5:15) or handkerchiefs touched to St. Paul (19:11-12).

Holy water and blessed salt are associated with exorcism. Remember that lay Catholics are not permitted to directly address evil spirits; only official exorcists should actually perform exorcisms as such. But laymen and women can still devoutly use holy water, blessed salt and other sacramentals (such as the **Saint Benedict Medal,** shown below) for spiritual protection. They can also pray, begging God to "deliver us from evil" or asking St. Michael the Archangel to defend us against the snares of the Devil.

Since we have so many weapons at our disposal, let us ask God to show us how and when to use them. *"Blessed be the Lord, my rock, who trains my hands for battle, my fingers for war"* (Ps. 143[144]:1).

Resolution: Make use of these weapons in your battle against temptation and impurity.

Saint Michael the Archangel, pray for us.

TRACK YOUR PROGRESS: *Since reading the last meditation, how many times have I:*

a) deliberately touched myself impurely while awake? ___0 _✓_1 ___2 ___3 or more times
b) deliberately viewed indecent pictures or movies? _✓_0 ___1 ___2 ___3 or more times
c) committed unchaste acts with others? _✓_0 ___1 ___2 ___3 or more times
d) deliberately entertained/enjoyed impure thoughts? _✓_0 ___1 ___2 ___3 or more times

e) When was the last time I went to Confession? _2 DAYS AGO_ to Mass? _YESTERDAY_

MEDITATION 27: HATRED OF SIN

Seek good and not evil, that you may live; then truly will the Lord, the God of hosts, be with you as you claim! Hate evil and love good, and let justice prevail at the gate - Amos 5:14-15

Prayer: *O Divine Spirit! penetrate my soul with true horror and loathing of sin. Grant that I may be more exact in the fulfillment of my duties, and strengthen my by Thy grace, that I may not again yield to temptation.*[lxxii]

Three of the "daughters of lust" are *self love, hatred toward God,* and *love of this world.* These are some of the undesirable traits that sins against purity develop in us. As we saw in the eighth meditation, Jesus says that we cannot serve two masters, for we will hate the one and love the other. If sin is our master, we will end up loathing God. In order for God to truly be Our Lord and Master, we must develop a deep, abiding hatred of sin and worldliness. A true disgust toward sins against purity is absolutely necessary in order to overcome them.

Regardless of what society tells us, sin is not a light matter. It alienates us from Our Creator and kills us spiritually. It is willful rebellion against Our Savior, which offends His Goodness and Majesty. We must stop treating our offenses lightly and start thinking about sin the way God thinks about it. Scripture compares sin to such vile things as bleeding sores, (Isa. 1:5-6), dog vomit and the mire a pig wallows in (2 Pet. 2:22). Though temptation makes sin seem attractive and pleasant, it is really a deceptive invitation to do something ugly and disgusting, which degrades our bodies and sickens our souls. This is especially true of sins of the flesh.

Pornography is evil. It is not a fun pastime or a "victimless crime"; it is simply evil. It distorts the image of God in man and woman, scoffs at Holy Matrimony, twists and degrades God's gift of sex, and leads to all kinds of sin, wickedness and perversion. It destroys marriages, devastates families, drains bank accounts, drives many to substance abuse and some even to despair and suicide. It saves no one but damns many. May God grant us a true, deep and holy hatred of pornography and all sins of the flesh.

> Lord, we have lost our sense of sin!
> Today a slick campaign of propaganda
> is spreading an inane apologia of evil,
> a senseless cult of Satan,
> a mindless desire for transgression,
> a dishonest and frivolous freedom,
> exalting impulsiveness, immorality and selfishness
> as if they were new heights of sophistication.
>
> Lord Jesus, open our eyes:
> let us see the filth around us
> and recognize it for what it is,
> so that a single tear of sorrow
> can restore us to purity of heart
> and the breadth of true freedom.
> Open our eyes, Lord, Jesus! [lxxiii]

Before Francis Xavier became a religious, while he was still attached to the things of the world, St. Ignatius of Loyola said to him one day: "Francis, reflect that the world is a traitor, which promises but does not perform. And though it should fulfil all its promises, it can never content your heart. But let us grant that it did make you happy, how long will this happiness last? Can it last longer than your life; and after death what will you take with you to eternity?" These words caused St. Francis Xavier to become a religious and later a saint.[lxxiv]

What St. Ignatius said of the world especially applies to sins against purity. They have betrayed you. They promised happiness, fulfillment and consolation, but did not deliver. The brief physical sensation that they caused dissipated very quickly, but it never gave you true happiness or contentment. Moreover, all physical gratification will end at your death; it is not eternal, though indulgence in them can endanger your immortal soul. Lust has failed you. It has *utterly* failed you. Despise it and let it go.

Now, part of hating sin involves hating any memories we may have of sinning in the past. Even after we have not sinned against purity in a long time, we may still enjoy - or even cherish - some of our memories of past sins and their illicit pleasures. Yet this is an attachment to sin, and can hinder our prayers: *"Were I to cherish wickedness in my heart, the Lord would not hear"* (Ps. 65 (66):18). Fond memories of sins of the past may even tempt us to sin again in the future. So if you truly want lasting purity of heart, you must also learn to hate your past sins and never allow your mind to dwell on them. You can't look back on your unchaste past with nostalgia; you must see it as God sees it.

O Wounds of Jesus! You are my hope. I should despair of the pardon of my sins, and of my eternal salvation, did I not behold you, the fountains of mercy and grace, through which a God has shed all His Blood, to wash my soul from the sins which I have committed. I adore you, then, O Holy Wounds, and trust in you. I detest a thousand times, and curse those vile pleasures by which I have displeased my Redeemer, and have miserably lost His friendship. Looking then at Thee, I raise up my hopes, and turn my affections to Thee. My dear Jesus, Thou deservest to be loved by all men, and to be loved with their whole heart. I have so grievously offended Thee, I have despised Thy love; but, notwithstanding my sinfulness, Thou hast borne with me so long, and invited me to pardon with so much mercy. Ah, my Saviour, do not permit me evermore to offend Thee, and to merit my own damnation. O, God! What torture should I feel in hell at the sight of Thy Blood and of the great mercies Thou hast shown me. I love Thee, and will always love Thee. Give me holy perseverance. Detach my heart from all love which is not for Thee, and confirm in me a true desire, a true resolution henceforth, to love only Thee, my sovereign good. O Mary, my Mother, draw me to God, and obtain for me the grace to belong entirely to him before I die. Amen. – St. Alphonsus[lxxv]

Resolution: Ask God for the grace to truly abhor sins of the flesh, and to love Him instead with all your heart, soul, mind and strength. If you still enjoy recalling any sins of your past, ask Him to help you grieve over their memory rather than enjoy it. Recall the spiritual darkness such sins plunged you into and how they alienated you from Jesus. Resolve, with the help of God's grace, to love your Divine Master above all else and to hate your former master, sin.

Saint Francis Xavier, pray for us.

TRACK YOUR PROGRESS: *Since reading the last meditation, how many times have I:*

a) deliberately touched myself impurely while awake? ___0 ___1 ___2 ✓3 or more times
b) deliberately viewed indecent pictures or movies? ___0 ___1 ___2 ✓3 or more times
c) committed unchaste acts with others? ✓0 ___1 ___2 ___3 or more times
d) deliberately entertained/enjoyed impure thoughts? ___0 ___1 ___2 ✓3 or more times

e) When was the last time I went to Confession?_____ to Mass?_____

MEDITATION 28: THE GIFT OF HOLY FEAR

"The fear of the Lord is to hate evil." - Proverbs 8:13

Prayer: *Come, O blessed Spirit of Holy Fear, penetrate my inmost heart, that I may set Thee, my Lord and God, before my face forever; help me to shun all things that can offend Thee, and make me worthy to appear before the pure eyes of Thy Divine Majesty in heaven.* - From the "Novena to the Holy Spirit for the Seven Gifts"[lxxvi]

Hatred of sin is related to the often-misunderstood Gift of the Holy Spirit known as *fear of the Lord.* This does not mean an abject terror of God; rather, Holy Fear is inspired by our love for God:

The gift of Fear fills us with a sovereign respect for God, and makes us dread nothing so much as to offend Him by sin. It is a fear that arises, not from the thought of hell, but from sentiments of reverence and filial submission to our heavenly Father. It is the fear that is the beginning of wisdom, detaching us from worldly pleasures that could in any way separate us from God. "They that fear the Lord will prepare their hearts, and in His sight will sanctify their souls."[lxxvii]

This wonderful Gift enables us to despise and turn away from what is evil. *"Come, children, hear me; I will teach you the fear of the Lord….Keep your tongue from evil and your lips from speaking guile. Turn from evil, and do good; seek peace, and follow after it."* (Ps. 33(34):12-15; see also Prov. 16:6)

Turning away from evil should be accompanied by doing what is good, so fear of God also involves obedience: *"And now, Israel, what does the Lord, your God, ask of you but to fear the Lord, your God, and follow his ways exactly, to love and serve the Lord, your God, with all your heart and all your soul, to keep the commandments and statutes of the Lord which I enjoin on you today for your own good?"* (Deut. 10:12-13)

Our Lord is infinitely lovely, deserving of all our love. He is also awesome and majestic, deserving of our reverence and holy fear. However, sin is repulsive, deserving of our hatred and horror. After developing a holy hatred for sin, the next step is to cultivate a *horror of sin,* that is, a healthy dread of ever sinning again. Sorrow for sin (compunction of heart) regrets and mourns over how ones past transgressions have offended God and negatively affected ones life. Hatred for sin pertains mostly to the present; it sees sin clearly as the ugly, loathsome, demonic thing it really is and deeply despises it. Horror of sin dreads the very thought of any future transgression of God's law, causing one to pray fervently for His grace to keep from offending Him. All of these help us sever our attachment to vice and overcome habitual sins.

Look past the attractive veneer and transient pleasures of vice and see it for what it truly is. Recognize the terrible effect it has had on you, your loved ones, and your Savior, Who endured such horrible torments because of your sins. This will dissolve your attachment to sin and help you to develop a true horror of it instead.

Resolution: Ask the Holy Spirit to stir up in you the gift of Holy Fear, which He strengthened in you at your Confirmation, so that you will dread nothing so much as to offend God by sin.

Spirit of God, grant us the gift of Holy Fear.

TRACK YOUR PROGRESS: *Since reading the last meditation, how many times have I:*

a) deliberately touched myself impurely while awake?   ✓0 ___1 ___2 ___3 or more times
b) deliberately viewed indecent pictures or movies?   ✓0 ___1 ___2 ___3 or more times
c) committed unchaste acts with others?   ✓0 ___1 ___2 ___3 or more times
d) deliberately entertained/enjoyed impure thoughts?   ✓0 ___1 ___2 ___3 or more times

e) When was the last time I went to Confession? *YESTERDAY* to Mass? *YESTERDAY*

MEDITATION 29: HOLY SOULS IN PURGATORY

It is therefore a holy and wholesome thought to pray for the dead, that they may be loosed from sins.
- 2 Maccabees 12:46

Prayer: *Eternal Father, I offer Thee the Most Precious Blood of Thy Divine Son, Jesus, in union with the Masses said throughout the world today, for all the holy souls in Purgatory, for sinners everywhere, for sinners in the Universal Church, those in my own home and within my own family. Amen*

Impurity is a grave matter, but in order for a sin to be mortal one must also have sufficient reflection and full consent of the will. If those two elements are absent, it is possible for a sin against purity to be venial. Also, every sin we commit, mortal or venial, carries with it some temporal punishment that must be remitted, either with penance or indulgences in this life or in Purgatory after death.

Many of the holy souls in Purgatory, therefore, may have died with unforgiven venial sins of the flesh, or with the temporal punishment incurred by unchastity, and some attachment to sins against purity. All of these imperfections must be removed before these souls can enjoy the Beatific Vision. So it is highly likely that sins against purity prolong many a person's stay in Purgatory.

Perhaps we in the Church Militant who struggle against this sin can pray especially for those in the Church Suffering who are in Purgatory because of impurity. We can even seek to gain indulgences, partial or plenary, and then ask that God apply them especially to these suffering souls. If our efforts succeed in releasing some of them from Purgatory, they will be most grateful to us and will in turn pray for our intentions before the throne of Grace as saints in the Church Triumphant.

Though the Church has not defined this, some saints believed and taught that the holy souls are able to pray for us even while they are still in Purgatory. Either way, if we help the holy souls we will gain more spiritual allies in our struggle against our besetting sins. Also, if we end up in Purgatory ourselves, God will have compassion on us to the same degree we showed compassion to them: *"Blessed are the merciful, for they shall obtain mercy"* (Mt. 5:7).

Resolution: Pray in a special way for the souls suffering in Purgatory because of sins against purity and seek to gain indulgences for them:

O God, Creator and Redeemer of all the faithful, grant to the souls of your servants departed full remission of all their sins, that, through the help of devout supplications, they may obtain the pardon of which they have always been desirous. Who lives and reigns, world with out end. Amen

Eternal rest grant unto them, O Lord, and let perpetual light shine upon them. May they rest in peace. Amen.

TRACK YOUR PROGRESS: *Since reading the last meditation, how many times have I:*

a) deliberately touched myself impurely while awake?	__0	__1	__2	✓ 3 or more times
b) deliberately viewed indecent pictures or movies?	__0	__1	__2	✓ 3 or more times
c) committed unchaste acts with others?	✓0	__1	__2	__3 or more times
d) deliberately entertained/enjoyed impure thoughts?	__0	__1	__2	✓ 3 or more times

e) When was the last time I went to Confession? _2 DAYS AGO_ to Mass? _YESTERDAY_

MEDITATION 30: FASTING AND ABSTINENCE

O Lord, Father and God of my life, do not give me haughty eyes, and remove from me evil desire. Let neither gluttony nor lust overcome me, and do not surrender me to a shameless soul. - Sirach 23:4-6 RSV

Prayer: *O Jesus, Teacher of abstinence, help me to serve you rather than my appetites. Keep me from gluttony the inordinate love of food and drink and let me hunger and thirst for your justice.*[lxxviii]

We mainly think of fasting as an obligation for certain days of the liturgical year. Yet since it is an act of bodily mortification (more on that tomorrow), fasting can aid Christians in overcoming sins of the flesh. Many saints knew of this fact. Here are some quotes from the Desert Fathers:[lxxix]

(Holy Syncletica said,) "Just as strong medicine can drive out bodily poisons, so fasting and prayer can drive out squalid thoughts from the soul."

(Abba Hyperichius said,) "Fasting serves the monk as a bridle against sin. If you put off fasting, you become like a stallion, overcome by sexual desire."

Again he said, "The monk's body is dried up by fasting, but his soul is drawn upwards from the depths. The fasting of the monk dries up the springs of desire."

The *Imitation of Christ* says: *"Bridle gluttony and you will the easier restrain carnal inclinations."*[lxxx] St. Alphonsus writes:

It is also necessary to abstain from superfluity of food. St. Jerome asserts that satiety of the stomach provokes (impurity). And St. Bonaventure says: "Impurity is nourished by eating to excess." ' But, on the other hand, fasting, as the holy Church teaches, represses vice and produces virtue: "O God, who by corporal fasting dost suppress vice, dost elevate the mind, and dost confer virtues and rewards." St. Thomas has written that when the devil is conquered by those whom he tempts to gluttony, he ceases to tempt them to impurity.[lxxxi]

St. Francis de Sales counsels us as follows:

If you are able to fast, you will do well to observe some days beyond what are ordered by the Church, for besides the ordinary effect of fasting in raising the mind, subduing the flesh, confirming goodness, and obtaining a heavenly reward, it is also a great matter to be able to control greediness, and to keep the sensual appetites and the whole body subject to the law of the Spirit; and although we may be able to do but little, the enemy nevertheless stands more in awe of those whom he knows can fast. The early Christians selected Wednesday, Friday and Saturday as days of abstinence. Do you follow therein according as your own devotion and your director's discretion may appoint.[lxxxii]

Fasting doesn't necessarily mean not eating anything at all. In fact, no one should undertake such an extreme fast without consulting ones physician first, since people with certain health conditions shouldn't attempt it at all!

There are many other *safer* forms of fast or abstinence. You could abstain from meat on Fridays, as a penitential act in honor of Christ's Passion. Or you could observe partial abstinence (eat meat at only one meal) on Fridays, and maybe on Wednesdays, too. During meals, refrain from taking seconds, or skip dessert, and refrain from snacking between meals. Or fast one day a week, either on bread and water, or by skipping one meal that day, or even using the same fast required on Ash Wednesday and Good Friday (eating one full meal plus two snacks, with no eating between meals).

Don't try to do all of the above; if you do too much in the beginning you may end up abandoning the whole plan! So start with just one - or two at the most. You might later add a long-term mortification, such as giving up sweets or alcohol entirely. Or explore other methods of fast, such as the Eastern Christian Lenten fast - no meat, dairy or eggs (it is a good idea to discuss major dietary changes with your doctor, though). These acts of self-denial may seem small, but they can help you gain more control over concupiscence.

Finally, let necessity, not pleasure, govern you in eating and drinking. I do not say that you must allow your body to want for nourishment. Oh, no; like any animal destined for the service of man, your body must be supported. All that is required is to control it, and never to eat solely for pleasure, We must conquer, not destroy, the flesh, says St. Bernard; we must keep it in subjection, that it may not grow proud, for it belongs to it to obey, not to govern.[lxxxiii]

Resolution: Start fasting and/or abstaining, perhaps using one of the above suggestions.

Saints Bonaventure and Francis de Sales, pray for us.

TRACK YOUR PROGRESS: *Since reading the last meditation, how many times have I:*

a) deliberately touched myself impurely while awake?   __0 ✓1 __2 __3 or more times
b) deliberately viewed indecent pictures or movies?   __0 __1 __2 ✓3 or more times
c) committed unchaste acts with others?   ✓0 __1 __2 __3 or more times
d) deliberately entertained/enjoyed impure thoughts?   ✓0 __1 __2 __3 or more times

e) When was the last time I went to Confession? 3 DAYS AGO to Mass? 3 DAYS AGO

69

MEDITATION 31: MORTIFICATION

"Therefore mortify your members, which are on earth: immorality, uncleanness, lust, evil desire and covetousness (which is a form of idol worship). Because of these things the wrath of God comes upon the unbelievers, and you yourselves once walked in them when they were your life. But now do you also put them all away: anger, wrath, malice, abusive language and foul-mouthed utterances."
- Colossians 3:5-8

Prayer: *O King of virgins and lover of chastity and innocence, with the heavenly dew of Thy blessing extinguish the tinder of burning desires within my body, so that there may abide an unbroken course of chastity in my body and soul. Destroy all the stings of the flesh and all lustful movements within my members, and give to me a true and lasting chastity, together with Thine other gifts, which are truly pleasing unto Thee.*[lxxxiv]

"Mortification" comes from the Latin verb *mortificare*, meaning "to kill." To "mortify the flesh" literally means to *put to death* inordinate desire for sin. This is a must for every Christian: *"For if you live according to the flesh you will die, but if by the spirit you put to death the deeds of the flesh, you will live"* (Rom. 8:13).

Our habitual sins have been pampering our flesh; catering to its every whim, fulfilling each desire as soon as possible. Like a spoiled child, we have come to expect such instant gratification. Mortification inflicts discomfort and difficulty on our flesh in order to re-train us to accept suffering and hardship rather than constantly looking for pleasure and ease.

We have already discussed some forms of mortification. Doing penance, getting rid of indecent objects, humbling oneself, denying oneself, embracing ones cross, taking custody of the senses, fleeing temptation, offering ones body as a living sacrifice and banishing impure thoughts are all types of mortification. They are all acts of self-denial that starve our sinful desires and overcoming bad habits. So if you've been reading these meditations and carrying out the resolutions, you have already begun practicing mortification.

Mortification can also mean accepting the pains or discomfort that life sends our way. The practice of "offering up" ones suffering to God, though often forgotten today, is quite spiritually beneficial. The next time you experience some kind of discomfort, illness or pain, offer it up to God through the hands of Mary, in union with Christ's suffering on the Cross, in reparation for your past sins against purity.

Another aspect of mortification involves denying oneself things that are not unlawful or sinful. Fasting and abstinence are examples of this; eating is not sinful, indeed it is necessary! But refraining from eating for a time, or avoiding certain foods, teaches us to accept delayed gratification and the hardship of hunger. If done as a penitential act, this can help bring concupiscence under control.

Mortification can even take the form of denying oneself certain comforts, such as wearing uncomfortable clothing (hair shirts, etc.), sleeping on a hard bed, or even directly inflicting pain on oneself. Though this type of mortification is rather controversial, the principle behind it is as follows: if something is bent, you fix it by bending it back the other way. Our concupiscence and years of self-gratification have "bent" us toward sin, so we can correct that by moving in the opposite direction. Past indulgence in unbridled pleasure can be countered and corrected by inflicting unpleasantness upon ones spoiled flesh.

Thus we read that saints like Francis of Assisi and Rose of Lima inflicted austerities on themselves to curb their disordered desires. Some of us who struggle with habitual sin may even wonder whether we should imitate the methods of physical mortification that these great saints used.

Well, let us first consider the potential pitfalls of such practices. As with all spiritual exercises, there is the danger of pride. The Devil loves to flatter us for our religious observances, in an effort to stir up the sins of vanity and self-righteousness! Excessive or imprudent mortification can also create an unhealthy attitude toward one's body, or even cause physical injury. St. Francis de Sales wrote:

I disapprove of long and immoderate fasting, especially for the young. I have learnt by experience that when the colt grows weary it turns aside, and so when young people become delicate by excessive fasting, they readily take to self-indulgence. The stag does not run with due speed either when over fat or too thin, and we are in peril of temptation both when the body is overfed or underfed; in the one case it grows indolent, in the other it sinks through depression, and if we cannot bear with it in the first case, neither can it bear with us in the last. A want of moderation in the use of fasting, discipline and austerity has made many a one useless in works of charity during the best years of his life, as happened to S. Bernard, who repented of his excessive austerity. Those who misuse the body at the outset will have to indulge it overmuch at last. Surely it were wiser to deal sensibly with it, and treat it according to the work and service required by each man's state of life.[lxxxv]

During one of her apparitions, Our Lady of Fatima told the children to make sacrifices for sinners. Shortly afterward, they discovered some very coarse rope, and decided that they could wear it as a sacrifice for sinners. The children cut it in three parts, one for each, and began wearing it around their waists all the time. This was extremely uncomfortable, especially at night when it interfered with their sleep. So much so that, during her last apparition, Our Lady had to tell them to stop wearing it at night.

Now, two of these children, Jacinta and Francisco are on their way to sainthood, and Sr. Lucia, who recently went to be with Our Lord, will also most likely be raised to the altar someday. Yet even these little saints were excessive in their physical mortification, and the Queen of Heaven herself had to correct them! How much more would we be likely to overdo mortification without proper guidance? This is why the Church warns that mortification by severe, self-inflicted austerities should only be done under the guidance of and obedience to a wise and prudent spiritual director.

Those who struggle with sins of the flesh have unique concerns when it comes to mortification. For instance, it would not be wise for people with masochistic tendencies to attempt self-flagellation. Also, the shame and self-loathing that sins against purity generate can easily cause one to slip from mortifying oneself to avoid sin to punishing oneself after sinning.

Yet there are a few relatively mild forms of mortification, often recommended for people who habitually sin against purity. A cold shower is one, another is wearing a rubber band on the wrist and snapping it whenever one has an impure thought. Some people find these helpful, while others report that they don't help at all. If they work well for you, you may wish to use them as part of your overall struggle for purity. If not, just stick with fasting and abstinence, along with the other the forms of self-denial outlined in these meditations. As for more severe acts of mortification, don't try them without knowledge, consent and supervision of a spiritual director.

Resolution: Offer up any suffering you experience in reparation for past sins of the flesh. Consider adopting a mild form of mortification, as described in the last paragraph. Continue with past resolutions.

Saint Rose of Lima, pray for us.

TRACK YOUR PROGRESS: *Since reading the last meditation, how many times have I:*

a) deliberately touched myself impurely while awake?   ___0 √1 ___2 ___3 or more times
b) deliberately viewed indecent pictures or movies?   √0 ___1 ___2 ___3 or more times
c) committed unchaste acts with others?   √0 ___1 ___2 ___3 or more times
d) deliberately entertained/enjoyed impure thoughts?   √0 ___1 ___2 ___3 or more times

e) When was the last time I went to Confession? *YESTERDAY* ____   to Mass? *YESTERDAY* ____

The night is far advanced, the day is at hand. Let us therefore lay aside the works of darkness, and put on the armor of light. Let us walk becomingly as in the day, not in revelry and drunkenness, not in debauchery and wantonness, not in strife and jealousy. But put on the Lord Jesus Christ, and as for the flesh, take no thought for its lusts. - Romans 13:12-14

Prayer: *Late have I loved you, O Beauty ever ancient, ever new, late have I loved you! You were within me, but I was outside, and it was there that I searched for you. In my unloveliness I plunged into the lovely things which you created. You were with me, but I was not with you. Created things kept me from you; yet if they had not been in you they would have not been at all. You called, you shouted, and you broke through my deafness. You flashed, you shone, and you dispelled my blindness. You breathed you fragrance on me; I drew in breath and now I pant for you. I have tasted you, now I hunger and thirst for more.*

Aurelius Augustine was born in AD 354, the son of a pagan father and a Christian mother. Though never baptized as an infant, his mother, St. Monica, taught him the tenets of Christianity. As a young man he abandoned those beliefs and soon gave himself over to a life of vice, particularly impurity. He associated with immoral people, read bad books, lived in sin for fifteen years with a woman and fathered a child by her.

For many years, his saintly mother kept praying for his conversion. Augustine eventually embraced a heresy of the time known as Manichaeism, but he still struggled with impurity. Once he even prayed, "God, give me chastity - but not yet!" At the age of thirty he abandoned Manichaeism and came under the influence of St. Ambrose, the Bishop of Milan. Yet Augustine still struggled with his faith for another three years. Monica continued to pray for her wayward son.

One day, while weeping over his past sins in his friend's garden in Milan, he heard a child's voice singing "Tolle lege, tolle lege," which is Latin for "Take up and read, take up and read." Augustine took it as a sign from God; he picked up the nearest book, which was a copy of St. Paul's Epistles he had been reading. He opened it up and read the first words on which his eyes fell:

Let us walk becomingly as in the day, not in revelry and drunkenness, not in debauchery and wantonness, not in strife and jealousy. But put on the Lord Jesus Christ, and as for the flesh, take no thought for its lusts. - Romans 13:12-14

Immediately, his anxiety and gloom were dispelled, his doubts disappeared. He knew exactly what God required of him. Augustine converted to Christianity and was baptized in AD 387, much to the delight of his long-suffering mother. He went on to become a bishop, a great Saint, a Father and Doctor of the Church and one of the most influential theologians in Church history. His feast day is August 28.

In St. Augustine's life story we see the power of the persevering prayers of another Christian. Be grateful for the spiritual help your accountability partner is providing for you by his or her prayers. Augustine's conversion also illustrates the power of Sacred Scripture to purify and transform the soul. The passage he read in Romans is particularly relevant to anyone who struggles against habitual sins of the flesh:

Let us walk becomingly… Live your life in a manner becoming a Christian. Remember, your body is a member of Christ and a temple of the Holy Spirit. You do not have a right to do as you please with a member of Christ's Body. Nor should you turn the temple of the Spirit into a place to worship idols of impurity. Glorify God in your body.

…as in the day. not in the darkness and secrecy of impurity, but in the Light of God. As discussed in Meditation Five, you do this in part by revealing your sins, temptations and struggles to the priest at Confession and to devout friends who will hold you accountable.

not in revelry and drunkenness, not in debauchery and wantonness... No longer live a life of impurity and sin, but live in His holy grace.

But put on the Lord Jesus Christ. You "put on Christ" at your Baptism (Gal. 3:27); now live according to your Baptism by renouncing sin, dying to yourself daily and living in and for Jesus.

And as for the flesh, take no thought for its lusts. Deny your flesh, starve your sinful desires, take up your cross and die to yourself, offering your body as a living sacrifice to God. This is the way to life in Christ.

This passage is as much a command to you as it was to St. Augustine. Ask him to pray for you, that you might live out this Scripture verse in your own life.

Resolution: Memorize Romans 13:12-14, ask for Sts. Augustine and Monica to pray for you to receive the grace to put that passage into practice. If anyone in your life has been praying for you the way St. Monica did for her son, thank him or her, and pray for that person's intentions as well.

Saint Augustine of Hippo, pray for us. Saint Monica, pray for us.

TRACK YOUR PROGRESS: *Since reading the last meditation, how many times have I:*

a) deliberately touched myself impurely while awake? ___0 ___1 ___2 ✓3 or more times
b) deliberately viewed indecent pictures or movies? ___0 ✓1 ___2 ___3 or more times
c) committed unchaste acts with others? ✓0 ___1 ___2 ___3 or more times
d) deliberately entertained/enjoyed impure thoughts? ___0 ✓1 ___2 ___3 or more times

e) When was the last time I went to Confession? 3 DAYS AGO to Mass? 2 DAYS AGO

Saints Augustine and Monica, by Ary Scheffer

73

MEDITATION 33: DEAD TO SIN

What then shall we say? Shall we continue in sin that grace may abound? By no means! For how shall we who are dead to sin still live in it? Do you not know that all we who have been baptized into Christ Jesus have been baptized in his death? For we were buried with him by means of Baptism into death, in order that, just as Christ has arisen from the dead through the glory of the Father, so we also may walk in newness of life. - Romans 6:1-4

Prayer: *Let my heart, O Lord, be made immaculate, that I may not be ashamed.* – Raccolta #712

The above passage from Holy Writ is very encouraging. You actually died to sin at Baptism! This wonderful Sacrament united you with Jesus Christ in His death and victory over sin. Through it you were nailed to the Cross along with Him, you died with Him to sin and rose with Him to live a new life, filled with His grace!

The Fall of Adam, among other things, put all his descendants under the dominion of sin. Baptism removes the soul from that dominion, it actually releases us from the power of sin. If we choose to indulge in sin after our Baptism, however, it can soon become a habit. When this happens, we have effectively "invited" sin back to become our master again! This is why habitual sin has dominated you for so long; not out of necessity as with those in a state of original sin, but by your own decision to gratify yourself rather than living to please God.

The grace of Christ, which comes to us through the Sacraments, can once again break sin's mastery over you. Once it is broken, the key is to never invite your old taskmaster back, to never again subject yourself to habitual sin. This does not mean that you will never, ever commit any sins for the rest of your life. Every Christian has faults and imperfections: *"If we say that we have no sin, we deceive ourselves, and the truth is not in us"* (1 John 1:8). Baptism does not remove concupiscence, so we must still struggle against our disordered passions. The key is to resist committing mortal sin and to not allow habitual sin to re-enslave you, to dominate your entire life again. This is possible by the grace of God.

For if we have been united with him in a death like his, we shall certainly be united with him in a resurrection like his. We know that our former man was crucified with him so that the sinful body might be destroyed, and we might no longer be enslaved to sin. For he who has died is freed from sin. But if we have died with Christ, we believe that we shall also live with him. For we know that Christ being raised from the dead will never die again; death no longer has dominion over him. The death he died he died to sin, once for all, but the life he lives he lives to God. - Romans 6:5-10 RSV

Realize that, if you are in a state of grace, your "old self" - your sinful nature - is dead. So although you may commit some venial sins in your ongoing struggle against your disordered passions, *sin itself* does not have mastery over you. You are no longer a slave to sin; you are united to Christ instead, so you must now live for God by His grace. You do not belong to yourself; you belong to God. So you must not live for yourself, for your own selfish gratification, but for the glory of Christ, learning over time to master concupiscence with His divine aid.

So you also must consider yourselves dead to sin and alive to God in Christ Jesus. Let not sin therefore reign in your mortal bodies, to make you obey their passions. Do not yield your members to sin as instruments of wickedness, but yield yourselves to God as men who have been brought from death to life, and your members to God as instruments of righteousness. For sin will have no dominion over you, since you are not under law but under grace. - Romans 6:11-14 RSV

So how can you keep yourself from becoming once again enslaved to habitual sin? First, *consider yourself to be dead to sin.* Tell yourself every day: "In Christ I have died to sins against purity. I must live a new life in and for Him. My body is not mine and I don't have a right to use it selfishly and impurely."

Next, *do not let sin reign in your body.* Don't allow it to rule you like a tyrant, enslaving you to your passions. Jesus has set you free from that dominion so that you no longer have to be ruled by sin. He has broken its power over you. He is your Master and King now; serve Him!

Finally, *do not yield your members to sin.* Don't obey your flesh's demands. Consecrate yourself to God instead; ask Him to fill you with His Holy Spirit, to inspire all your thoughts, to fill your heart with love for Him, that you may use your hands only for His glory and never again offend him by thought, word or action. In short, offer your body as a living sacrifice, as described in Meditation 17.

Remember, you can only do all this by God's grace, which gives us the ability to be holy and obey Him. *"You are not under law but under grace."* The Law could only tell us what is wrong with us, but it could not give us the ability to do what is right. Grace enables us to conquer sin rather than be mastered by it.

Now, the Enemy will most likely try to make you doubt that you are truly dead to sin. He will tell you, "You haven't really changed, you know. Sooner or later you will return to your old ways; it's inevitable!" Remember, though, that Jesus gave us the Sacraments to transform us, to make us new creatures, living and growing in His grace. You certainly cannot remake yourself, but the One who made you in the first place can. Humbly trust in His grace to keep you free from habitual sins of the flesh.

Another trick the Tempter may use involves creating a "nostalgia" for your sinful past. He will recall to your mind certain magazines you read, movies you watched, or web sites you frequented. He wants you to dwell on these things, in hopes that you will eventually return to those activities "for old times sake."

The truth is, none of your past transgressions are even worth remembering now. Such memories are near occasions of sin, so treat them as such by dismissing them from your mind. If you must "feel" anything toward them, let it be remorse for how you forfeited sanctifying grace in order to wallow in the foul slime of impurity - but don't even dwell on that for long. The past is gone, forget about it and press on toward your goal of Heaven.

> But one thing I do: forgetting what is behind, I strain forward to what is before, I press on towards the goal, to the prize of God's heavenly call in Christ Jesus. - Philippians 3:13-14

Resolution: Prayerfully meditate on Romans 6 today, asking God to help you live it. Memorize any portion(s) of that chapter that inspire or encourage you to reject sin and live purely. Continue with ongoing resolutions.

Saint John the Baptist, pray for us.

TRACK YOUR PROGRESS: *Since reading the last meditation, how many times have I:*

a) deliberately touched myself impurely while awake? ___0 ___1 ___2 ⎵3 or more times
b) deliberately viewed indecent pictures or movies? ___0 ___1 ___2 ⎵3 or more times
c) committed unchaste acts with others? ___0 ___1 ___2 ___3 or more times
d) deliberately entertained/enjoyed impure thoughts? ___0 ___1 ___2 ⎵3 or more times

e) When was the last time I went to Confession? *2 DAYS AGO* to Mass? *YESTERDAY*

MEDITATION 34: ALIVE IN CHRIST JESUS

In (Christ), too, you have been circumcised with a circumcision not wrought by hand, but through putting off the body of flesh, a circumcision which is of Christ. For you were buried together with him in Baptism, and in Him also rose again through faith in the working of God who raised him from the dead. And you, when you were dead by reason of your sins and the uncircumcision of your flesh, he brought to life along with him, forgiving all your sins – Colossians 2:11-13

Prayer: *Lord Jesus Christ, I consecrate myself today anew and without reserve to your divine Heart. I consecrate to you my body with all its senses, my soul with all its faculties, my entire being.* - From the "Act of Consecration to Jesus"

A Christian is not just a member of a particular world religion, but of a new, redeemed humanity. As Adam is the head of fallen mankind and Eve the "mother of all the living" (Gen. 3:21), so Jesus the New Adam is the Head of this new Humanity redeemed by His Blood, while Mary and the Church constitute the New Eve, Mother of all who live in Christ. We are not just a bunch of lonely individuals wandering this earth; we are one with Our Lord Who lives in us: *"With Christ I am nailed to the cross. It is now no longer I that live, but Christ lives in me. And the life that I now live in the flesh, I live in the faith of the Son of God, who loved me and gave himself up for me"* (Gal. 2:20).

As we have seen, this begins with our Baptism, when we are identified with Jesus Christ in His death and resurrection. We are incorporated into Him, so to speak; we die with Him to sin and rise with Him to a new life. We literally become a new creation, a new humanity infused with sanctifying grace:

For the love of Christ urges us on, because we are convinced that one has died for all; therefore all have died. And he died for all, that those who live might live no longer for themselves but for him who for their sake died and was raised.... Therefore, if any one is in Christ, he is a new creation; the old has passed away, behold, the new has come. - 2 Corinthians 5:14-17 RSV

As this verse tells us, now we must not live for ourselves, but for Our Savior. For we belong entirely to Him; our bodies are members of Christ, and we are one spirit with Him (1 Cor. 6:15-17). This mystical union is most powerfully evident when we receive His Body, Blood, Soul and Divinity in the Blessed Sacrament of the Altar:

"So Jesus said to them, "Truly, truly, I say to you, unless you eat the flesh of the Son of man and drink his blood, you have no life in you; he who eats my flesh and drinks my blood has eternal life, and I will raise him up at the last day. For my flesh is food indeed, and my blood is drink indeed. He who eats my flesh and drinks my blood abides in me, and I in him. As the living Father sent me, and I live because of the Father, so he who eats me will live because of me." - St. John 6:53-57

Note all the things that the Holy Eucharist does for us. It infuses us with eternal life (v. 53-54), gives assurance of the eventual resurrection of our body (v. 54) and is our true spiritual food and drink (v. 55). It also causes us to abide in Christ and He in us (v. 56) and to draw our life from Him even as He draws His life from God the Father (v. 57).

So the Sacraments incorporate us into the Mystical Body of Christ: the Church. Though we were sinners, we receive His own righteousness and holiness by grace: *"For our sake he made him to be sin who knew no sin, so that in him we might become the righteousness of God"* (2 Cor. 5:21 RSV). We have already begun to partake in His Divine Nature (2 Pet. 1:4). Yet greater things are in store; if we persevere in grace, we are destined to one day be glorified and divinized in Him:

"For those whom he has foreknown he has also predestined to become conformed to the image of his Son, that he should be the firstborn among many brethren. And those whom he has predestined, them he has also called; and those whom he has called, them he has also justified; and those whom he has justified, them he has also glorified." - Romans 8:29-30

"Beloved, we are God's children now; it does not yet appear what we shall be, but we know that when he appears we shall be like him, for we shall see him as he is. And every one who thus hopes in him purifies himself as he is pure. Every one who commits sin is guilty of lawlessness; sin is lawlessness. You know that he appeared to take away sins, and in him there is no sin. Any one who abides in him does not sin; Any one who sins has not seen him, nor has he known him." - 1 John 3:2-6 RSV

Of course, this will never happen if we forfeit grace and die in mortal sin, as the last passage shows. Because we hope to be divinized we must purify ourselves and abandon habitual sin. As long as the seed of sanctifying grace remains in us, we can know that we will be divinized. But if we lose this grace by mortal sin and die in that state, we are lost.

So let us not forfeit the tremendous graces God lavished on us in His Beloved Son. Let us regard them as our greatest treasure, to be kept at all costs. No earthly pleasure, no fleeting fleshly gratification is worth the loss of eternal life.

Blessed be the God and Father of our Lord Jesus Christ, who has blessed us in Christ with every spiritual blessing in the heavenly places, even as he chose us in him before the foundation of the world, that we should be holy and blameless before him. He destined us in love to be his sons through Jesus Christ, according to the purpose of his will, to the praise of his glorious grace which he freely bestowed on us in the Beloved. In him we have redemption through his blood, the forgiveness of our trespasses, according to the riches of his grace which he lavished upon us. - Ephesians 1:3-8 RSV

Resolution: Ask God to help you to know and appreciate your status before Him in Christ. Ask Him to help you to never again lose sanctifying grace by grievous sin. Continue to draw close to Jesus in prayer and devotion, and with previous resolutions.

Sacred Heart of Jesus, I place my trust in You.

TRACK YOUR PROGRESS: *Since reading the last meditation, how many times have I:*

a) deliberately touched myself impurely while awake?   ✓0 ___1 ___2 ___3 or more times
b) deliberately viewed indecent pictures or movies?   ✓0 ___1 ___2 ___3 or more times
c) committed unchaste acts with others?   ✓0 ___1 ___2 ___3 or more times
d) deliberately entertained/enjoyed impure thoughts?   ✓0 ___1 ___2 ___3 or more times

e) When was the last time I went to Confession? 3 DAYS AGO   to Mass? 2 DAYS AGO

MEDITATION 35: SAINT MARGARET OF CORTONA

I chastise my body and bring it into subjection, lest perhaps after preaching to others I myself should be rejected. – 1 Corinthians 9:27

Prayer: *O glorious Saint Margaret of Cortona,....Guide us with the strength of your example, support us with your constant protection, be our companion we beg you, till we reach our Father's house. Amen.* - Pope John Paul II

Margaret of Cortona was born in Tuscany in AD 1247. Her mother died when she was seven years old, and two years later her father remarried. Her stepmother acted very cold and harsh toward her. Margaret's temperament was such that she felt she needed love and affection, so her stepmother's treatment left the young girl feeling rejected and unloved.

Margaret was a very beautiful girl, so when she entered adolescence men really began to take notice of her. She, in turn, began to appreciate their attention, and soon developed a very bad reputation in her hometown. When she was seventeen years old she left there to become a servant in a castle in Montepulciano, where she caught the eye of her master, a dashing young nobleman. For the next nine years she lived in sin with him in his castle and bore a son with him.

Yet even in the midst of her sinful life, God kept drawing Margaret's heart to Himself. She would sometimes wander into the forest and wonder what her life would have been like had she dedicated it to God. She often asked her lover to legitimize their relationship by marrying her. Though he continually promised her that he would, he never did. For in that society, a nobleman such as himself could not marry a peasant and former servant. She could become his mistress, but never his wife.

One day, while on a journey, he was murdered. When his dog returned to the castle without his master, Margaret knew something was wrong. She followed the dog, which led her to the shallow grave in which his decomposing body lay.

Grieving his death and disturbed by the thought that he might have been damned in part because of her, Margaret decided it was time to get right with God. She confessed her sin publicly, gave all her lover's gifts back to his family, dressed as a penitent, took her son and returned to her father's humble farmhouse. He wanted to welcome her, but his wife refused to allow such a notorious sinner, who had brought shame upon her family with her wanton ways, to live under her roof.

So Margaret and her son were sent away, with nowhere else to go. During this dark time she was tempted to return to life at the castle, but she prayed for strength and wisdom instead. She then heard an inner voice telling her to go to the Franciscan Friars Minor at Cortona, so she sought refuge there. The Friars took her and her son under spiritual direction.

Margaret wanted to become a Franciscan Tertiary, but had to wait three years before receiving the habit. During that time she struggled with difficult temptations. She was still young, spirited and beautiful, and the pleasures of the world kept calling to her. But she fasted, practiced strict self-discipline and mortification; she was sometimes so harsh to herself that her confessor, Friar Giunta, had to restrain her!

She finally did join the Third Order of St. Francis, and her son became a Franciscan soon afterward. She supported herself for a while working as a nurse, taking care of sick women. She eventually started a congregation called the Poverelle and founded a hospital. As she advanced spiritually, Margaret began to have visions of Jesus. At one point Our Lord told her:

I have made you a mirror for sinners. From you will the most hardened learn how willingly I am merciful to them, in order to save them. You are a ladder for sinners that they may come to me through your example. My daughter, I have set you as a light in the darkness, as a new star that I give to the world, to bring light to the blind, to guide back again those who have lost the way, and to raise up those who are broken down under their sins. You are the way of the despairing, the voice of mercy.

She preached vigorously against vice at every opportunity; many sinners came to her seeking help and counsel. She directed them to her confessor who restored them to the Church.

Her impure past still affected her, though; she experienced temptations of the flesh to the very end of her life, and was well aware of her human weakness. In 1289, some gossips in Cortona even started a vicious rumor that Margaret was having an affair with Friar Giunta. He was transferred elsewhere as a result, but investigations later showed that these rumors were nothing but evil calumny. Margaret continued to preach against impurity, and to mortify herself with fasting and self-discipline. She also became renowned for her holiness and ecstasies. God even revealed to her the date on which she would die.

That day finally came on February 22, 1297, and she was buried in a church in Cortona. Many miracles occurred around her tomb. She was canonized in 1728. Her feast day is February 22.

There is so much we can learn from the life of St. Margaret of Cortona, and so much to which we can relate. She was a woman who first sought love and happiness in sins against purity, but in the end found it only in Jesus Christ. Perhaps you can relate to how she was drawn in two directions: downward to lust and upward to God.

Yet she was able to turn from her selfish ways and live a life of service to others in a hospital. Her sins cost her dearly: her family, her reputation, and even years after she had abandoned her life of sin Margaret was still the subject of malicious gossip. Yet God still used her to bring other sinners back to the Sacraments. Know that Our Lord has a plan for your life as well. Also, her past sins did not prevent her from rising to a high level of sanctity by the grace of God. This should inspire hope in those who wish to abandon sins against purity.

Finally, she had to deal with temptation for her entire life, yet she was able to resist by the grace of God and become a saint. How encouraging to know that, even if you are tempted against purity for the rest of your life, you can still resist it with Our Lord's help and get to Heaven.

Resolution: Cultivate a devotion to St. Margaret of Cortona, asking her to help you overcome sins against purity.

Saint Margaret of Cortona, pray for us.

TRACK YOUR PROGRESS: *Since reading the last meditation, how many times have I:*

a) deliberately touched myself impurely while awake? ✓0 ___1 ___2 ___3 or more times
b) deliberately viewed indecent pictures or movies? ✓0 ___1 ___2 ___3 or more times
c) committed unchaste acts with others? ✓0 ___1 ___2 ___3 or more times
d) deliberately entertained/enjoyed impure thoughts? ✓0 ___1 ___2 ___3 or more times

e) When was the last time I went to Confession? 4 DAYS AGO to Mass? YESTERDAY

MEDITATION 36: WALK IN THE SPIRIT

"But I say: Walk in the Spirit, and you will not fulfill the lusts of the flesh. For the flesh lusts against the spirit, and the spirit against the flesh; for these are opposed to each other, so that you do not do what you would. But if you are led by the Spirit, you are not under the Law." - Galatians 5:16-18

Prayer: *Breathe in me O Holy Spirit, that my thoughts may all be holy; Act in me O Holy Spirit, that my work, too, may be holy; Draw my heart O Holy Spirit, that I love but what is holy; Strengthen me O Holy Spirit, to defend all that is holy; Guard me, then, O Holy Spirit, that I always may be holy.* – St. Augustine

In order to stifle the lusts of the flesh one must walk in the Spirit. As long as we are in a state of grace, God the Holy Spirit dwells within us at all times. Yet we are not always completely led and empowered by Him, surrendered to His will, abandoned to His providence. Too often, we go our own way, ignoring His Divine Presence, living more to please ourselves than to please God. So He allows us to fall into sin after sin, even sins against purity:

Now the works of the flesh are manifest, which are immorality, uncleanness, licentiousness, idolatry, witchcrafts, enmities, contentions, jealousies, anger, quarrels, factions, parties, envies, murders, drunkenness, carousings, and suchlike. And concerning these I warn you, as I have warned you, that they who do such things will not attain the kingdom of God. - Galatians 5:19-21

But if we ask Him to lead and strengthen us, if we submit to His guidance, we can walk in the Spirit. He will help us starve our sinful desires and cultivate holy virtues in their place. His Divine Power flowing through us will cause our lives to bear righteous fruit:

But the fruit of the Spirit is, charity, joy, peace, patience, kindness, goodness, faith, modesty, continency. Against such things there is no law. And they who belong to Christ have crucified their flesh with its passions and desires. If we live by the Spirit, by the Spirit let us also walk. - Galatians 5:22-26

So how do we walk in the Spirit? Begin by consecrating yourself to God the Holy Spirit. Pray this traditional *Act of Consecration to the Holy Spirit* with all your heart:

On my knees I before the great multitude of heavenly witnesses I offer myself, soul and body to You, Eternal Spirit of God. I adore the brightness of Your purity, the unerring keenness of Your justice, and the might of Your love. You are the Strength and Light of my soul. In You I live and move and am. I desire never to grieve You by unfaithfulness to grace and I pray with all my heart to be kept from the smallest sin against You. Mercifully guard my every thought and grant that I may always watch for Your light, and listen to Your voice, and follow Your gracious inspirations. I cling to You and give myself to You and ask You, by Your compassion to watch over me in my weakness.

Holding the pierced Feet of Jesus and looking at His Five Wounds, and trusting in His Precious Blood and adoring His opened Side and stricken Heart, I implore You, Adorable Spirit, Helper of my infirmity, to keep me in Your grace that I may never sin against You. Give me grace O Holy Spirit, Spirit of the Father and the Son to say to You always and everywhere, "Speak Lord for Your servant heareth." Amen.

Then, each morning when you wake up, ask the Holy Spirit to lead you for the rest of that day. This must be a daily choice to surrender control of your life to Him

The Secret of Sanctity.

Cardinal Mercier was once asked during a retreat what is the "secret of sanctity." He replied:

If every day during five minutes you will keep your imagination quiet, shut your eyes to all the things of sense, and close your ears to all the sounds of earth, so as to be able to withdraw into the sanctuary of your baptized soul, which is the temple of the Holy Spirit, speaking there to that Holy Spirit saying:

> O Holy Spirit, Soul of my soul, I adore You.
> Enlighten me, guide me, strengthen me, console me.
> Show me what I ought to do and command me to do it.
> I promise to be submissive to You in everything that you permit to happen to me.
> Merely show me what is Your Will.

If you do this, your life will pass happily and serenely. Consolation will about even in the midst of troubles. Grace will be given in proportion to the trial, as well as strength to bear it, bringing you to the Gates of Paradise full of merit.

This submission to the Holy Spirit is: *the secret of sanctity.*

Don't expect to always feel His presence and leading. Sometimes you may sense Him, sometimes you will not, but just because you can't "feel" anything doesn't mean He isn't there. Remember, He is always present in your soul as long as you are in a state of grace. You can trust in His promise: *"If you then, who are evil, know how to give good gifts to your children, how much more will the heavenly Father give the Holy Spirit to those who ask him!"* (Lk. 11:13)

Resolution: Consecrate yourself to the Holy Spirit, and pray the "Secret of Sanctity" every morning, as Cardinal Mercier recommended. Say this prayer before the devotion to Our Lady outlined in the second meditation.

God the Holy Spirit, have mercy on us.

TRACK YOUR PROGRESS: *Since reading the last meditation, how many times have I:*

a) deliberately touched myself impurely while awake? ✓0 ___1 ___2 ___3 or more times
b) deliberately viewed indecent pictures or movies? ✓0 ___1 ___2 ___3 or more times
c) committed unchaste acts with others? ✓0 ___1 ___2 ___3 or more times
d) deliberately entertained/enjoyed impure thoughts? ✓0 ___1 ___2 ___3 or more times

e) When was the last time I went to Confession? 5 DAYS AGO to Mass? YESTERDAY

81

MEDITATION 37: THE TABLE OF DEVILS

The cup of blessing which we bless, is it not the sharing of the blood of Christ? And the bread that we break, is it not the partaking of the body of the Lord? Because the bread is one, we though many, are one body, all of us who partake of one bread. Behold Israel according to the flesh, are not they who eat of the sacrifices partakers of the altar? What then do I say? That what is sacrificed to idols is anything, or that an idol is anything? No, but I say that what the Gentiles sacrifice, "they sacrifice to devils and not to God"; and I would not have you become associates of devils. You cannot drink the cup of the Lord and the cup of devils; you cannot be partakers of the table of the Lord and of the table of devils. Or are we provoking the Lord to jealousy? Are we stronger than he? - 1 Corinthians 10:16-22

Prayer: *O Blood and Water which gushed forth from the Heart of Jesus as a fountain of Mercy, I trust in You.*

In Meditation Eight we saw that sin against purity is tantamount to idolatry. It is "worship" offered up on the false altar of impurity. As St. Jerome says: "A vice in the heart is an idol on the altar."

In the passage above, St. Paul tells us that Christians cannot partake of both the Sacrifice of the Mass and pagan sacrifices, since the latter are actually offered to demons! So we who have been given the incredible privilege of eating Christ's Flesh and drinking His Blood cannot also partake of the pagan altar of sins of the flesh. Otherwise we will provoke Our Lord to jealousy, for He is the mystical Bridegroom of the Church. We must be faithful to Him alone and not bow the knee adulterously before other gods.

While the children of Israel wandered in the wilderness, their only bread was the manna God gave them, and their only drink was water from the rock which Moses struck (1 Cor. 10:4). The Manna clearly foreshadows Jesus, the true Bread from Heaven (Jn. 6:32-35). The Rock foreshadows Him as well, for when His side was pierced on the Cross, Blood and Water flowed forth to heal, cleanse and revive us. As the Israelites were completely dependent on God for their nourishment in the desert, so our only spiritual nourishment during this earthly exile must come from Our Lord: the Bread of Life, the Precious Blood of Jesus in the Blessed Sacrament, the word of God and the living water of the Holy Spirit:

Now on the last, the great day of the feast, Jesus stood and cried out, saying, "If anyone thirst, let him come to me and drink. He who believes in me, as the Scripture says, 'From within him there shall flow rivers of living water.'" He said this, however, of the Spirit whom they who believed in him were to receive. - St. John 7:37-39

In the past you turned to other sources, seeking to fill the emptiness within your soul, only to end up spiritually poisoned and sickened by the garbage you so eagerly consumed. Now that you have abandoned vice for the true nourishment that God gives, it is imperative that you stay away from impurity *permanently!* If you ever again seek to fill your hunger with sins against purity, you will place yourself in great danger. For those who refrain from these sins for a while, only to return to them, often end up sinking deeper into vice than they were before!

Our Lord explains why this occurs:

"But when the unclean spirit has gone out of a man, he roams through dry places, in search of rest, and finds none. Then he says, 'I will return to my house which I left'; and when he has come to it, he finds the place unoccupied, swept, and decorated. Then he goes and takes with him seven other spirits more evil than himself, and they enter in and dwell there; and the last state of that man becomes worse than the first." - St. Matthew 12:43-45

This is no light matter. If we clean up our lives by penitence, but then become careless and fail to replace our sin with devotion to Jesus and Mary, frequenting the Sacraments, study of Sacred Scripture, mortification, etc., we leave a vacuum into which vice may return. Then we will be even worse off than before!

> If a man again touches a corpse after he has bathed, what did he gain by the purification? So with a man who fasts for his sins, but then goes and commits them again: Who will hear his prayer, and what has he gained by his mortification? - Sirach 34:25-26

So let us not return like a dog to its vomit or a pig to wallow in the mud (2 Pet. 2:20-22), but let us ask God for the grace to persevere in devotion, mortification and good works, and to leave no room for the Devil. As Pope St. Leo the Great says:

> Let then us put off the old man with his deeds, and having obtained a share in the birth of Christ, let us renounce the works of the flesh. Christian, acknowledge your dignity; having become a partaker in the Divine Nature, refuse to return to your old base condition by degenerate conduct. Remember the Head and the Body of which you are a member. Recall that you were rescued from the power of darkness and brought out into God's light and Kingdom. By the mystery of Baptism you were made the temple of the Holy Spirit; do not drive away so great a Guest by base acts and subject yourself once more to the devil's servitude. For you were bought by the Blood of Christ, and He Who ransomed you in mercy will judge you in truth, Who with the Father and the Holy Spirit reigns for ever and ever. Amen. *(Pope St. Leo the Great, Homily XXI on the Feast of the Nativity, III)[†]*

Resolution: Resolve to never again seek to satisfy your spiritual hunger at the altar of impurity, and ask God for the grace to always turn to Him rather than vice.

Virgin Most Pure, pray for us.

TRACK YOUR PROGRESS: *Since reading the last meditation, how many times have I:*

a) deliberately touched myself impurely while awake?   ✓0 ___1 ___2 ___3 or more times
b) deliberately viewed indecent pictures or movies?   ✓0 ___1 ___2 ___3 or more times
c) committed unchaste acts with others?   ✓0 ___1 ___2 ___3 or more times
d) deliberately entertained/enjoyed impure thoughts?   ✓0 ___1 ___2 ___3 or more times

e) When was the last time I went to Confession? 6 DAYS AGO   to Mass? YESTERDAY

---

† Thanks to David Morrison for this quote, which he posted on his *Sed Contra* blog (davidmorrison.typepad.com/sed_contra).

MEDITATION 38: SAINT MARY OF EGYPT

Strive for peace with all men, and for that holiness without which no man will see God. - Hebrews 12:14

Prayer: *Having escaped the fog of sin and having illumined your heart with the light of penitence, O glorious one, you came to Christ and offered to Him His immaculate and holy Mother as a merciful intercessor. Hence you have found remission of transgressions, and with the Angels you ever rejoice.*[lxxxvi]

Mary of Egypt was born sometime around AD 344. At the age of twelve she ran away from home to the city of Alexandria, where she became a singer and actress. Like many actresses of the time, she was also involved in prostitution. Mary lived a debauched life there for seventeen years, wallowing in impurity; in her own words, she "had an insatiable desire and an irrepressible passion for lying in filth."

One day, she overheard some pilgrims saying that they were going to visit Jerusalem to venerate the True Cross of Christ. Always adventurous, Mary decided to go along and prostitute herself in Jerusalem. She couldn't afford to pay for the voyage, so she offered herself to the sailors as payment for the trip.

When she arrived in Jerusalem, she continued to prostitute herself. On the Feast of the Exaltation of the Holy Cross, Mary saw a huge crowd of people heading for a church in which the True Cross was venerated. Out of curiosity, she joined the throng. But when she got to the doors of the church, she was suddenly unable to go inside. While the crowds around her had no difficulty entering, it was as though an invisible force held Mary back, not allowing her to pass over the threshold.

Mary realized that she was being prevented from entering because of her sinful life. She suddenly felt deep remorse and began to weep over her sins. She then looked toward an icon of the Mother of God hanging over the door, and humbly prayed:

O Lady, Mother of God, who gave birth to God the Word according to the flesh; I know well that it is no honor or praise to you when one so impure and depraved as I look up to your icon, O Ever-Virgin, who kept your body and soul in purity. Rightly do I inspire hatred and disgust before your virginal purity. But I have heard that God Who was born of you became man to call sinners to repentance. Help me, then, for I have no other help. Order the entrance of the church to be opened to me. Allow me to see the venerable Tree on which He Who was born of you suffered in the flesh and on which He shed His holy Blood for the redemption of sinners and for me, unworthy as I am. Be my faithful witness before your Son that I will never again defile my body by the impurity of fornication, but as soon as I have seen the Tree of the Cross I will renounce the world and its temptations and will go wherever you lead me.

She then approached the door of the church again, and this time had no problem entering. She venerated the True Cross, kissed the ground humbly, then left the church and went to pray before the icon again, for guidance. She then heard a voice telling her that she would find peace if she crossed the Jordan River. So she traveled to the Jordan, where she found a church dedicated to St. John the Baptist. There she received Holy Communion for the first time in her life.

The next day, she set out for the desert, carrying only three loaves of bread. There she lived all alone for the next forty-seven years, cut off from human contact, living first on those loaves of bread and then whatever plants she could forage. For the first seventeen years, she experienced strong temptations to return to her sinful ways, but she kept reminding herself of her vow. She would then think about the icon before which she had prayed, and ask Our Lady to drive away the temptations. Eventually, they would subside.

When Mary was around seventy-six years old, a priest named Zozimas discovered her living alone in the desert. He was deeply impressed by her obvious holiness and amazing life story. She even knew passages from Sacred Scripture, though she could not read and did not own a Bible. She said that God had taught it to her.

Mary also asked Zozimas to return a year later to bring her Holy Communion. When he did, she received Communion for only the second time in her life. Shortly afterward she went to be with Our Lord in Heaven. Portions of her relics are kept in a variety of places, including Naples, Cremona, Antwer and Rome. Her feast is April 3 in the West and April 1 in the East.

St. Mary of Egypt is an excellent example of true penitence with affliction of spirit and mortification. The Catechism's definition of repentance sounds like a description of her post-conversion actions:

> Interior repentance is a radical reorientation of our whole life, a return, a conversion to God with all our heart, an end of sin, a turning away from evil, with repugnance toward the evil actions we have committed. At the same time it entails the desire and resolution to change one's life, with hope in God's mercy and trust in the help of his grace. This conversion of heart is accompanied by a salutary pain and sadness which the Fathers called *animi cruciatus* (affliction of spirit) and *compunctio cordis* (repentance of heart). (CCC 1431)

Note also that St. Mary of Egypt only received the Blessed Sacrament twice in her life. Yet her first reception filled her with enough grace to sustain her interior life for *forty six years* alone in the desert! What a tremendous illustration of the power of the Holy Eucharist, which we Catholics receive much more often yet tend to take for granted.

Resolution: Ask St. Mary of Egypt to pray that you gain a spirit of true penitence and benefit from the abundant graces available to you in the Blessed Sacrament.

Saint Mary of Egypt, pray for us.

TRACK YOUR PROGRESS: *Since reading the last meditation, how many times have I:*

a) deliberately touched myself impurely while awake?   ✓0 ___1 ___2 ___3 or more times
b) deliberately viewed indecent pictures or movies?   ✓0 ___1 ___2 ___3 or more times
c) committed unchaste acts with others?   ✓0 ___1 ___2 ___3 or more times
d) deliberately entertained/enjoyed impure thoughts?   ✓0 ___1 ___2 ___3 or more times

e) When was the last time I went to Confession? 7 DAYS AGO   to Mass? YESTERDAY

MEDITATION 39: THE VIRTUE OF MODESTY

Among you there must not be even a mention of fornication or impurity in any of its forms, or promiscuity; this would hardly become the saints! There must be no coarseness or salacious talk and jokes - all this is wrong for you; raise your voices in thanksgiving instead. - Ephesians 5:3-4 JB

Prayer: *Come Spirit of Modesty and fill the hearts of your faithful. Come, Holy Spirit, come by means of the powerful Intercession of the Immaculate Heart of Mary, your well beloved spouse.*

St. Paul states that there must not even be a mention of impurity among Christians - not even a *hint* of it existing in our midst! That may sound like a virtual impossibility in our sex-saturated society. Yet remember that St. Paul wrote this to Christians in the pagan town of Ephesus; their surrounding culture wasn't really better than ours. God never requires the impossible; if they could remain pure by His grace, so can we. The virtue of *modesty* will help us, and those around us, remain pure.

Modesty is often called "the guardian of chastity." This virtue moderates how we appear, speak and behave toward others, so that we do not present an occasion of sin to them. Practicing modesty will help keep you pure as well as prevent others from sinning because of your bad example. We are our brother's keeper, and so should be very careful, as much as is in our power to do so, to not cause others to stumble.

The *Catechism* says the following about modesty:

2521 Purity requires modesty, an integral part of temperance. Modesty protects the intimate center of the person. It means refusing to unveil what should remain hidden. It is ordered to chastity to whose sensitivity it bears witness. It guides how one looks at others and behaves toward them in conformity with the dignity of persons and their solidarity.

2522 Modesty protects the mystery of persons and their love. It encourages patience and moderation in loving relationships; it requires that the conditions for the definitive giving and commitment of man and woman to one another be fulfilled. Modesty is decency. It inspires one's choice of clothing. It keeps silence or reserve where there is evident risk of unhealthy curiosity. It is discreet.

Today's meditation will focus on modesty in speech. Meditation 44 will address modesty in dress.

Modesty in Speech

"So the tongue is a little member and boasts of great things. How great a forest is set ablaze by a small fire! And the tongue is a fire. The tongue is an unrighteous world among our members, staining the whole body, setting on fire the cycle of nature, and set on fire by hell." - St. James 3:6

We can sin by our words in many ways: lies, gossip, insults, bearing false witness, etc. Today we will focus on the use of obscenities - crude terms for venereal or scatological matters. People with soiled hearts often use bad language, for *"The good man out of the good treasure of his heart produces good, and the evil man out of his evil treasure produces evil; for out of the abundance of the heart his mouth speaks"* (Lk. 6:45). So there is a good possibility that many readers of this book also have a foul mouth. Since the words we speak can cause others to stumble, one aspect of modesty involves watching ones speech.

Some of the principles you've already learned apply to curbing obscene speech as well. First of all, believe that you can break this habit with God's help. As with other sins against purity, the Devil wants you to think it is hopeless; you've been using obscenities so long that you could never break the habit. But the virtue of hope tells us that with God all things are possible. Pray for the grace to let go of this habit. If you have been praying these meditations regularly for many weeks now, you may already have begun to notice a change in your language. The purer your heart becomes, the cleaner your speech will become. The more you think holy, positive and uplifting thoughts, the less angry and frustrated you will be, which will also lead to less obscenity. Letting go of anger through prayer, forgiveness and developing a positive attitude toward life will also help.

If you use obscenities, you most likely think them as well. Try to change your thought processes. When you think an obscene word, stop yourself and think of a clean word that expresses the same thought. Repeat the sentence over and over in your mind using the substitute word instead. Pretend your mind is a tape recorder and you are "recording over" the foul language, replacing it with a clean substitute. Try to delete the word from your mind.

Avoid hearing obscene conversations as much as possible, to starve your mind of such words (custody of the senses). If you happen to hear one, ask God for the grace to hate what you hear (hatred of sin). If possible, ask the person politely to please stop using those words.

Consider whether there any bad words that you would never say because you hate them. Perhaps certain racial or ethnic slurs, for instance. Remember the disgust you feel when you hear someone use such words. If you can teach yourself to hate obscenities as much as you hate those slurs, you wouldn't use them either. Think of obscenities as slurs against God's holy gift of procreation, by which we become co-creators of new life with Him. Ask God for the grace to hate hearing them spoken as much as you hate to hear racial or ethnic slurs.

Here's an exercise: when you feel angry, write down or type up your feelings, including the bad language. Put what you wrote away for a day or so, then read it again. Do you like the way you sounded? Could you have said it differently?

Another strategy: listen more than you speak. Certain religious orders take a "vow of silence" for good reason: if you stop using your tongue, you will never sin with it. This is not practical for most of the laity in the world, but we can always refrain from talking for a short time, especially if we are not in a good mood. How much better it would be to pray silently than complain about your problems and turn other people off: *He who spares his words is truly wise, and he who is chary of speech is a man of intelligence. Even a fool, if he keeps silent, is considered wise; if he closes his lips, intelligent* (Prov. 17:27-28) CAUTIOUS, CAREFUL

Resolution:. Prayerfully read Sections 2514 through 2533 of the *Catechism of the Catholic Church* (the context of the above quoted sections on the virtue of modesty.) Begin to practice modesty in speech.

Make my heart and my body clean, holy Mary. – Raccolta #713

TRACK YOUR PROGRESS: *Since reading the last meditation, how many times have I:*

a) deliberately touched myself impurely while awake?   ___0 ___1 ___2 ___3 or more times
b) deliberately viewed indecent pictures or movies?   ___0 ___1 ___2 ___3 or more times
c) committed unchaste acts with others?   ___0 ___1 ___2 ___3 or more times
d) deliberately entertained/enjoyed impure thoughts?   ___0 ___1 ___2 ___3 or more times

e) When was the last time I went to Confession? 8 DAYS AGO to Mass? YESTERDAY

MEDITATION 40: MAKING UP FOR THE PAST

I will restore to you the years which the swarming locust has eaten, the hopper, the destroyer, and the cutter, my great army, which I sent among you. You shall eat in plenty and be satisfied, and praise the name of the LORD your God, who has dealt wondrously with you. And my people shall never again be put to shame. - Joel 2:25-26 RSV

Prayer: *O my God! Source of all Mercy! I acknowledge Your sovereign power. While recalling the wasted years that are past, I believe that You, Lord, can in an instant turn this loss to gain. Miserable as I am, yet I firmly believe that You can do all things. Please restore to me the time lost, giving me Your grace, both now and in the future, that I may appear before You in "wedding garments." Amen.* [lxxxii] ST, TERESA of AVILA

It is consoling to know that God offers to restore to us the time we have wasted on sin when we should have been growing in grace. Let us ask Him for this grace. Here are some ways to make up for our impure past:

The Divine Mercy Promise

During Our Lord's apparitions to St. Faustina Kowalska, He asked on many occasions for the Church to designate the Second Sunday of Easter (or the Octave Day of Easter) as the Feast of Divine Mercy. Pope John Paul II granted this request in the year 2000, at the canonization of St. Faustina; so the Sunday after Easter is now officially known as Divine Mercy Sunday.

Jesus, Who is Love and Mercy personified, made some amazing promises for those who observe the Feast of Divine Mercy. Here is an excerpt from St. Faustina's diary:

On one occasion, I heard these words: My daughter, tell the whole world about My Inconceivable mercy. I desire that the Feast of Mercy be a refuge and shelter for all souls, and especially for poor sinners. On that day the very depths of My tender mercy are open. I pour out a whole ocean of graces upon those souls who approach the fount of My mercy. The soul that will go to Confession and receive Holy Communion shall obtain complete forgiveness of sins and punishment. On that day all the divine floodgates through which grace flow are opened. Let no soul fear to draw near to Me, even though its sins be as scarlet. My mercy is so great that no mind, be it of man or of angel, will be able to fathom it throughout all eternity. Everything that exists has come forth from the very depths of My most tender mercy. Every soul in its relation to Me will I contemplate My love and mercy throughout eternity. The Feast of Mercy emerged from My very depths of tenderness. It is My desire that it be solemnly celebrated on the first Sunday after Easter. Mankind will not have peace until it turns to the Fount of My Mercy. (*Diary* 699)

Notice Christ's incredible statement: "The soul that will go to Confession and receive Holy Communion shall obtain *complete forgiveness of sins and punishment.*" Later in the Diary we find a similar promise: "I want to grant *complete pardon* to the souls that will go to Confession and receive Holy Communion on the Feast of My mercy" (*Diary* 1109).

This promise is different from a plenary indulgence, which only removes all temporal punishment that results from sin. Our Merciful Lord also promises complete pardon of sins, along with removal of their punishment. In effect, Jesus is offering to thoroughly clean our souls again as He did when we were baptized! This is an incredible offer, but perhaps understandable when we consider the times in which we live, with sins of the flesh rampant in our world. Foreseeing the vice and corruption into which we would soon sink, Christ offered this full pardon during the 1930's, as if to confirm Sacred Scripture when it says: "*But where sin increased, grace abounded all the more*" (Rom. 5:20 RSV).

On June 29, 2002, the Church issued a plenary indulgence for Divine Mercy Sunday. This indulgence does not change or negate Christ's promise of complete forgiveness, but instead shows that the Church fully approves of this apparition and its message. We would do well to try to gain both the plenary indulgence and Christ's Divine Mercy Promise, and so take full advantage of that feast day. Jesus' Promised pardon will remit all our sins and punishments, thus cleansing us completely of our past transgressions against purity. We can then ask Blessed Mother to apply the indulgence to a soul who is in Purgatory because of sins of the flesh.

Prayer for Daily Neglects

According to a pious tradition, a certain poor Clare nun who had recently died, one day appeared to her abbess. The abbess had been praying for her soul, but the nun told her, " I went straight to heaven, for by means of this prayer, which I recited every evening, I paid all my debts." Here is the prayer that the nun said every night:

Eternal Father, I offer Thee the Sacred Heart of Jesus with all Its Love, all Its sufferings and all Its merits:

First - To expiate all the sins I have committed this day and during all my life. *Glory be to the Father...*etc.

Second - To purify the good I have done badly this day and during all my life. *Glory be...*

Third - To supply for the good I ought to have done, and that I have neglected this day and during all my life. *Glory be...*[lxxxviii]

Though this prayer cannot substitute for the Sacrament of Reconciliation, it is still an excellent prayer to help atone for our sins of omission and human failings. You may wish to say it every night after making a general examination of conscience, to recall any sins or failings of that day.

Resolution: Pray the above *Prayer for Daily Neglects* every night, and take advantage of the Divine Mercy Promise on the next Divine Mercy Sunday.

Merciful Jesus, I trust in You!

TRACK YOUR PROGRESS: *Since reading the last meditation, how many times have I:*

a) deliberately touched myself impurely while awake? ✓0 ___1 ___2 ___3 or more times
b) deliberately viewed indecent pictures or movies? ✓0 ___1 ___2 ___3 or more times
c) committed unchaste acts with others? ✓0 ___1 ___2 ___3 or more times
d) deliberately entertained/enjoyed impure thoughts? ✓0 ___1 ___2 ___3 or more times

e) When was the last time I went to Confession? _9 DAYS AGO_ to Mass? _YESTERDAY_

But thou, O man of God, flee these things; but pursue justice, godliness, faith, charity, patience, mildness. Fight the good fight of the faith; lay hold on the life eternal, to which thou hast been called, and hast made the good confession before many witnesses. - 1 Timothy 6:11-12

Prayer: *Dearest Jesus! I know well that every perfect gift, and above all others that of chastity, depends upon the most powerful assistance of Thy Providence, and that without Thee a creature can do nothing. Therefore, I pray Thee to defend, with Thy grace, chastity and purity in my soul as well as in my body. And if I have ever received through my senses any impression that could stain my chastity and purity, do Thou, Who art the Supreme Lord of all my powers, take it from me, that I may with an immaculate heart advance in Thy love and service, offering myself chaste all the days of my life on the most pure altar of Thy Divinity. Amen.* – St. Thomas Aquinas

Thomas Aquinas was the son of a count and countess. From his youth, he was drawn to prayer and study of the Catholic Faith. At sixteen years of age he decided to become a Dominican friar - a decision which greatly displeased his aristocratic family. While traveling from Naples to Paris to study for his vocation, two of his brothers (who were soldiers) captured and imprisoned him in a cell in the fortress of Monte San Giovanni. There his two sisters visited him regularly, attempting to convince him to abandon his vocation. Yet Thomas refused to change his mind, and spent his imprisonment praying and memorizing Scripture.

Seeing that their sisters' pleas were to no avail, his brothers decided to take matters into their own hands. They sent a beautiful young prostitute into Thomas' cell to seduce him, figuring that if he broke his vow of chastity he might abandon the religious life. Yet once Thomas realized her intention, he prayed for strength, grabbed a hot firebrand from the fireplace and drove her right out of his cell!

Disturbed by this brazen temptation, he traced a cross on his door with the glowing firebrand, prostrated himself before it and said the prayer at the top of this meditation, begging God for the grace to remain chaste. He then fell asleep, and two angels appeared to him in a dream, telling him God had heard his prayers. They tied a white cord around his waist, saying, "Thomas, on God's behalf, we gird you with the cincture of chastity, which no attack will ever destroy."

Thomas Aquinas wore this miraculous cincture for the rest of his life. On his deathbed he confided in his confessor, Father Reginald, that he had never experienced a temptation against purity while wearing the cord. Today this precious relic is preserved in a reliquary in the Dominican convent at Chieri, Italy. St. Thomas' feast day is celebrated on January 28.

The virtue of chastity was so important to St. Thomas Aquinas that he actually fought aggressively to preserve it! May God grant us the same fervent zeal for purity.

There is a lesson here for us as well. Earlier in this course we learned to flee from temptation, a strategy that remains valuable. Yet, like St. Thomas, there are times when we must turn and fight against impurity. This is especially true of near occasions of sin, which we must aggressively cut off and root out of our lives, as we have seen. Rejecting impure thoughts, practicing self-denial and mortification are other aggressive steps against vice.

Again, let us not envy saints like Thomas Aquinas who were reportedly spared further temptations against purity. He undoubtedly struggled in other areas of his life, for the Devil tempts everyone. He may have even gone through more severe trials than we will ever experience. Our crosses are each tailored for us alone.

Angelic Warfare Confraternity

Because of his love for holy purity, St. Thomas has been venerated and invoked for centuries as a patron saint of virginity and chastity. After he died, some people adopted the pious practice of wearing a white cincture called the "cord of St. Thomas," in memory of the miraculous cincture given him by the angels. They would also ask the Angelic Doctor to obtain for them the virtue of purity by his prayers. In the seventeenth century, a Dominican priest named Fr. Francis Duerwerdes established the *Militia Angelica*, a Confraternity dedicated to spreading this devotion and promoting purity. Many popes sanctioned this confraternity, enriching it with indulgences; St. Aloysius of Gonzaga belonged to it. In English it is commonly called the *Angelic Warfare Confraternity*.

Members are enrolled in the confraternity and given a white linen cincture with fifteen knots on one end, on which they pray fifteen Ave's every day, in honor of St. Thomas Aquinas. They are also given a special medal to wear, and say the following prayer:

Chosen Lily of innocence, pure St. Thomas, who kept chaste the robe of baptism, and became an angel, I implore you to commend me to Jesus, the Immaculate Lamb, and to Mary, Queen of Virgins, Gentle protector of my purity, ask them that I who wear the holy sign of your victory of the flesh may also share your purity and that after imitating you on earth, I may at last come to be crowned with you among the angels. Amen.

For more information about the Angelic Warfare Confraternity, check the Resources and Bibliography section in the back of this book.

Resolution: Ask St. Thomas to pray for you to learn how to attack against impurity with holy zeal. Consider joining the Angelic Warfare Confraternity. Continue with past resolutions.

Saint Thomas Aquinas, pray for us.

TRACK YOUR PROGRESS: *Since reading the last meditation, how many times have I:*

a) deliberately touched myself impurely while awake? ✓0 ___1 ___2 ___3 or more times
b) deliberately viewed indecent pictures or movies? ✓0 ___1 ___2 ___3 or more times
c) committed unchaste acts with others? ✓0 ___1 ___2 ___3 or more times
d) deliberately entertained/enjoyed impure thoughts? ✓0 ___1 ___2 ___3 or more times

e) When was the last time I went to Confession?__YESTERDAY__ to Mass?_____TODAY_____

St. Thomas Aquinas receives the miraculous cincture from the holy angels

91

MEDITATION 42: THE HUMAN BODY IN THE DIVINE PLAN

Then the Lord God said, "It is not good that the man is alone; I will make him a helper like himself." … The Lord God cast the man into a deep sleep and, while he slept, took one of his ribs and closed up its place with flesh. And the rib which the Lord God took from the man, he made into a woman, and brought her to him. Then the man said, "She is now bone of my bone, and flesh of my flesh; she shall be called Woman, for from man she has been taken." For this reason a man leaves his father and mother, and clings to his wife, and the two become one flesh. Both the man and his wife were naked, but they felt no shame. – Genesis 2:18, 21-25

Prayer: *O most holy and immaculate Mary, Virgin of virgins and our most loving Mother, keep clean my heart and my soul through all my days; beseech for me the fear of the Lord and a lively distrust of myself.*[lxxxix]

Cleanness of heart involves understanding the Creator's intention for the marital act[†]. In the beginning, God created man in His image. This means Adam had intellect and will, which reflect God's infinite Intellect and Divine Will. It also means that he was a person made to relate to other persons - a created copy of how the Three Persons of the Trinity live in an eternal Communion of persons. This is why Our Lord said of him *"It is not good that the man is alone."* Adam lived in what Pope John Paul II called "original solitude"; he was a solitary person, with no other human person with whom he could relate or commune. God and the angels were above him, the animals below him, but no one stood by his side.

While angels are pure spirits, and animals exist in the material realm only, man is *spiritual and material*, both soul and body. We are not spirits trapped in a body, for our bodies are as much a part of us as our souls. God intends for the human soul to relate to the material world through the body. This is how the first man related to his world: his soul expressed itself through his body, his body was formed and animated by a spiritual soul.

When God brought all the animals before him, Adam could not find among them a suitable partner for himself. None were a unity of a physical body and a spiritual soul, none were made in the image of God, and none were persons made for communion with him. God then created a woman from the man's side. She shared his flesh and bone, had an immortal soul and was created in the image of God like Adam. She was a person with intellect and will, made to relate to another person. When Adam recognized in her a suitable partner, he exclaimed: *"She is now bone of my bone, and flesh of my flesh; she shall be called Woman, for from man she has been taken."*

Then the Creator officiated at the first marriage: *God blessed them and said to them, "Be fruitful and multiply; fill the earth and subdue it"* (Gen. 1:28). He gave the man and woman the awesome privilege of becoming co-creators with Himself by bringing more created "images of God" into existence. This is the primary purpose of marriage. Man and woman do this through an act in which *"the two become one flesh,"* their bodies become joined in the private marital act, and later a new human life formed of their cells is born as a manifestation of their one-flesh union. Coitus, by its very nature, is ordered toward bringing new life into the world.

We do not know whether Adam and Eve consummated their marriage before the Fall. If so, it would have been a perfect union, untainted by sin. Adam would have given his entire self to Eve, soul and body, without reserve, and she would have responded to his self-gift by giving her whole self to him. The act would have united them physically, emotionally, intellectually and spiritually. Their innocence and unselfishness would have fostered total trust and love between them; neither would have ever sought to *use* the other for selfish gratification.

John Paul II said that this is the meaning of *"Both the man and his wife were naked, but they felt no shame."* We feel shame when we know that someone wants to sinfully use us as an object for gratification. We instinctually respond to this threat to our human dignity by covering ourselves up to prevent such a vile use of

---

† This meditation and the next are partially based on Pope John Paul II's "Theology of the Body."

our person. Prior to the Fall, our first parents had no such desire to use one another, only to love and give themselves to each other.

Had they procreated before the Fall, their children would have been born filled with the same sanctifying grace their parents enjoyed as a gift from God. Yet this was not to be, for when God tested their loyalty Adam and Eve disobeyed Him. Thus Adam forfeited sanctifying grace for himself and his descendants, along with certain other gifts of God, such as control over their passions, freedom from suffering and physical immortality.

Immediately after their disobedience, *"the eyes of both were opened, and they realized that they were naked; so they sewed fig leaves together and made themselves coverings"* (Gen. 3:7). Until then, our first parents' physical desires were governed by the soul through reason, which kept them in moderation. After reason no longer controlled their passions, they tended toward excess known as *concupiscence*. As the man and woman looked at one another, each now saw the other's body as a thing that he or she could use for selfish gratification. When they each became aware of the other's lustful gaze, they experienced shame and their first instinct was to cover the parts of their body that distinguished them from each other. We continue to clothe ourselves to this day, because the original sin of Adam still infects and influences the human race.

The first sin would have profound consequences on the procreative act. Its primary end would be accompanied by pain and peril for the woman, and its unitive element would be distorted by selfishness and lust: *"for your husband shall be your longing, though he have dominion over you"* (Gen. 3:16). Though he was already Eve's head, Adam was not supposed to dominate her, but to exercise a servant leadership over her. Something like what Our Lord later described to His disciples: *"Whoever wishes to become great shall be your servant; and whoever wishes to be first among you shall be the slave of all; for the Son of Man also has not come to be served but to serve, and to give his life as a ransom for many"* (Mk 10:43-44)

This is Our Creator's ideal for leadership: to make decisions for the good of those led rather than for selfish gain. Adam would have done this for Eve and their children had there been no Fall, and Eve would have been able to trust him. But the Fall shattered their innocence and trust, causing discord between them.

Over time, the sinful descendants of Adam and Eve would continue to distort the procreative act by using outside its divinely-ordained context of the marriage covenant (fornication, adultery), thwarting its procreative purpose (sodomy, masturbation, contraception) and distorting it into a commodity for monetary gain (pornography, prostitution). What God intended to be an intimate act of communion of persons is now too often reduced to selfishly using another human being for personal gratification.

Yet, despite all these sinful distortions, the marital act remains good in itself as a creature of God. Marriage gained a third end as a *remedy for concupiscence*, in addition to its other ends: *the procreation and education of children* and *mutual aid of the spouses*. Though we cannot completely rid ourselves of disordered desire in this life, grace enables us to resist our inclination to sin caused by our darkened intellect, weakened will and disordered passions. The Sacrament of Matrimony in particular gives us grace to help regulate our passions somewhat, although it is hardly an instant cure; we must still develop self-control over time.

Resolution: Prayerfully read Sections 2331 through 2350 of the *Catechism of the Catholic Church*. Ask God to help you gain a truly Catholic understanding of sexuality.

Most Holy Trinity, One God in Three Persons, have mercy on us.

TRACK YOUR PROGRESS: *Since reading the last meditation, how many times have I:*

a) deliberately touched myself impurely while awake? ✓0 ___1 ___2 ___3 or more times
b) deliberately viewed indecent pictures or movies? ✓0 ___1 ___2 ___3 or more times
c) committed unchaste acts with others? ✓0 ___1 ___2 ___3 or more times
d) deliberately entertained/enjoyed impure thoughts? ✓0 ___1 ___2 ___3 or more times

e) When was the last time I went to Confession? 2 DAYS AGO to Mass? YESTERDAY

MEDITATION 43: THE GOODNESS OF MARITAL LOVE

And Tobias said: Lord God of our fathers, may the heavens and the earth, and the sea, and the fountains, and the rivers, and all thy creatures that are in them, bless thee. Thou madest Adam of the slime of the earth, and gavest him Eve for a helper. And now, Lord, thou knowest, that not for fleshly lust do I take my sister to wife, but only for the love of posterity, in which thy name may be blessed for ever and ever. Sara also said: Have mercy on us, O Lord, have mercy on us, and let us grow old both together in health. - Tobias 8:5-8

Prayer: *Almighty Father, Maker of my soul and body, help me to appreciate the human body as Your masterpiece and its procreative powers as Your gift. Lord Jesus Christ, Savior of my soul and body, please heal the damage I have inflicted upon myself by sin and teach me to crucify my selfishness and lust. Holy Spirit, Sanctifier of my soul and body, grant me the grace to be truly chaste and to ever glorify God in my body. Glory to You, O Blessed Trinity, now and forever. Amen.*

Contrary to popular misconception, Catholicism does not despise the body and the procreative act. We believe that the human body is God's beautiful work of art, in and through which the human soul expresses itself. Nor is it merely a temporary vehicle which the soul permanently discards at death, for we also believe in the *resurrection of the body.* Since our bodies are as much a part of us as our souls, physical death is a temporary and unnatural state that God will reverse on the Last Day. When soul and body are reunited, both will partake in the same divinization or punishment, even as both participated in the same virtues and sins during life.

We also believe that the marital act is essentially good, designed by God for the purpose of bringing children into the world (procreative) and bringing a man and women together in a one-flesh union (unitive). Husband and wife express their love and union bodily in the conjugal union, which naturally results in a new life who is "the two become one flesh." Spouses "own" each other's bodies, so to speak, and so cannot refuse each other their marital rights *"except perhaps by agreement for a season, that you may devote yourselves to prayer"* (1 Cor. 7:1-7).

The pleasure of the act is a means to the ends of the act, not an end in itself. It is a gift each gives to the other, not to be sought selfishly or used by ones self. Yet it is perfectly licit for spouses to enjoy the marital act: *"Find joy with the wife you married in your youth, fair as a hind, graceful as a fawn. Let hers be the company you keep, hers the breasts that ever fill you with delight, hers the love that ever holds you captive"* (Prov. 5:18-19 JB).

In fact, we believe that God created human marriage as an earthly image of the mystical union between Christ and His Church. Jesus the Bridegroom gives Himself entirely to His Bride through His Death and in the graces of the Sacraments. She responds by giving herself entirely to Her Divine Bridegroom. Because of their mysterious union, the Church becomes the spiritual Mother of millions of souls in the Sacrament of Baptism.

Though their union is not carnal, but spiritual, God intended the one-flesh union of man and woman as a sign of this mysterious heavenly reality. The marriage of Adam and Eve at the beginning of Scripture mirrors this mystical union of the New Adam and Eve at the end of Scripture in the "marriage supper of the Lamb."

If marriage is intended to be an earthly image of the union between Christ and His Church, what does this tell us about the sanctity of Holy Matrimony? Since we must reverence holy things, all Christians should have great reverence for marriage: *"Let marriage be held in honor with all, and the marriage bed be undefiled. For God will judge the immoral and adulterers"* (Heb. 13:4).

To "profane" is to desecrate something sacred. Pornography profanes the Sacrament of Matrimony, and, along with all other sins against purity, it distorts what God designed to be a loving self-gift to ones spouse alone. The procreative act is a beautiful, life-giving act that should not be degraded for pleasure or exploited for money. Pornography is absolutely contrary to the Creator's design for marital love and so should be hated and shunned by all mankind, and particularly by Christians.

Conjugal relations are also intended to be, at least implicitly, the renewal of the marriage covenant.[†] Thus they are reserved for the marriage bond. All sex outside of marriage is essentially a lie, for one cannot renew a covenant that does not exist. It is also an implicit negation of the union between Christ and the Church, of which the marital bond is an earthy image. This is why all sex outside of marriage is morally unacceptable.

Moreover, since the primary end of conjugal relations is the procreation and education of children, artificial contraception thwarts the very purpose of sex. It also distorts the image of the fruitful union between Christ and the Church; there is no "barrier" between them. This is why artificial methods of birth control are wrong.

Once we understand these principles, we can see what was so wrong with sins of the flesh. They distort the true meaning and thwart the divinely-ordained purpose of the procreative act, and obscure its function as an earthly icon of Christ the Bridegroom and the Church His Bride. We were settling for a cheap imitation of a beautiful gift. May God grant us the grace to no longer indulge in the desecration of the procreative act.

Of course, being what we are, our marriages are not perfect. Human marriages are unions of imperfect persons wounded by the Fall, and so may not always live up to God's perfect plan. This is why we have the Sacrament of Reconciliation to receive forgiveness. But let us not forget that the Sacrament of Matrimony bestows graces upon the couple to help them live out their vocation as a married couple. Though we suffer the effects of the Fall, it is still possible for husband and wife to grow in grace and holiness together, which over time will permeate and purify all aspects of their relationship, including conjugal union. Then the couple may possibly enjoy a small taste of what the marital act would have been like in the Garden of Eden.

Under such circumstances, conjugal relations can be a grace-filled act for both husband and wife, but the spouses must both have clean hearts. So if you are married, this is all the more reason to seek a clean heart.

Now you may be wondering, "If marriage is so terrific, what about consecrated virginity? Doesn't the Church teach that this is a higher calling than marriage?" Yes, consecrated virginity is a higher calling than marriage, not because it forfeits something bad (marriage and sex) for something good (no sex), but because it sacrifices something good (marriage and sex) for something better – celibacy for the Kingdom of God. As good as marriage is, it is only a temporal state which ends at death. But the reality it signifies – the union between Christ and the Church – endures for all eternity. In Heaven we will *"neither marry nor be given in marriage"* to one another, because all will be eternally united to the Divine Bridegroom!

A consecrated virgin doesn't wait for the end of time, but seeks to be married to Our Lord *right now*. She forgoes the earthly image in order to seize the heavenly reality. So her virginity is a sign and foretaste of what we shall all experience, God willing, in the World to Come. This is why virginity is superior to the married state. An appreciation of the meaning and goodness of marriage helps us better appreciate the great sacrifice made by celibate clergy and religious.

Resolution: Read Sections 2351 through 2400 of the *Catechism of the Catholic Church*, which come right after yesterday's reading. Continue with previous resolutions.

All you holy virgins, pray for us.

TRACK YOUR PROGRESS: *Since reading the last meditation, how many times have I:*

a) deliberately touched myself impurely while awake?   ✓0 ___1 ___2 ___3 or more times
b) deliberately viewed indecent pictures or movies?   ✓0 ___1 ___2 ___3 or more times
c) committed unchaste acts with others?   ✓0 ___1 ___2 ___3 or more times
d) deliberately entertained/enjoyed impure thoughts?   ✓0 ___1 ___2 ___3 or more times

e) When was the last time I went to Confession? 3 DAYS AGO   to Mass? YESTERDAY

[†] See John F. Kippley's "covenant theology of sex," outlined in Sex and The Marriage Covenant, (Cincinnati: Couple to Couple League, 1991).

MEDITATION 44: MODESTY IN DRESS

In like manner I wish women to be decently dressed, adorning themselves with modesty and dignity, not with braided hair or gold or pearls or expensive clothing, but with good works such as become women professing godliness. - 1 Timothy 2:9-10

Prayer: *Mary, loving Spouse of the Holy Spirit, I give my body to your care. Let me always remember that my body is a home for the Holy Spirit who dwells in me. Let me never sin against Him by any impure actions alone or with others, against the virtue of purity.*

A pious tradition holds that Jesus endured being stripped of His garments on Calvary to expiate for our lack of modesty in dress. According to Blessed Jacinta Marto, Our Lady of Fatima once predicted that "Certain fashions will be introduced which will offend my Son very much." Sure enough, the last century saw a tremendous increase in immodest fashions, alongside a rise in sins against purity that continues even today.

How often we hear people try to justify their lack of modesty by saying, "Well, I'm not ashamed of my body!" As though modest people are somehow *ashamed* of their bodies! Contrary to popular opinion, modesty in dress does not arise from disgust for the body; rather, it is a form of self-defense against objectification by others - a tragic yet utterly inescapable result of the Fall of Adam.

As we saw in Meditation 42, in their state of original innocence, Adam saw his wife, Eve, as a person to love, to whom he could give himself wholly and completely. She, in turn, saw her husband the same way. After the Fall, however, they experienced shame because they now viewed one another as objects they could use for selfish gratification. This was the beginning of the vice of lust. As a result, they each sought to retain a sense of personal dignity by hiding the parts of their bodies where they differed most from each other - hence the fig-leaf clothing (Gen 3:7).

Not much has changed since then. Lust still infects the human race, so some people still want to use others selfishly and sinfully. Immodest clothing only exacerbates this situation. Consider this: when one sees someone who is dressed immodestly, where are ones eyes immediately drawn? Are they not drawn toward the person's body, toward the parts revealed (or partially revealed) by the cut of the clothing? By focusing attention on the body and away from the face, immodest attire invites the viewer to lust, to treat the one viewed as a mere object for gratification. Diverting attention from the face and eyes makes it easier to ignore that this is a *person* rather than a thing - ever hear the old saying, "The eyes are the windows of the soul?"

Modest clothing, on the other hand, sufficiently covers the private areas of the body, so that attention is naturally drawn to the face instead†. Therefore, modest apparel tends to emphasize the *personhood* of the wearer while diminishing the possibility of objectification. This does not mean that no one will ever have impure thoughts about a modestly-dressed person, but that such thoughts will not occur quite as easily when the body is sufficiently covered.

So modesty in dress is not just an act of charity toward others that eliminates an occasion of sin. It also preserves the human dignity of the wearer. Far from degrading the body, it exalts the whole person. Such apparel tells others, "Don't look upon me as an object, but relate to me as a person, a fellow human being."

Now we can understand why immodesty offends God. Not because the human body is disgusting or evil but because revealing clothes diminish the dignity of a human person created in the image of God, as well as pose an occasion of sin for others. Note that He Himself confirmed Adam and Eve's instinct to cover their bodies by clothing them in animal skin (Gen. 3:21) - a more permanent garment than leaves and one which most likely concealed more of their bodies. God clearly wants us to wear modest clothes after the Fall of Man.

---

† Christian modesty has never required fashions which hide the face, such as the burqua.

How to Dress Modestly

Though the verse at the beginning of this meditation is directed at women, modesty is important for men as well. Contrary to popular belief, some women *are* attracted by the male form, and men with same-sex attraction who strive to remain chaste as the Church teaches would be greatly helped if other men dressed modestly. Here are some guidelines for both men and women of what to wear in public in order to preserve your dignity and avoid being an occasion of sin for others:

For Men: Shirts without sleeves should not be worn in public. It is also not modest to go outside without a shirt. Shorts should be knee-length or lower.

For Women: Dresses and skirts should be knee-length or lower. No back-less shirts or dresses, halter tops, tube tops, strapless fashions or low-rise pants.

For both Men and Women: Collars should dip no more than two inches below the neckline. No bare shoulders; sleeves should preferably be about elbow-length, though quarter-length is okay for summer and warm climates. Avoid tight clothing and bare midriffs; conceal undergarments thoroughly. Transparent fabrics such as lace, tulle or mesh must be backed by opaque fabrics.

In short, aim at concealing the body more than revealing it[†]. When you are getting dressed, ask yourself: "Does this garment conceal or reveal? Does it draw attention toward or away from my face? Do I want to wear it to attract the lustful attention of others? Could this garment be an occasion of sin for others?" If the weather is hot where you live, buy only modest clothes made of 100% natural fabrics such as cotton. Avoid synthetic fabrics since they cause more perspiration and will prove uncomfortable in hot weather.

Resolution: Begin dressing modesty, as described above. Continue with past resolutions.

Make my heart and my body clean, holy Mary. – Raccolta #713

TRACK YOUR PROGRESS: *Since reading the last meditation, how many times have I:*

a) deliberately touched myself impurely while awake?   ✓0 ___1 ___2 ___3 or more times
b) deliberately viewed indecent pictures or movies?   ✓0 ___1 ___2 ___3 or more times
c) committed unchaste acts with others?   ✓0 ___1 ___2 ___3 or more times
d) deliberately entertained/enjoyed impure thoughts?   ✓0 ___1 ___2 ___3 or more times

e) When was the last time I went to Confession? 4 DAYS AGO to Mass? YESTERDAY

[†] These modesty guidelines are based on the "Marylike Standards for Modesty in Dress" pamphlet, which, as far as I know, is in the public domain. I have updated the standards to address current fashion issues and to include guidelines for men.

MEDITATION 45: SAINT MARIA GORETTI

Truly, truly, I say to you, unless a grain of wheat falls into the earth and dies, it remains alone; but if it dies, it bears much fruit. He who loves his life loses it, and he who hates his life in this world will keep it for eternal life. – St. John 12:24-25

Prayer: *Most lovable little Saint, who valued your purity above any earthly gain, and who sealed this choice with a martyr's death, obtain for me also a strong love of this virtue, so consoling to the Sacred Heart of Jesus and to the Immaculate Heart of Mary. The pleasures of the world create many temptations for me. I turn to your powerful intercession in Heaven, so that with this help I may remain ever loyal to God, no matter what the price. In danger inspire me to repeat with you. "No, it is a sin!" Amen.*[xci]

Maria Teresa Goretti was born on October 16 1890, in Ancona, Italy, to two poor yet devout farmworkers named Luigi Goretti and Assunta Carlini. From a young age, Maria was very cheerful and devout, for Assunta had instilled in her a deep love of God, the Catholic Faith and of virtue.

After Luigi died of malaria, the Goretti family worked as sharecroppers on the farm of a count, under the stern authority of a man named Giovanni Serenelli. His nineteen year-old son, Alessandro, was in some ways the opposite of the devout Maria. Brought up with little parental guidance, Alessandro was sullen and spent much time alone in his room, pouring over his collection of obscene literature. It is said that he also had indecent pictures hanging on the wall of his room.

His mind polluted by impurity, Alessandro soon developed an unchaste interest in eleven year-old Maria. He began flattering her, then later propositioning her. Maria rebuffed him many times, yet since Alessandro had threatened to kill her and her mother if she told anyone about his advances, she kept quiet about it. The poor girl suffered long in silence and fear. Assunta noticed her daughter's cheerfulness give way to sorrow, but did not know why.

Alessandro eventually decided to force Maria to submit to his evil designs. On July 5, 1902, while Assunta worked in the fields, he hid a knife in his clothes and confronted Maria on the steps of her house, where she was watching her little sister, Teresita. He grabbed Maria by the arm, dragged her into the bedroom and bolted the door. She screamed and struggled, telling Alessandro "No, no, it is a sin, God does not will it, you will go to Hell!" He tried to choke her, but she continued resisting him. In his fury, he pulled out the knife and stabbed her fourteen times. He then fled and locked himself in his room, leaving Maria for dead.

Teresita woke up and began crying, which caused Alessandro's father to go upstairs to see what was wrong. When he found Maria lying in a pool of blood, he yelled to her mother and another farmhand to come quickly. Still alive, Maria told everyone that Alessandro had killed her because she refused to submit to his lust. She was rushed to the hospital, but the damage to her internal organs was so extensive there was little the doctors there could do. Yet she somehow clung to life for nearly 20 hours after the brutal assault.

The next day, Maria's parish priest, Father Signori, brought her Viaticum in the hospital. He reminded her of how Our Lord had pardoned His executioners on the Cross, and asked whether she forgave Alessandro. She focused her gaze on a crucifix on the wall and replied "Yes, for the love of Jesus I forgive him, and I want him to be with me in Paradise." She then received Last Rites and Viaticum, and died soon afterward.

Meanwhile, Alessandro was arrested and charged with murder. At first he denied everything, but the evidence against him was overwhelming and he was sentenced to thirty years hard labor. Though he would later admit that he had felt remorse for the murder from the start, for many years he concealed it out of pride, sometimes even bragging about his crime to his fellow inmates.

One night, about eight years into his sentence, Alessandro dreamed that he was in a beautiful flower garden. Maria came walking toward him dressed in a pure white gown; she was gathering an armful of white lilies. She then offered him a lily from the bouquet she held, but when he took it from her it transformed into a white flame. She then offered him another lily, which also turned into a flame as he took it. In that manner she offered him fourteen flowers in all - one for each stab wound he had inflicted on her years before. She then smiled and said "Alessandro, as I have promised, your soul shall someday reach me in Heaven."

When he awoke from the dream, he felt a deep peace along with profound penitence. He called to the prison guard to bring him a priest, to whom he confessed and received absolution for his sin. From then on, Alessandro became a model prisoner, so much so that he was released from prison three years early. The first thing he did when freed was ask Assunta's forgiveness, which she granted. He spent the rest of his life doing penance in reparation for his terrible sins. Alessandro testified during Maria's Cause of Beatification, and both he and Assunta were reportedly present when Maria was beatified in 1948. Two years later she was canonized by Pope Pius XII. Her feast day is July 6.

This terrible, yet beautiful, true story contains many lessons for us. St. Maria valued purity so highly that she was willing to lay down her life rather than lose it. As saints through the ages have said, "Death before mortal sin!" A pure, grace-filled soul is an immense treasure, to be fiercely guarded.

Alessandro, however, was a porn addict, which many reading this book have been in the past or may still be. His obsession with impurity eventually led him to murder an innocent twelve year old girl - which is probably *worse* than anything most readers of this book have done! Yet even he was not beyond redemption; the prayers of a saint saved his soul. There is hope for you as well, dear reader. No matter how far you have sunk into depravity, you can make it to Heaven through heartfelt repentance, prayer and penance, along with frequent reception of the Sacraments and relying on the prayers of the saints.

On 5 May 1961, Alessandro wrote the following personal testimony:

> "I'm nearly 80 years old. I'm about to depart. Looking back at my past, I can see that in my early youth, I chose a bad path which led me to ruin myself. My behavior was influenced by print, mass-media and bad examples which are followed by the majority of young people without even thinking. And I did the same. I was not worried…. When I was 20 years-old, I committed a crime of passion. Now, that memory represents something horrible for me. Maria Goretti, now a Saint, was my good Angel, sent to me through Providence to guide and save me. I still have impressed upon my heart her words of rebuke and of pardon. She prayed for me, she interceded for her murderer. Thirty years of prison followed….

> "I hope this letter that I wrote can teach others the happy lesson of avoiding evil and of always following the right path, like little children. I feel that religion with its precepts is not something we can live without, but rather it is the real comfort, the real strength in life and the only safe way in every circumstance, even the most painful ones of life.'[xcii]

A few days before his death in 1970, he wrote and signed his last message to the youth of the world: "I sincerely beg pardon of God and of the entire world for the outrage which I committed against the martyr Maria Goretti and against purity. With all my heart I urge you to avoid all immoral displays and all the dangerous occasions that can lead you to sin."

Resolution: Meditate on Maria's story and on Alessandro's words.

Saint Maria Goretti, patroness of purity, pray for us.

TRACK YOUR PROGRESS: *Since reading the Introduction, how many times have I:*

a) deliberately touched myself impurely while awake? ✓0 ___1 ___2 ___3 or more times
b) deliberately viewed indecent pictures or movies? ✓0 ___1 ___2 ___3 or more times
c) committed unchaste acts with others? ✓0 ___1 ___2 ___3 or more times
d) deliberately entertained/enjoyed impure thoughts? ✓0 ___1 ___2 ___3 or more times

e) When was the last time I went to Confession? 5 DAYS AGO to Mass? YESTERDAY

As a closing prayer today, instead of the *Prayer for Purity* you may wish to pray the *Prayer to St. Maria Goretti, Martyr for Purity,* found in Appendix IV.

MEDITATION 46: LOVE OF PURITY

As obedient children, do not conform to the lusts of former days when you were ignorant; but as the One who called you is holy, be you also holy in all your behavior; for it is written, "You shall be holy, because I am holy." - 1 Peter 1:14-16

Prayer: *O Jesus, Lover of purity, remove all lust from my heart, so that I may serve you with a pure mind and a chaste body.*[xciii]

We tend to pursue what we love and avoid what we hate. If we have pursued sins of the flesh in the past, it was because, on some level, we actually loved them – or at least the gratification we received from them. Once we uproot the love of sin from our hearts, turning it into bitter hatred, we must also replace our former love by sowing new loves there.

Since the beginning of this program we have seen the importance of love and devotion to Christ for regaining a clean heart. This continues to be true. Yet along with a love for God, we should also seek to cultivate a deep love for the virtue of holy purity; one at least as strong as our former love for impurity, if not stronger! For if we love and delight in purity, we will seek it with all our hearts and shun anything that would thwart our pursuit of purity.

This is the secret to long-term victory over sin: to establish in ones soul a deep hatred and horror of sins of the flesh, along with a fervent love for the virtue of holy purity. As St. John Cassian wrote: *"Chastity does not consist, as you think, in austere preventions, but rather in the love and in the delight of purity itself."*[xciv]

How does one cultivate a love for this virtue? First - as always - ask God to give you a fervent love for purity. Ask Him to grant you the grace to pursue it with all your heart. Second, meditate often on the beauty of purity and the benefits you will receive from practicing this virtue:

1. Purity will give you a clean conscience before God and others. It will set you free from guilt. You will no longer feel like a hypocrite who "talks holy" in public while offending God in private. Purity will also set you free from the fear that your secret sins will become known to others. For the first time in a long time, you will have nothing to hide.

2. Purity means you will not need to confess the same sins over and over again to the priest. Imagine what it would be like to go to confession and not have to tell the priest you touched yourself impurely – because you didn't do it this week! That is what purity will bring about in your life. It will enable you to walk in the light; living more consistently in a state of grace rather than in a state of mortal sin and spiritual darkness.

3. Purity will give you a greater appreciation for the world God created and for the simple joys of life. It will also draw you closer to Our Lord, enlighten your soul and deepen your interior life. Purity will remove hindrances to your prayers and break the Devil's stronghold in your life and (if you're married) in your family.

4. Purity will conform your life more perfectly to that of Christ, for Jesus Himself has a great love for the virtue of holy purity. In fact, two of His many beautiful titles are "Lover of purity" and "Lover of chastity." The *Imitation of Christ* puts these words on our Savior's lips: "I am the lover of purity, and the giver of all holiness. I seek a pure heart; and there is the place of my rest."[xcv] The Litany of the Holy Name of Jesus invokes Him as "Jesus, lover of chastity."

5. Purity will also make you more like the Blessed Virgin Mary, for she also loves chastity and purity, as St. John Damascene notes:

She is a virgin and a lover of virginity. She is pure and a lover of purity. If we purify our mind with the body, we shall possess her grace. She shuns all impurity and impure passions. She has a horror of intemperance, and a special hatred for fornication. She turns from its allurements as from the progeny of serpents.... In a word, she grieves over every sin, and is glad at all goodness as if it were her own. If we turn away from our former sins in all earnestness and love goodness with all our hearts, and make it our constant companion, she will frequently visit her servants, bringing all blessings with her, Christ her Son, the King and Lord who reigns in our hearts.[xcvi]

The more you love holy purity, the cleaner your heart will become. The cleaner your heart is, the more it will resemble the Immaculate Heart of Mary and be conformed to the Sacred Heart of Jesus. In short, purity will make you a better Christian.

Meditate also upon St. Alphonsus' high praise of the virtue of chastity:

No price is worthy of a continent soul. (Sir. 26:20) In comparison with a chaste soul, all the riches, all the titles and dignities of the earth are contemptible. Chastity is called by St. Ephrem the life of the spirit; by St. Peter Damian, the queen of virtues; and by St. Cyprian, the acquisition of triumphs. He who conquers the vice opposed to chastity, easily subdues all other vices; and, on the other hand, the man who submits to the tyranny of impurity, easily falls into many other vices, into hatred, injustice, sacrilege, etc.

Chastity, says St. Ephrem, changes a man into an angel. St. Bernard says, "Chastity makes an angel of man." And according to St. Ambrose, "he who has preserved chastity is an angel: he who has lost it is a devil." The chaste, who live at a distance from all carnal pleasures, are justly assimilated to the angels: *They shall be as the angels of God in Heaven.* (Mt. 22:30) The angels are pure by nature, but the chaste are pure by virtue.

"Through the merit of this virtue," says Cassian, "men are like unto angels." And St. Bernard asserts that a chaste man differs from an angel only in felicity, not in virtue; and although the chastity of the angel is more blissful, that of man is stronger. St. Basil adds, that chastity renders man like to God, Who is a pure spirit.... St. Athanasius, then, had reason to call chastity the house of the Holy Ghost, the life of angels, and the crown of Saints. And St. Jerome has justly called it the honor of the Church and the glory of priests.[xcvii]

The virtue of holy purity may not be easy to obtain, especially for those in the sorry habit of violating it. But it is more than worth the struggle! Whatever you might "lose" in giving up sins of the flesh is *worthless* compared with the treasures you will gain from a clean heart.

Resolution: Renew your resolve to hate sins against purity and to love God above all things. Pray earnestly for a deep love of holy purity and chastity, and meditate often on the many benefits of these virtues.

Jesus, Lover of chastity, have mercy on us.... From the spirit of fornication, deliver us, O Jesus.

TRACK YOUR PROGRESS: *Since reading the Introduction, how many times have I:*

a) deliberately touched myself impurely while awake? ___0 ___1 ___2 ___3 or more times
b) deliberately viewed indecent pictures or movies? ___0 ___1 ___2 ___3 or more times
c) committed unchaste acts with others? ___0 ___1 ___2 ___3 or more times
d) deliberately entertained/enjoyed impure thoughts? ___0 ___1 ___2 ___3 or more times

e) When was the last time I went to Confession?_____6_____ to Mass? YESTERDAY

MEDITATION 47: THE FOUR LAST THINGS   DEATH

In all you do, remember the end of your life, and then you will never sin. – Sirach 7:36 RSV

Prayer: *"I must die, I know not when, nor where, nor how, but if I die in mortal sin, I am lost forever. O Jesus, have mercy on me!"*

The "Four Last Things" are four future events that mankind will experience: *Death, Judgment, Hell* and *Heaven.* The Church teaches that we can benefit spiritually from meditation on these Four Last Things, for they inspire us to turn away from sin and seek to live a holy life. The first, *Death,* is the subject of this meditation; later meditations will cover the other three.

The thought of Death is unpleasant, so much so that some people may find this meditation difficult to read. The thought of ones own death is so distasteful, even frightening, that we tend to live our entire lives in denial about the fact that we will die someday. Yet death is the one sure thing in life; the only thing that we know for certain we will all endure. We make plans for tomorrow, for next week, next month, next year - but how do we know we will live long enough to fulfill them? We could die tomorrow, or even tonight in our sleep. We may not know exactly when, but we can be absolutely sure that, eventually, our earthly lives will end.

The above quote from the Book of Sirach states that reflection on ones mortality can actually help one to avoid sin. For this reason, the Church reminds us of the fleeting nature of this life, with all its pleasures and delights, when we receive ashes on our heads on Ash Wednesday and hear the sobering words: "Remember that you are dust, and to dust you shall return."

Some saints in the past used *"Memento mori"* - visual reminders of the reality of death[†] - to keep the thought of their future demise constantly before them. The most common momento mori were skulls or skeletons, but they were not limited to that. St. Alphonsus de Liguori once painted a watercolor portrait of the decomposed corpse of Alexander the Great for this purpose. Such graphic images were not meant to frighten or entertain, like modern Halloween decorations or horror movies. Nor were they based on a fascination with the macabre. They simply reminded the owner of his or her own mortality and so inspire humility before God, true repentance and avoidance of sin.

St. Alphonsus writes:

My brother, in this picture of death behold yourself and what you must one day become. "Remember that dust thou art, and unto dust thou shalt return." Consider that in a few years, and perhaps in a few months or days, you will become rottenness and worms.... All must end; and if, after death, you lose your soul, all will be lost for you. Consider yourself already dead, says St. Laurence Justinian, since you know that you must necessarily die. If you were already dead, what would you not desire to have done? Now that you have life, reflect that you will one day be among the dead. St. Bonaventure says that to guide the vessel safely, the pilot must remain at the helm; and in like manner, to lead a good life, a man should always imagine himself at the hour of death. "Look to the sins of your youth, and be covered with shame," says St. Bernard. "Remember the sins of manhood and weep." Look to the present disorders of your life; tremble, and hasten to apply a remedy.[xcviii]

Not only will we die, but all those centerfolds and porn stars who have been the objects of your lust will also die. Indeed, many have already departed this life. Some spiritual writers of the past actually suggested that one counter temptations against purity by mentally "peeling away" the skin of an attractive person and imagining the blood and bones underneath! Or by considering that the attractive physical form before their eyes would one day be reduced to a moldering corpse.

---

† Thanks to David Morrison for this information, which he posted on his *Sed Contra* blog (davidmorrison.typepad.com/sed_contra)

This book has not recommended such methods, since it is better to prayerfully flee a temptation than to mull it over - even in an attempt to refute it. Yet, bizarre as such counsel might seem to modern ears, it does provide some food for thought. Physical attractiveness and "sex appeal" are fleeting, yet your soul lasts forever. Why endanger your immortal soul for something that will someday perish and decompose?

St. Francis de Sales asks us to consider that, when we die:

the world is at end as far as you are concerned, there will be no more of it for you, it will be altogether overthrown for you, since all pleasures, vanities, worldly joys, empty delights will be as a mere fantastic vision to you. Woe is me, for what mere trifles and unrealities I have ventured to offend my God? Then you will see that what we preferred to Him was nought. But, on the other hand, all devotion and good works will then seem so precious and so sweet:--Why did I not tread that pleasant path? Then what you thought to be little sins will look like huge mountains, and your devotion will seem but a very little thing.[xcix]

There is an old Irish Catholic practice before going to sleep to fold ones arms over ones chest in the form of a cross and say the prayer at the beginning of this meditation: *"I must die, I know not when, nor where, nor how, but if I die in mortal sin, I am lost forever. O Jesus, have mercy on me!"* (This was often done right before a general examination of conscience). Again, though not a pleasant thought, it is a salutary one. It should inspire us to turn away from sin and the pleasures of this world, and instead pursue devotion, mortification, good deeds and holiness during our short time on this earth. For these we shall be rewarded someday; everything else we have pursued in life will be a loss.

Jesus, may I lead a good life, may I die a holy death. May I receive thee before I die. May I say when I am dying: "Jesus, Mary and Joseph, I give you my heart and my soul." Amen.

Resolution: Meditate upon your own demise. How might the thought of death change your attitude toward sins against purity? Remember to examine your conscience every night and ask forgiveness for any sins committed during the day.

Jesus, Mary, Joseph, assist me in my last agony! Jesus, Mary, Joseph, may I breathe forth my soul in peace with You!

TRACK YOUR PROGRESS: *Since reading the Introduction, how many times have I:*

a) deliberately touched myself impurely while awake? ___✓0 ___1 ___2 ___3 or more times
b) deliberately viewed indecent pictures or movies? ___✓0 ___1 ___2 ___3 or more times
c) committed unchaste acts with others? ___✓0 ___1 ___2 ___3 or more times
d) deliberately entertained/enjoyed impure thoughts? ___✓0 ___1 ___2 ___3 or more times

e) When was the last time I went to Confession?___8___ to Mass?_2 DAYS AGO_

MEDITATION 48: THE FOUR LAST THINGS   JUDGMENT

"The Lord knows how to deliver the God-fearing from temptation, and to reserve the wicked for torment on the day of judgment, but especially those who follow the flesh in unclean lust and despise authority." - 2 Peter 2:9-10

Prayer: *O Sovereign Judge of the living and the dead! Who, at the moment of our death, will decide our eternal doom, remember that Thou art our Savior as well as our Judge, and that as much as our sins have provoked Thee to wrath, Thy sacred Wounds have inclined Thee to mercy. Look, therefore, on those Wounds inflicted on Thee for our sins, and on the Blood which Thou hast shed for their expiation, and by those precious pledges of salvation we conjure Thee to pardon our manifold transgressions. Amen.*

The Church teaches that, at the moment of our death, we will each go to stand before the judgment seat of Christ. He will judge our entire life and declare our eternal destiny, after which we will go immediately either to Heaven, Purgatory, or Hell. This is called the *Particular Judgment.*

The *General Judgment*, also called the Last Judgment, will occur after the Second Coming of Christ at the end of time. God will resurrect every human being who ever existed and bring them to stand before Our Lord Jesus Christ, to receive an eternal sentence for how they lived on earth. Christ will divide humanity into two groups, the just and the damned, placing the former at His right hand and the latter at His left. Then our whole lives, our relationship with God (or lack thereof), the good things we have done or failed to do, the sins we have committed and the consequences of all our actions will be laid bare for all to see.

For the just this will be a day of vindication, but for the damned a day of terror and humiliation. All transgressions in deed, word and thought - including all secret sins - will be revealed for everyone to see (1 Cor. 4:4-5). Sinners will have nowhere to hide on that horrible day, and no hope of appeal when they are sentenced to the eternal flames. Let us pray earnestly that we do not end up in their number!

We may think our sins against purity are our own little secret, known to us alone. But this is an illusion. They are known to God, to His holy angels, to the infernal Enemy of our souls and to his minions. Plus, on the Day of Judgment they will be made known to all mankind: *"But I tell you, that of every idle word men speak, the shall give account on the day of judgment. For by thy words thou wilt be justified, and by thy words thou wilt be condemned"* (Mt. 12:36-37). Venerable Louis of Granada comments:

If we must render an account of idle words which harm no one, how severe will be the account exacted of us for impure words, immodest actions, sinful glances, bloodstained hands, for all the time spent in sinful deeds? We could hardly credit the severity of this judgment, did not God Himself affirm it. Oh! Sublime religion, how great are the purity and perfection thou teachest!

What shame, then, and what confusion will overwhelm the sinner when all his impurities, all his excesses, all his iniquities, hidden in the secret recesses of his heart, will be exposed, in all their enormity, to the eyes of the world! Whose conscience is so clear that he does not blush, does not tremble, at this thought? If men find it so difficult to make known their sins in the secrecy of confession, if many prefer to groan under the weight of their iniquities rather than declare them to God's minister, how will they bear to see them revealed before the universe?

On Judgment Day *"Nothing is covered up that will not be revealed, or hidden that will not be known. Whatever you have said in the dark shall be heard in the light, and what you have whispered in private rooms shall be proclaimed upon the housetops"* (Lk. 12:2-3 RSV). This is a good reason for you to confess all your past sins of the flesh, overcome this terrible habit and avoid such sins for the rest of your life! You don't want to end up at the left hand of the Just Judge; you don't want to hear those terrible words: "Depart from me, you cursed, into everlasting fire" addressed to *you.*

To avoid that, you must abandon sin and pursue holiness. St. Francis de Sales writes:

Abhor your sins, which alone can cause you to be lost when that fearful day comes. Surely I will judge myself now, that I be not judged; - I will examine my conscience, accuse, condemn, punish myself, that the Judge may not condemn me then. I will confess my faults, and follow the counsels given me.... Thank God for having given you means of safety in that terrible Day, and time for repentance. Offer Him your heart, and ask for grace to use it well.[cii]

Even if this means enduring temptations against purity every day for the rest of your life, it is worth it. For if you resist them with the help of God's grace, a special reward will await you at the Judgment Seat of Christ: *"Blessed is the man who endures temptation; for when he has been tried, he will receive the crown of life which God has promised to those who love him"* (Jas. 1:12). As the *Imitation of Christ* says:

'Be careful at present and sorry for your sins, that in the Day of Judgment you may be secure with the blessed. For then shall the just stand with great constancy against those that have afflicted and oppressed them' (Wis. 5:1). Then he who now humbly submits himself to the judgment of men, will stand to judge. Then the poor and humble will have great confidence, and the proud will fear on every side.

Then it will appear that he who learned for Christ's sake to be a fool and to be despised was a wise man in this world. Then all tribulation suffered patiently will be pleasing and "all iniquity shall stop her mouth" (Ps. 106:42). Then every pious person will rejoice and the irreligious will be sad.

Then the flesh that has been mortified will triumph more than if it had been nourished in delights. Then will the lowly habit shine and fine clothing appear dingy. Then will the poor cottage be praised more than the gilded palace. Then constant patience will be of more use than all the power of the world. Then simple obedience will be more valued than all worldly craftiness.

Then a pure and good conscience will bring more joy than the knowledge of philosophy. Then contempt for riches will weigh more than all the treasures of the children of earth. Then will you be more comforted that you had prayed devoutly than that you had feasted daintily. Then will you rejoice more that you had kept silence than that you had made long speeches or talked much. Then will holy works be of greater value than many fair words. Then will a strict life and hard penance be more pleasing than all the joys of the earth.[ciii]

Resolution: Read what the Catechism says about the Judgment (#1021-1022 and #1038-1041). Pray for your salvation and the grace to avoid sins against purity for the rest of your life. Make a good Confession often.

My sweetest Jesus, be not my Judge, but my Saviour.

TRACK YOUR PROGRESS: *Since reading the Introduction, how many times have I:*

a) deliberately touched myself impurely while awake? ___0 ✓1 ___2 ___3 or more times
b) deliberately viewed indecent pictures or movies? ✓0 ___1 ___2 ___3 or more times
c) committed unchaste acts with others? ✓0 ___1 ___2 ___3 or more times
d) deliberately entertained/enjoyed impure thoughts? ___0 ✓1 ___2 ___3 or more times

e) When was the last time I went to Confession?__9_____ to Mass? _YESTERDAY_

MEDITATION 49: THE FOUR LAST THINGS   HELL

But as for the cowardly, the faithless, the polluted, as for murderers, fornicators, sorcerers, idolaters, and all liars, their lot shall be in the lake that burns with fire and sulphur - Apocalypse 21:15

Oh my God I am heartily sorry for having offended Thee, and I detest all my sins because I fear the loss of heaven and I dread the pains of hell…

Presumption is assuming that you will make it to Heaven no matter what you do. Thinking that you can sin all you like because God will just keep forgiving you, and that you will surely get a chance to repent before death and make it to Heaven.

While it is true that some great sinners have repented on their deathbed and made it to Heaven, we cannot presume that we will also get that chance. Many sinners have also had their lives end suddenly, leaving them no time to repent. We don't know when we will die, and a sudden death is as much a possibility as a long, drawn-out deathbed ordeal.

Presumption is a sin because it postpones repentance, ignores the justice of God and so sends many souls to Hell. The sin of presumption often seems to go hand-in-hand with habitual sins against purity. When the Tempter whispers, "Go ahead, God will forgive you; after all, you can always confess it later," he is tempting you to presume upon the mercy of God while disregarding His justice and hatred of sin. Believing and acting on this demonic lie will further reinforce ones sinful habits, causing one to sin again and again: "God is merciful; He understands. I can enjoy this sin now because He'll forgive me later."

Sacred Scripture dispels this illusion by informing us that habitual sins of the flesh exclude people from Heaven. *"Do not err; neither fornicators, nor idolaters, nor adulterers, nor the effeminate, nor sodomites, nor thieves, nor the covetous, nor drunkards, nor the evil tongued, nor the greedy will possess the kingdom of God"* (1 Cor. 6:9-10). How common these sins are in the world! How common they are even among Christians. It has been said that, as pride has filled Hell with angels, so impurity has filled it with men.[civ] How foolish to treat mortal sins so lightly! How many times have we endangered our immortal souls for a few empty moments of physical gratification?

You can begin to counter the sin of presumption by convincing yourself of the awful reality of Hell and that you could very well end up there. Imagine for a moment being a state of eternal alienation from God, deprived of grace and the Beatific Vision, suffering unspeakable torment as just punishment for ones sins. Consider that if you ever end up in such a state, it will not be by accident or some divine cruelty, but entirely your own fault. Jesus died a horrendous death to save you from sin, gave you sanctifying grace in the Sacrament of Baptism and numerous graces throughout your life. He gave you every blessing and opportunity for salvation, but you preferred to be His servant in name only while living a self-centered, pleasure-seeking life, postponing repentance, presuming upon His mercy while blithely ignoring His holiness and justice. You refused to take up your cross and follow Him; you have damned yourself.

If men who sin so rashly would weigh this truth, they would know the terrible burden that they lay upon themselves. Those who earn their living by carrying burdens first estimate the weight they are to bear, that they may know whether it is beyond their strength. Why, then, O rash man, will you – for a passing pleasure – so lightly assume the terrible burden of sin, without considering your strength to bear it? Will you not reflect on the heavy weight you thus condemn yourself to bear for all eternity?[cv]

Yes, you could end up in Hell, but do not allow this thought to drive you to despair. While the sin of presumption ignores Divine Justice, the sin of despair forgets about the Divine Mercy. God wants you to be happy with Him forever in Heaven, and gives you sufficient grace to achieve that end. So give thanks to Him for your salvation and ask Him to deliver you from the twin sins of presumption and despair.

Now, some readers might object, "Why all this talk of Hell? Doesn't the Church teach that perfect contrition is superior to imperfect contrition? Shouldn't we avoid sin out of pure love for God rather than fear of hell-fire?" Yes, perfect contrition is far superior to imperfect contrition, and our love for God should be strong enough to cause us to shun sin. Indeed, a perfect love for God would even expel from our souls all fear of eternal punishment (1 John 4:17-18).

Yet how many of us truly have a perfect love for God? If we are honest with ourselves, we will realize that our love for Him is often weak and inconstant. This is why we may sometimes need to fall back on fear of damnation to keep us from sin. Many saints and spiritual writers have said as much in the past, as in this quote from the *Imitation of Christ:*

> For he who loves God with his whole heart fears neither death, nor punishment, nor judgment, nor hell; because perfect love gives certain access to God. But he who is still delighted with sin, no wonder if he fears death and judgment. It is good, however, that if love, as yet, reclaim you not from evil, that at least the fear of hell check you. But he who lays aside the fear of God will not be able to persevere long in good, But will quickly fall into the snares of the devil.[cvi]

So do not despise this possible weapon in your struggle. If a healthy fear of Hell helps you to avoid sin, make use of it. Yet make sure that you are not driven to despair; trust always in God's Mercy and continually ask the Holy Ghost to perfect your love for Him.

One possible way to fight presumption is to recall St. Maria Goretti's warning to her would-be rapist and murderer: "No, no, it is a sin...you will go to Hell!" Simple words, spoken by a child - yet so full of wisdom and truth! Make this little saint's words your own. Tell yourself over and over again, "Pornography is a sin, I will go to Hell if I view it," or "Masturbation is a sin, I will go to Hell if I do that." Say the same about any besetting sin of the flesh. Ask St. Maria to pray that the truth of those words may really sink in to your mind and heart. Learn from her words to never take sins of the flesh lightly or your salvation for granted.

Resolution: Read what the Catechism says about Hell (#1033-1037). Recall St. Maria Goretti's words often in relation to sins against purity.

O my Jesus, forgive us our sins, save us from the fires of Hell.

TRACK YOUR PROGRESS: *Since reading the Introduction, how many times have I:*

a) deliberately touched myself impurely while awake?   ___0 ___1 ___2 ✓3 or more times
b) deliberately viewed indecent pictures or movies?   ___0 ___1 ___2 ✓3 or more times
c) committed unchaste acts with others?   ✓0 ___1 ___2 ___3 or more times
d) deliberately entertained/enjoyed impure thoughts?   ___0 ___1 ___2 ✓3 or more times

e) When was the last time I went to Confession?_10_____ to Mass?_YESTERDAY_____

MEDITATION 50: THE FOUR LAST THINGS   HEAVEN

Or do you not know that the unjust will not possess the kingdom of God? Do not err; neither fornicators, nor idolaters, nor adulterers, nor the effeminate, nor sodomites, nor thieves, nor the covetous, nor drunkards, nor the evil-tongued, nor the greedy will possess the kingdom of God. And such were some of you, but you have been washed, you have been sanctified, you have been justified in the name of the Lord Jesus Christ and in the Spirit of our God. - 1 Corinthians 6:9-11

Prayer: *O good Jesus, hear me. Within Thy wounds hide me. Permit me not to be separated from Thee. From the malignant enemy defend me. In the hour of my death call me and bid me come unto Thee, that with Thy saints I may praise Thee forever and ever. Amen.* – from the Anima Christi

Yesterday, we briefly considered the first part of the above Scripture passage. Those who have struggled with habitual sins against purity may find this quote rather frightening. Yet, let's not forget about the second part: *"And such were some of you, but you have been washed, you have been sanctified, you have been justified in the name of the Lord Jesus Christ and in the Spirit of our God."*

Note the word *were* - past tense. You *were* a fornicator, or an adulterer, or a sodomite - or a viewer of indecent images, or a self-abuser. Yet if you have sincerely and deeply repented, rejected those activities and relied on the grace of God to keep you pure, then you no longer are a fornicator, an adulterer, a sodomite, a viewer of indecent images, a self-abuser. You no longer engage in those practices now.

This does not mean that you will never again fall back into such behavior. You could very well return to them if you are not vigilant. After all, God set you free from the domination of sin at your Baptism, yet you became a slave to it again later through bad choices and actions. It could certainly happen again, especially since, barring a miracle, you will likely carry a proclivity toward such sins for the rest of your life. So never become puffed up with pride; remember that any victory you have gained over sin comes from God and not from yourself. Remain humble before Our Lord and rely on His grace always.

While frightening in one sense, 1 Corinthians 6:9-11 is reassuring as well. For if you are no longer a fornicator, adulterer, etc., if you have been sanctified and justified, then you have a real chance of someday possessing the kingdom of God. If you remain in a state of grace and victory over sin for the rest of your life, you will ultimately attain to Heaven. *"For once you were darkness, but now you are light in the Lord. Walk, then, as children of light (for the fruit of the light is in all goodness and justice and truth), testing what is well pleasing to God"* (Eph. 5:8-10). If a once-foul sinner like Alessandro Serenelli can now stand in the glory of Heaven, next to the pure young girl he murdered in a fit of lust, there is hope for you as well!

Even if you fall sometime in the future, you can regain His grace through the Sacrament of Penance, and if you die in a state of grace you will go to Heaven. This is the goal of every Christian, and the bliss of the Beatific Vision is by far greater than any earthly pleasure or delight or physical gratification.

The belief that the procreative act is evil or sinful is not Christian, but an error characteristic of heterodox groups such as the Manichaeans and Shakers. An opposite error involves the divinization of sex, as is found in certain forms of paganism which either profess that their gods have physical relations or that humans can use venereal acts to "achieve union with the Divine." This is also not a Christian belief.

Our Catholic Faith avoids either extreme, teaching instead that conjugal relations are a *natural good* reserved for the marriage bond. Though its misuse is sinful, sex is not innately evil, but part of God's good creation. On the other hand, although it is an earthly sign of the union of Christ and the Church, the marital act does not divinize us - that is the work of the Sacraments.

The teaching that virginity is superior to marriage also helps keep sex in its proper perspective. The marital act is but a temporal good that does not exist in the World to Come. In Heaven, all are celibate, yet they are deprived of nothing because they enjoy the Beatific Vision - to which no earthly pleasure can compare.

So sex, though an earthly good, is not the greatest good. The pleasure that accompanies it is not the best or highest or most perfect experience, nor is it something that one "cannot live without." If one dies a virgin, one will not necessarily have died "unfulfilled," for how many saints have preserved their virginity until death? It is important for all Christians to keep this perspective in the pathetically sex-saturated culture in which we live.

St. Aloysius Gonzaga, a young saint renowned for his purity of heart, is said to have judged everything in life according to the saying, *Quid hoc ad aeternitatem?* This translates as, *"What is this to eternity?"* meaning: What is this matter in light of eternity? How does this act, thing or event compare with eternity, and what may be the eternal consequences of what I do?

Let us learn to judge physical gratification this way. If you see an attractive, immodestly dressed person, turn away and ask yourself, *Quid hoc ad aeternitatem?* Think about Heaven instead. Or if you are tempted to touch yourself impurely, think, *Quid hoc ad aeternitatem?* Is the momentary gratification I may get from the act anything to compare with the eternal joy and bliss and consolation of Paradise? Is it worth the loss of Paradise?

It would be helpful for us to learn more about and meditate often on Heaven, and so gain a great love for it. St. Francis de Sales encourages us to think about Heaven as follows:

1. Represent to yourself a lovely calm night, when the heavens are bright with innumerable stars: add to the beauty of such a night the utmost beauty of a glorious summer's day, - the sun's brightness not hindering the clear shining of moon or stars, and then be sure that it all falls immeasurably short of the glory of Paradise. O bright and blessed country, O sweet and precious place!

2. Consider the beauty and perfection of the countless inhabitants of that blessed country; - the millions and millions of angels, Cherubim and Seraphim; the glorious company of Apostles, martyrs, confessors, virgins, and saints. O blessed company, any one single member of which surpasses all the glory of this world, what will it be to behold them all, to sing with them the sweet Song of the Lamb? They rejoice with a perpetual joy, they share a bliss unspeakable, and unchangeable delights.

3. Consider how they enjoy the Presence of God, Who fills them with the richness of His Vision, which is a perfect ocean of delight; the joy of being for ever united to their Head. They are like happy birds, hovering and singing for ever within the atmosphere of divinity, which fills them with inconceivable pleasures. There each one vies without jealousy in singing the praises of the Creator. "Blessed art Thou for ever, O Dear and Precious Lord and Redeemer, Who dost so freely give us of Thine Own Glory," they cry; and He in His turn pours out His ceaseless Blessing on His Saints. "Blessed are ye, - Mine own for ever, who have served Me faithfully, and with a good courage."[xvii]

Such meditations should cause us to love our heavenly homeland, to despise sinful gratification that can prevent us from attaining it, and to aspire toward Heaven, abandoning anything that hinders us.

Resolution: Read what the Catechism says about Heaven (#1023-1029) and about the New Heaven and New Earth (#1042-1050). Start to consider things in the light of eternity: *Quid hoc ad aeternitatem?* Meditate often on Heaven and resolve to abandon anything that might hinder your going there.

All you holy angels and saints in heaven, pray for us.

TRACK YOUR PROGRESS: *Since reading the Introduction, how many times have I:*

a) deliberately touched myself impurely while awake?	___0 ✔1 ___2 ___3 or more times
b) deliberately viewed indecent pictures or movies?	✔0 ___1 ___2 ___3 or more times
c) committed unchaste acts with others?	✔0 ___1 ___2 ___3 or more times
d) deliberately entertained/enjoyed impure thoughts?	___0 ✔1 ___2 ___3 or more times

e) When was the last time I went to Confession?___11_____ to Mass?_2 DAYS AGO_

MEDITATION 51: FINAL ADVICE

This, therefore, I say and testify in the Lord, that henceforth you are not to walk as the Gentiles walk, in the futility of their mind, having their understanding clouded in darkness, estranged from the life of God through the ignorance that is in them, because of the blindness of their heart. For they have given themselves up in despair to sensuality, greedily practicing every kind of uncleanness. But you have not so learned Christ…. As regards your former manner of life you are to put off the old man, which is being corrupted through its deceptive lusts. But be renewed in the spirit of your mind, and put on the new man, which has been created according to God in justice and holiness of truth. - Ephesians 4:17-24

Prayer: *Grant, we beseech Thee, Almighty and everlasting God, that we may attain to purity of mind and body through the inviolate virginity of the most pure Virgin Mary. Amen.* – Raccolta #715

Reread and ponder the quote from Ephesians that begins this final meditation. This is St. Paul's charge to you. You must no longer live like an unbeliever, but like a Christian. Their minds are darkened by sin, your mind must be renewed and enlightened by Christ. They are estranged from God, you possess His life in your soul and must seek intimacy with Him. They live in despair, you have hope; they give themselves over to impurity, you must shun impurity and sanctify yourself to the service of Our Lord in righteousness and holiness. Let this be the way you live your life in Christ Jesus from now on.

Now that you have completed these meditations, it is highly recommended that continue praying the three Ave's and *O Domina Mea* prayer every morning and evening, which you began after the second meditation. If you choose not to continue praying them, make sure to replace them with some other form of spiritual discipline: the Liturgy of the Hours, perhaps joining a third order, confraternity, sodality or other such group. The Catholic Faith has a rich and diverse spiritual tradition; do not fail to take advantage of it.

Continue to *always*, **always** look to Jesus rather than vice. These meditations should have helped sever your ties to habitual sins of the flesh, and build spiritual ties with Our Lord. Do not slip backward, but keep moving forward, for you have only begun your journey on the road to sanctity and union with God.

Always remember the ugliness of sin and the three attitudes you must have toward it: *Sorrow, Hatred* and *Horror.* Do not dwell on your sinful past, but if you ever happen to remember it, greet the memory with profound remorse rather than fondness, then dismiss it. Ask God for the grace to keep loathing the very thought of sin and feeling deep revulsion over the thought of ever sinning again. You are not likely to do something that you regret, hate and dread with all your heart!

Here is some more advice to help you persevere in purity:

1. **Beware of Pride**. The cardinal sin of Pride is a constant, crafty enemy. It will keep trying to slip back into your life in various ways. Sooner or later, you will find yourself thinking, "Well, I haven't sinned in so many months, I must be over it now; I have beaten the problem." Do not entertain this thought! No matter how long you resist sin, your strength and victories will always come from God, not yourself. Do not forget that fact, and keep humbling yourself before Him. Never consider yourself "over it," *never* believe you have beaten the problem.

2. **Keep away from near occasions of sin.** After remaining pure a long time, you also may be tempted to relax your vigilance. You may even start to toy with occasions of sin, by watching questionable TV shows again or reading bad books, magazines or web sites, thinking, "I'm stronger now, I can handle it." **Beware,** for this is one of the Devil's favorite tricks. Such overconfidence has caused many devout souls to fall, even people more spiritually advanced than you are! *"Can a man carry fire in his bosom and his clothes not be burned? Or can one walk upon hot coals and his feet not be scorched?"* (Prov. 6:27-28) Never overestimate your own strength. Keep the blocking software on the computer, keep the adult channels blocked on your cable or satellite service, continue to avoid all near occasions of sin as you have throughout this course.

110

3. **Be especially vigilant during trying times**. We all experience times of profound loss, such as the death of a loved one, unemployment, chronic illness, financial difficulties, etc.. During such times, the Devil might try to take advantage of your pain by suggesting the stolen pleasure of sin as a temporary "high." He may use the pathetic voice of self-pity: "Your life is so difficult, you're suffering so much. Don't you deserve just a little pleasure? How could God begrudge you that?" Yet sins of the flesh solve nothing and only cause more problems. So turn instead to Jesus for solace in difficult times, and offer up your suffering, uniting it with His. Deny yourself and embrace you cross, as He did.

4. **Join the fight against impurity**. Pornography is ruining our youth, our families, our society. A whole generation of young people is absorbing a distorted view of human sexuality from cyberporn, which will negatively affect their future relationships. Families are being torn apart by divorce when one partner becomes deeply ensnared in sins against purity, children are viewing the most disgusting hardcore images at younger and younger ages. Porn is quickly becoming mainstreamed, infecting other forms of entertainment media such as movies, music and television. Something must be done about this satanic plague before it consumes our society in darkness.

Have you ever asked yourself "Why?" Why did God ever allow you to become enslaved to sins of the flesh in the first place? After all, we believe that Our Lord is in control of our lives. Nothing happens to us in life unless He wills or permits it, and even the negative experiences He permits us to endure work out somehow for our good in His ultimate plan. What purpose, then, could your enslavement to sins against purity play in His greater plan for you?

Though we ultimately cannot know His mind, perhaps God allowed you to fall into this sin because He wanted you to gain victory over it by His grace and then *help others* to gain victory as well. Perhaps God is calling you to make known to others the truths that have set you free, to show others by word and example the beauty of a clean heart, and so help restore purity to our impure society.

So if you have gained victory over this sin by His grace, consider joining the fight against the sins which once ensnared you. If you know of others struggling with this sin, introduce them to this book. If you make sacramentals, learn how to make Cords of St. Joseph or Immaculate Conception chaplets. You could start a pro-purity web site or join a group like the *Angelic Warfare Confraternity* or the *Serenellians* for adults, *St. Joseph's Covenant Keepers* or *True Knights* for men, or the *Pure Love Club* for young people (you will find contact information for these groups in the **Resources and Bibliography** section at the end). In the spirit of St. Thomas Aquinas, let us seize the firebrand and drive vice from the lives of our brothers and sisters in Christ.

Resolution: Take this final advice to heart, and never forget it. Most of all, stay humble and rely on God's grace. If you have not done so, obtain a copy of the book Sex and the Mysteries, by John M. Haffert (AMI Press, 1970) and read it as a follow-up to the Clean of Heart program.

God our Father and Creator, have mercy on us.

Instead of the *Prayer for Purity,* say this Closing Prayer today:

> O Sovereign and Eternal God, I thank Thee for having created me; for having redeemed me by means of Jesus Christ; for having made me a Christian by calling me to the true Faith, and giving me time to repent after the many sins I have committed. O Infinite Goodness, I love Thee above all things; and I repent with all my heart of all my offenses against Thee. I hope Thou hast already pardoned me; but I am continually in danger of again offending Thee. For the love of Jesus Christ, I beg of Thee holy perseverance till death. Thou knowest my weakness; help me, then, and permit me never again to separate myself from Thee. Rather let me die a thousand times, than ever again to lose Thy grace. O Mary, my Mother, obtain for me holy perseverance! Amen. - St. Alphonsus[cviii]

Now one of the Pharisees asked Jesus to dine with him; so He went into the house of the Pharisee and reclined at table. And behold, a woman in the town who was a sinner, upon learning that He was at table in the Pharisee's house, brought an alabaster jar of ointment; and standing behind Him at his feet, she began to bathe His feet with her tears, and wiped them with the hair of her head, and kissed His feet, and anointed them with ointment.

Now when the Pharisee, who had invited Him, saw it, he said to himself, "This man, were He a prophet, would surely know who and what manner of woman this is who is touching Him, for she is a sinner."

And Jesus answered and said to him, "Simon, I have something to say to thee." And he said, "Master, speak."

"A certain money-lender had two debtors; the one owed five hundred denarii, the other fifty. As they had no means of paying, he forgave them both. Which of them, therefore, will love him more?"

Simon answered and said, "He, I suppose, to whom he forgave more." And He said to him, "Thou hast judged rightly."

And turning to the woman, He said to Simon, "Dost thou see this woman? I came into thy house; thou gavest Me no water for My feet; but she has bathed My feet with tears, and has wiped them with her hair. Thou gavest Me no kiss; but she, from the moment I entered, has not ceased to kiss My feet. Thou didst not anoint My head with oil; but she has anointed My feet with ointment. Wherefore I say to thee, her sins, many as they are, shall be forgiven her, because she has loved much. But he to whom little is forgiven, loves little."

And He said to her, "Thy sins are forgiven." Then they who were at table with him began to say within themselves, "Who is this man, who even forgives sins?" But He said to the woman, "Thy faith has saved thee; go in peace."

- Saint Luke 7:6 50

Merciful Jesus, I Trust in You!

APPENDIX I: MORE LIES AND EMPTY PROMISES

Here are some more lies the Tempter might tell you to try to convince you to sin:

LIE: **"You are married, so it's okay to use indecent images as a 'marital aid'."**

TRUTH: Viewing indecent images is sinful even for married couples. Nothing sinful can "aid" the holy covenant and Sacrament of Matrimony; in fact using that stuff will only prove detrimental to your marriage in the long run. Indecent pictures make people feel inadequate about themselves and dissatisfied with their spouses, since few can measure up to the unrealistic images found in porn. You will soon find yourself desiring your spouse less - and pornography more!

Scripture says that marriage must be held in honor by all, and the marriage bed kept undefiled (Hebrews 13:4). Pornography fails on both counts. Rather than holding marriage in honor, it deceptively portrays all sorts of infidelity and extramarital sex as being normal and fun, which reveals a profound *disrespect* for marriage! It also defiles the marriage bed by putting images of other men and women in the minds of the spouses, thus turning their focus away from each other. These things all tend to undermine a marriage, not "aid" it.

LIE: **Pornography has become mainstream and acceptable now, so it's perfectly okay to view it.**

TRUTH: Mainstream or not, it is still harmful. Its greater acceptance today only enables it to do even more harm to countless men, women and children. How many more marriages, families, careers and lives have to be ruined by porn before our culture finally wakes up and recognizes its fundamentally evil nature?

LIE: **Just look at photos of naturists; that's not real porn so it's okay.**

TRUTH: If you have a problem in this area, such pictures can still be occasions of sin if they put more impure images in your head. So fill your mind with holy things instead by gazing at icons and memorizing Scripture.

LIE: **"Pornography and masturbation are okay because sex is a good gift of God."**

TRUTH: Sex is indeed a good gift of God, but we must use it as God intended. Any *abuse* of His good gift is certainly *not* good, but sinful.

LIE: **Lust is normal; there's absolutely nothing wrong with it.**

TRUTH: While sexual desire is a normal physical urge (though even that must be kept under control), lust is an *illicit* craving for carnal gratification. It is a sin (Matthew 5:28; 1 John 2:15-17), in fact, one of the seven cardinal sins. As we will discuss in Meditation Four tomorrow, God does not want us to live in sin, so He does not want us to indulge our lust.

LIE: **Sex is the most important thing in your life; you need it! You can't live without it!**

TRUTH: Your Creator is more important than anyone or anything else; you need Him, not sin. You certainly don't need something as distorted as lust. It is only hurting you and will continue to hurt you as long as you indulge in it. You do not need sins of the flesh and, by the grace of God, you *can* live without them!

LIE: **"You only do that stuff when you're all by yourself; you're not hurting anyone."**

TRUTH: Sins against purity engender bad habits and endanger your immortal soul, so you are definitely hurting yourself. If you are married, your activities are affecting your family as well, whether you realize it or not. If your spouse ever finds out, he or she may feel very hurt and may never trust you again. If your children ever find your stash of porn, it may start them on the path to habitual sins of the flesh that could ultimately lead to their damnation. Your family will most likely discover your "secret" activities sooner or later, so you are setting a terrible example for your kids. Also, if you are purchasing this stuff, that means less money for your family and more going to support the porn industry, which sexually exploits many men, women and children. You are probably hurting a lot more people than you realize....

LIE: **"You're not a kid anymore, you're an adult; you can handle programs with mature themes now."**

TRUTH: This lie is tailored to appeal to your pride. The Tempter may also want you to recall how you felt as a minor when you couldn't watch certain movies or programs, so you may want to "make up for" your previous "deprivation." Yet sinful forms of entertainment will still negatively affect your soul, regardless of your age. Refusing to view them will not *deprive* you of anything, rather it will help foster purity of heart, which will in turn help you *gain* a deeper communion with God.

LIE: **"This is a natural physical urge, how can you resist something natural?"**

TRUTH: Another lie intended to cause despair; don't fall for it. "Natural" does not mean irresistible, for many celibates resist the same natural urges all their lives with the help of grace. Again, pray for the virtue of hope.

LIE: **"It's no use, you'll never overcome your sins. You've been committing them for too long.**

TRUTH: Once again we hear the voice of despair. Yet nothing is impossible with God! Jesus died to save you from sin, and He is more powerful than evil. He can give you the victory; ask Him for the grace to overcome your habitual sin. Humble yourself before Him and trust in Him, not in yourself.

LIE: **If others knew the real you they wouldn't like you.**

TRUTH: God knows every sinful thing you do yet He still loves you. So does your Guardian Angel. Many other people have struggled or continue to struggle with this compulsion and would be compassionate and understanding towards you. You are not alone.

APPENDIX II: RENEWAL OF BAPTISMAL VOWS

1. If holy water is available, get it now before you start. You will use it later.

2. Place yourself in the awesome Presence of Christ the King, and pray one of these prayers:

> O Christ Jesus, I acknowledge Thee as Universal King. All that has been made, was created for Thee. Exercise over me all the rights that Thou hast. I renew my Baptismal promises, renouncing Satan, his pomps, and his works, and I promise to live as a good Christian. Especially do I pledge myself, by all the means in my power, to bring about the triumph of the rights of God and of Thy Church.
>
> Divine Heart of Jesus, I consecrate all my poor actions to the cause of Thy Kingship, that all hearts may recognize Thee their Ruler and thus establish the kingdom of Thy peace in all the world. Amen[cix]

OR:

> I, N. N., who through the tender mercy of the Eternal Father was privileged to be baptized "in the name of the Lord Jesus" (Acts 19, 5) and thus to share in the dignity of his divine Sonship, wish now in the presence of this same loving Father and of his only-begotten Son to renew in all sincerity the promises I solemnly made at the time of my holy Baptism.
>
> I, therefore, now do once again renounce Satan; I renounce all his works; I renounce all his allurements.
>
> I believe in God, the Father almighty, Creator of heaven and earth. I believe in Jesus Christ, his only Son, our Lord, who was born into this world and who suffered and died for my sins and rose again. I believe in the Holy Spirit, the Holy Catholic Church, the communion of Saints, the forgiveness of sins, the resurrection of the body and life everlasting.
>
> Having been buried with Christ unto death and raised up with him unto a new life, I promise to live no longer for myself or for that world which is the enemy of God but for him who died for me and rose again, serving God, my heavenly Father, faithfully and unto death in the holy Catholic Church.
>
> Taught by our Savior's command and formed by the word of God, I now dare to say:
>
> Our Father, who art in heaven, hallowed be thy name; thy kingdom come; thy will be done on earth as it is in heaven. Give us this day our daily bread; and forgive us our trespasses as we forgive those who trespass against us; and lead us not into temptation, but deliver us from evil. Amen.[cx]

3. Now bless yourself with the holy water, if you have it. You may also wish say this prayer: *"By this holy water and by Thy Precious Blood, wash away all my sins, O Lord."*

4. You may now wish to meditate on Romans 6:2-10, which explains how you died to sin at Baptism:

> How can we who died to sin still live in it? Do you not know that all of us who have been baptized into Christ Jesus were baptized into his death? We were buried therefore with him by baptism into death, so that as Christ was raised from the dead by the glory of the Father, we too might walk in newness of life. For if we have been united with him in a death like his, we shall certainly be united with him in a resurrection like his. We know that our former man was crucified with him so that the sinful body might be destroyed, and we might no longer be enslaved to sin. For he who has died is freed from sin. But if we have died with Christ, we believe that we shall also live with him. For we know that Christ being raised from the dead will never die again; death no longer has dominion over him. The death he died he died to sin, once for all, but the life he lives he lives to God. (RSV-SCE)

APPENDIX III: EXAMINATION OF CONSCIENCE

Have I entertained and delighted in impure thoughts and fantasies?
Have I read impure books, magazines, comics, etc.?
Have I viewed suggestive or indecent TV shows, movies, web sites, etc.?
Have I drawn, photographed or written anything obscene?
Do I own indecent reading material or movies?
Have I shown, lent or sold them to others?
Have I done anything to provoke impure thoughts in other people?
Have I destroyed another person's innocence?
Do I dress immodestly in public?
Have I willfully lusted after someone?

Have I used obscene words, told immodest stories, off-color jokes, etc.?
Have I enjoyed hearing immodest words, songs, stories, jokes, conversations, etc.?
Have I boasted about my sins against purity?
Have I committed acts of self-abuse?
Have I kissed or touched someone in an impure manner? (Normal conjugal relations don't count.)
Have I permitted someone to do that to me? (Normal conjugal relations don't count.)
Have I deliberately caused someone to climax apart from coitus?
Have I committed fornication?
Am I cohabiting with someone apart from marriage?
Have I committed adultery?
Have I solicited prostitutes?
Have I worked in a sex trade?
Have I committed incest?
Have I committed pedophilia?
Have I engaged in transvestitism?
Have I committed any homosexual activity?
Have I committed any other unnatural acts?

Do I try to control my thoughts and imagination?
Do I immediately seek to banish impure thoughts?
Do I pray immediately to resist temptation?
Do I try to avoid near occasions of sin?
Do I seek to be chaste in my words and actions?
Do I turn away from immodest images or people?
Am I careful to dress modestly myself?
Do I treat other human beings as objects?
Do I respect all members of the opposite sex as persons made in God's image?
Do I have a reverent attitude toward love, marriage, family, motherhood and fatherhood?

For the Married:
Have I been faithful to my marriage vows in both thought and deed?
Have I engaged in sexual activity outside of marriage?
Have I used artificial contraception in my marriage?
Have I denied my spouse his or her marriage rights?
Did we cohabit prior to marriage?
Have we viewed indecent images together?
Have we engaged in "swinging" or wife swapping?
Do we have an "open marriage"?

APPENDIX IV: MORE PRAYERS AND DEVOTIONS FOR PURITY

Prayer against Lust

O Lord Jesus Christ, Guardian of chaste souls, and lover of purity, who wast pleased to take our nature and to be born of an immaculate Virgin: mercifully look upon my infirmity. Create in me a clean heart, O God: and renew a right spirit within me; help me to drive away all evil thoughts, to conquer every sinful desire, and so pierce my flesh with the fear of Thee that, this worst enemy being overcome, I may serve Thee with a chaste body and please Thee with a pure heart. Amen.[cxi]

An Act of Contrition

O Lord Jesus Christ, most ardent lover of our souls, Who, through the exceeding charity wherewith Thou lovest us, wouldst not the death of a sinner, but rather that he should be converted and live; I grieve from my inmost heart that I have ever offended Thee, my loving Father, and most gracious Redeemer, to Whom all sin is grievously displeasing; for Thou hast so much loved me that Thou didst shed Thy Precious Blood for me--a worthless sinner, and didst suffer for me a most bitter death. O my God! O Infinite Goodness! would that I had never offended Thee. Pardon, Lord Jesus, pardon me, most humbly imploring Thy mercy. Have pity upon a sinner for whom Thy Blood is pleading before the Face of Thy Father.

O most merciful and forgiving Lord, for the love of Thee I forgive all who have ever offended me. I firmly resolve to forsake all sin, and to avoid the occasions of it; and to confess in bitterness of soul, all those sins which I have committed against Thy Divine Goodness, and to love Thee, O my God, for Thine Own Sake, above all things, and for ever. Grant me grace so to do, O most gracious Lord Jesus.[cxii]

Prayer for the Feast of the Immaculate Conception
(Pray after Meditation 21)

Most holy Virgin, who, being predestined to become the Mother of God, was preserved by a singular privilege from original sin and filled with grace, confirmed in grace and enriched with all the gifts of the Holy Ghost, do thou accept, we pray, the homage of our most lively admiration and of our most profound veneration, the expression of our intense and reverent affection.

Beholding in thee a relic of the earthly paradise that was lost to man, purer and more spotless than the snowy splendor of mountain tops bathed in light, in that magnificent act of treading upon the proud head of the infernal serpent, the heavens exulted, earth was filled with joy and hell trembled with fear. With thee came the bright dawn of man's redemption from sin, and when the children of men, having for centuries anxiously scanned the horizon in expectation of a fairer day, raised their heads, they discovered thee on high like a radiant vision of paradise and saluted thee with a cry of holy enthusiasm: "Thou art all fair, O Mary, and in thee there is no original stain."

At our feet, O Mary, the muddy torrent of lust did not halt, as it did before thine, that torrent still flows across the world and threatens continually to submerge our souls also. We bear about within us and perceive around us countless deadly incentives that cease not to urge us on to savor the foul pleasures of sensual passion. O good Mother, enfold us under thy mantle, protect us from the snares of the infernal enemy, renew in us our love of the angelic virtue, and grant that, by ever keeping vivid in our hearts the reflections of thy heavenly brightness, we may be able one day to sing to thee a hymn of love and glory in the world to come. Amen. -Raccolta #373

Prayer to Our Lady for Purity

O Mary, Virgin Mother, thy purity of body and mind suffered not the slightest stain during thy entire life. I desire to imitate this virtue, that gave added glory to thine already illustrious greatness. But I am beset on all sides with temptations. They are so strong that I cannot possibly overcome them without the assistance of grace. To whom shall I go but to thee, Mary most Pure? Behold, my sincerity and my weaknesses! Give me an active horror for the sin of impurity so detested by thy Divine Son. Direct my footsteps from the pathway of dangerous companions, and set them toward the tribunal of penance and the celestial banquet table where I may receive new graces and the Body of my Lord and Saviour. I believe, O Mother, that receiving the Body of Jesus Christ under the sacramental species I shall extinguish the fires of passion, and strengthen the virtue of holy purity. Give me the courage to begin and to persevere in this salutary practice. O Lady of the Miraculous Medal, pray for me. Amen.[cxiii]

Prayer to Our Lady and St. Joseph
(Pray after Meditation 22)

Mary, Mother most pure, and Joseph, chaste guardian of the Virgin, to you I entrust the purity of my soul and body. I beg you to plead with God for me that I may never for the remainder of my life soil my soul by any sin of impurity. I earnestly wish to be pure in thought, word and deed in imitation of your own holy purity.

Obtain for me a deep sense of modesty, which will be reflected in my external conduct. Protect my eyes, the windows of my soul, from anything that might dim the luster of a heart that must mirror only Christlike purity. And when the "Bread of Angels" becomes my food in Holy Communion, seal my heart forever against the suggestions of sinful pleasures.

Finally, may I be among the number of those of whom Jesus spoke, "Blessed are the pure of heart for they shall see God." Amen. – *Fr. Lovasik*[cxiv]

Prayer to One's Guardian Angel
(Pray after Meditation 23)

My dear Guardian Angel, I beg you to plead with God for me that I may always keep my life pure and happy. Protect me from the many dangers that confront me on my journey through life. Strengthen me in my struggle against the temptations of the world, the flesh, and the devil.

My loving angel-friend, help me to be pure in thought, desire, word, and deed, in imitation of Jesus, the Lover of pure souls, and of Mary, the Virgin of virgins. Obtain for me a deep sense of modestly which will be reflected in my external conduct.

I beg you, gentle angel, to be the guardian of my purity. For your great love for Jesus, the King of the Angels, and for Mary, the Queen of the Angels, keep me from all uncleaness, and grant that my mind may be untainted, my heart pure, and my body chaste. Help me always to serve Jesus and Mary in perfect chastity, so that one day I may merit to belong to those of whom Jesus spoke: "Blessed are the pure of heart for they shall see God." Amen. – *Fr. Lovasik*[cxv]

Prayer to St. Maria Goretti, Martyr for Purity
(Pray after Meditation 45)

O Saint Maria Goretti, who, strengthened by God's grace, did not hesitate, even at the age of eleven, to shed your blood and sacrifice life itself to defend your virginal purity, deign to look graciously on the unhappy human race which has strayed far from the path of eternal salvation. Teach us all, and especially our youth, the courage and promptness to flee for love of Jesus, anything that could offend Him or stain our souls with sin. Obtain for us from Our Lord and Our Lady Immaculate, victory in temptation, comfort in the sorrows of life, and the grace which we earnestly beg of thee - a clean heart, a pure soul and a chaste body - so that we may one day enjoy with thee the imperishable glory of heaven. Amen.

Chaplet of the Immaculate Conception

This sacramental may prove helpful in your struggle for purity. St. John Berchmanns composed this *Chaplet of the Immaculate Conception* and prayed it daily to obtain, through Mary's intercession, the grace to never commit a sin against purity.

It consists of 3 groups of 4 beads each, A large bead separates each set, and a medal of the Immaculate Conception (the Miraculous Medal) hangs on the end. The beads are typically blue but sometimes white, in which case it is called the "Purity Chaplet."

You can purchase Immaculate Conception chaplets from religious articles dealers or rosary makers. There are two ways of praying it:

First Method:

Begin with the Sign of the Cross

O God, come to my aid; O Lord make haste to help me.

On the single bead: I thank You, O Eternal Father because of Your power, You preserved Mary, Your most Blessed Daughter, from the stain of original sin. Our Father, who art in heaven... *etc.*

On each of the four small beads: Hail Mary, full of grace... *etc.*, *adding after each one:* "Blessed be the pure, holy and Immaculate Conception of the Blessed Virgin Mary."

On the second single bead: I thank You, O Eternal Son, because of Your wisdom You preserved Mary, Your most Blessed Mother, from the stain of original sin.

Then a Paternoster (Our Father) *and four Ave's as before.*

On the third single bead: I thank You, O Holy Spirit, because by Your love You preserved Mary, Your most Blessed Spouse, from the stain of original sin.

One Paternoster *and four* Ave's *as before.*

Conclude with the Gloria Patri *in honor of the purity of Saint Joseph.*

Shorter Method:

Begin with the Sign of the Cross

On the First bead: Blessed be the Holy and Immaculate Conception of the Blessed Virgin Mary.

Then one Paternoster, *four* Ave's *and one* Gloria Patri.

Repeat the same prayers on subsequent sets of beads.

GLOSSARY

Aspirations: Brief prayers, sometimes called "ejaculations."

Ave: A term for the *Hail Mary*, because in Latin it begins with the word "Ave."

Beatific Vision: The direct Vision of God that the blessed will enjoy forever in Heaven.

Chastity: The virtue that moderates our desires and actions so we use sex properly according to our state in life. For the unmarried this means abstinence from all sexual activity; for the married, monogamous conjugal relations. Chastity is required of all human beings, not just the unmarried.

Concupiscence: Disordered passions after the Fall. Lust is one form of concupiscence, gluttony another, etc..

Conjugal relations: Coitus within marriage, the only morally legitimate use of intercourse.

Gloria Patri: A term for the *Glory Be*, because in Latin it begins with "Gloria Patri…"

Gratification: Another term for a climax or orgasm.

Habitual sins: Besetting sins; sins we commit frequently no matter how much we try to stop.

Indecency, Indecent pictures/images: Pornography

Lust: The inordinate desire for venereal pleasure; one of the Seven Cardinal Sins.

Marital act, the: a synonym for *conjugal relations*.

Marital rights: The right spouses have to conjugal relations with one another, according to 1 Cor. 7:2-5.

Modesty: The virtue that moderates how we appear, speak and behave toward others, so that we do not present an occasion of sin to them. Modesty is the guardian of chastity.

Occasion of sin: Any person, place, or thing that tempts us to sin, which we must avoid as much as possible.

Paternoster: A term for the *Our Father*, because in Latin it begins with the words "Pater noster…"

Procreative act: Coitus, since it is naturally ordered toward procreation. *See conjugal relations.*

Purity: The virtue that moderates our interior thoughts, beliefs and intentions, keeping them consistent with the Church's teaching on the proper use of sex.

Self abuse: Masturbation.

Sins against purity, Sins of the flesh: Sexual sins.

Temptation: An invitation or enticement to sin. Temptation is not a sin as long as one does not delight in or yield to it.

Unnatural acts: Sexual acts that are not procreative and so thwart the purpose of intercourse, such as homosexual activity, self-abuse, sodomy, bestiality, etc.

RESOURCES AND BIBLIOGRAPHY

Angelic Warfare Confraternity

United States:

> St. Martin de Porres Lay Dominican Community
> 3050 Gap Knob Rd.
> New Hope KY 40052
> web site: http://www.newhope-ky.org/index.html
>
> Archive of defunct page from the St. Antoninus Institute site:
> http://snipurl.com/awc_archived

Nigeria:

> Angelic Warfare Confraternity
> Dominican Community,
> P.M.B. 5361, Ibadan
> Oyo State, Nigeria.
> http://uk.geocities.com/angelicwarfareconfraternity/

Catholic Support Group for Sexual Addiction Recovery: http://www.saint-mike.org/csgsar/default.asp

Courage Apostolate (for Catholics with same sex attraction): http://www.couragerc.net/

Family Life Center/ St. Joseph's Covenant Keepers (for men): http://www.familylifecenter.net/

Generation Life (promotes chastity for young people): http://www.generationlife.org/

Pure Love Club (promotes chastity for young people): http://www.pureloveclub.org/index.htm

Serenellians: http://www.pornnomore.com/

True Knights Apostolate (for men): http://www.trueknights.org/

WORKS CITED

Catechism of the Catholic Church. New York: Doubleday, 1994.

Congregation for the Doctrine of the Faith. The Message of Fatima.

Guardian Angels: Our Heavenly Companions. Rockford, IL: TAN, 1996.

Haydock's Douay-Rheims Catholic Bible. Rev. Father George L. Haydock. 2 vols. Monrovia, CA: Catholic Treasures, reprint of 1859 edition.

Holy Bible Confraternity -Douay Version. Washington, DC: Confraternity of Christian Doctrine, 1961.

Holy Bible Revised Standard Version - Second Catholic Edition. San Francisco: Ignatius, 2006.

Jerusalem Bible, The. New York: Doubleday and Co., 1967.

John XXIII. Journal of a Soul. Dorothy White, trans. New York: McGraw Hill, 1964.

Pius XII, encyclical, Mediator Dei.

St. Michael and the Angels: A Month with St. Michael and the Holy Angels. Rockford, IL: TAN, 1983.

Thomas Aquinas, Summa Theologica.

Prayer books:

Dougherty, Rev. Daniel M. Pearls of Prayer. New York: Benziger, 1927.

Enchiridion of Indulgences: Norms and Grants. William T. Barry, trans. New York: Catholic Book Publishing
   Co., 1969.

Holy Trinity Book of Prayers. NY: P.J. Kenedy, 1952.

Lasance, Fr. Francis X. My Prayer Book. New York: Benziger, 1923.

Little Treasury of Leaflets. 4 vols. Dublin: Gill, 1914.

Lovasik, Rev. Lawrence G. Treasury of Prayer. St Paul, MN: Catechetical Guild, 1954.

Our Lady's Book: prayers for numerous occasions seeking the intercession of the Mother of God. Ed. Rev.
   James Cashman, C.M. St. Louis, MO: Vincentian Foreign Mission Society, 1942.

Prayers and Heavenly Promises: Compiled from Approved Sources by Joan Carrol Cruz. Rockford IL: TAN,
   1990.

The Precious Blood and Mother: A Compilation of Prayers from Approved Sources by the Sister Adorers of
   the Precious Blood, Edmonton, Canada. Manchester, NH: Monastery of the Precious Blood.

The Raccolta, or A Manual of Indulgences: Prayers and Devotions Enriched with Indulgences. New York:
   Benziger, 1952.

Stedman, Fr. Joseph F. Triple Novena Manual of Jesus, Mary and Joseph. Brooklyn, NY: Confraternity of
the
   Precious Blood, 1943.

Guides to Christian Living and Overcoming Temptation:

Alphonsus de Liguori. Dignity and Duties of the Priest. Brooklyn, NY: Redemptorist Fathers, 1927.
..... Glories of Mary. Brooklyn, NY: Redemptorist Fathers, 1931.
..... Holy Eucharist. Brooklyn, NY: Redemptorist Fathers, 1934.
..... Passion and Death of Jesus Christ. Brooklyn, NY: Redemptorist, 1927.
..... Preparation for Death. Brooklyn NY: Redemptorist, 1926.
..... Way of Salvation and Perfection. Brooklyn, NY: Redemptorist, 1926.

Francis de Sales. Introduction to the Devout Life. Grand Rapids, MI: Christian Classics Ethereal Library, 2002.

Vianney, John Baptist Mary. The "Eucharistic Meditations of the Curé d'Ars." Carmelite Publications: 1961.

Louis of Granada. The Sinner's Guide. Rockford, IL: TAN Books, 1985.

Robinson, Jonathan. Spiritual Combat Revisited. San Francisco: Ignatius, 2003. (Excellent, especially ch. 6)

Scupoli, Lorenzo. The Spiritual Combat and a Treatise on Peace of Soul. Rockford, IL: TAN Books, 1990.

Tanquerey, Adolphe. The Spiritual Life: A Treatise on Ascetical and Mystical Theology. Herman Branderis, trans. Tournai, Belgium: Desclee, 1930.

Thomas à Kempis. Following of Christ, The: A New Translation from the Original Latin to which Are Added Practical Reflections and a Prayer at the End of Each Chapter. New York: Benziger Brothers, 1929.
….. Imitation of Christ. New York: Alba House, 1995.

Chastity Issues:

Cavins, Jeff. The Pornography Plague (CD). Ascension Press, West Chester PA, 2004.

Cleveland, Mike. Pure Freedom: Breaking the Addiction to Pornography. Bemidji, MN: Focus, 2002. *An Evangelical Bible study; the online version is now called "The Way of Purity". Not recommended for Catholics because of doctrinal errors and numerous explicit personal testimonies that may be an occasion of sin for those struggling against lust.*

Curran, Tom. For Men Only (CD set). Trinity Formation Resources, Federal Way, WA.

Groeschel, Fr. Benedict J. The Courage to be Chaste. New York: Paulist, 1985. *Recommended especially for singles.*

Haffert, John M. Sex and the Mysteries. Washington: AMI, 1970. *Highly recommended.*

John Cassian. Cassian on Chastity. Terrence G. Kardong, trans. Richardton, ND: Assumption Abbey, 1993.

Kippley, John F. Sex and the Marriage Covenant. Cincinnati: Couple to Couple League, 1991.

Lovasik, Rev. Lawrence G. Sex is Sacred: Youth at Prayer. Tarentum, PA: Rev. Lawrence G. Lovasik, S.V.D.

Remler, Fr. Francis J. How to Resist Temptation. Manchester, NH: Sophia Institute Press, 2001. *An excellent book, contains lots of great advice. Highly recommended!*

Von Hildebrand, Deitrich. In Defence of Purity. New York: Sheed & Ward, 1935.

West, Christopher. A Crash Course in the Theology of the Body: Naked Without Shame 2nd Edition. GIFT Foundation, Carpentersville IL, 2002.

….. Winning the Battle for Sexual Purity: Straight Talk with Men about Love and Life (CD set). Ascension Press, West Chester PA, 2002.

Wood, Steve. Breaking Free: 12 Steps to Sexual Purity for Men. Port Charlotte, FL: Family Life Center, 2003.

Wood, Steve et.al. Breaking Free Audio Series on CD. Family Life Center, Port Charlotte FL, 2004.

ENDNOTES

i "Act of Perfect Contrition" Triple Novena Manual of Jesus, Mary and Joseph, Fr. Joseph F. Stedman (Brooklyn, NY: Confraternity of the Precious Blood, 1943) 51.

ii "My Body," Triple Novena Manual, 111-112.

iii St. Francis de Sales, Introduction to the Devout Life, III:12, 11 June 2004
<http://www.ccel.org/d/desales/devout_life/htm/v.xii.htm#v.xii>.

iv St. Alphonsus relates this story in both The Glories of Mary, (Brooklyn, NY: Redemptorist, 1931) 371-372; and Dignity and Duties of the Priest, (Brooklyn, NY: Redemptorist, 1927) 264.

v From the "Chaplet of the Holy Spirit," 11 June 2004 <http://www.miraclerosarymission.org/chs.htm>.

vi From the "Prayer for the Virtue of Chastity," Holy Trinity Book of Prayers, (New York: P.J. Kenedy, 1952) 259.

vii Adolphe Tanquerey, The Spiritual Life: A Treatise on Ascetical and Mystical Theology, Herman Branderis, trans. (Tournai, Belgium: Desclee, 1930) 103-104.

viii Introduction to the Devout Life, VI:7, 11 June 2004
<http://www.ccel.org/d/desales/devout_life/htm/vi.vii.htm#vi.vii>.

ix Thomas Aquinas, Summa Theologica, Bk IIb, Q.153, Art. 5.

x Alphonsus de Liguori, Dignity and Duties of The Priest, 113.

xi John M. Haffert, Sex And The Mysteries, (Washington: AMI, 1970) 8, 22-23.

xii Alphonsus de Liguori, The Passion and Death of Jesus Christ, (Brooklyn, NY: Redemptorist, 1927) 459.

xiii Footnote to Matthew 5:27-30, Haydock's Douay-Rheims Catholic Bible, Rev. Father George L. Haydock, 2 vols., (Catholic Treasures, 1859), 1495.

xiv Alphonsus de Liguori, Preparation for Death, (Brooklyn, NY: Redemptorist, 1926) 157.

xv Alphonsus de Liguori, The Way of Salvation and Perfection, (Brooklyn, NY: Redemptorist, 1926) 162-163.

xvi "Prayer to be Freed of the Seven Deadly Sins," 11 June 2004 <http://www.catholic-forum.com/saints/pray0486.htm>.

xvii Dignity and Duties of The Priest 260-261.

xviii Dignity and Duties of The Priest 261.

xix Vitae Patrum, Book V, Section 5, verses 10-11.

xx Thomas à Kempis, The Imitation of Christ, 1:XXI:6 (New York: Alba House, 1995) 75-76.

xxi Triple Novena Manual, 51.

xxii Imitation of Christ, 1:XXI:1-4; 73-75.

xxiii Venerable Louis of Granada, O.P.. The Sinner's Guide, (Rockford, IL: TAN Books, 1985) 279. The word "dealings" was substituted for the archaic meaning of the term "intercourse."

xxiv Sinner's Guide, 279.

xxv From the "Litany to Our Lady of Fatima," traditional.

xxvi Introduction to the Devout Life, IV:5, 11 June 2004
<http://www.ccel.org/d/desales/devout_life/htm/vi.v.htm#vi.v>.

xxvii Alphonsus de Liguori, The Holy Eucharist, (Brooklyn, NY: Redemptorist, 1934) 450.

xxviii Introduction to the Devout Life, IV:3, 11 June 2004
<http://www.ccel.org/d/desales/devout_life/htm/vi.ii.htm#vi.iii>.

xxix Introduction to the Devout Life, IV:4, 11 June 2004
<http://www.ccel.org/d/desales/devout_life/htm/vi.ii.htm#vi.iv>.

xxx From the "Chaplet of the Holy Spirit," 11 June 2004 <http://www.miraclerosarymission.org/chs.htm>.

xxxi Sinner's Guide, 278-279.

xxxii Holy Eucharist 450-1.

xxxiii Holy Eucharist 452-453.

xxxiv Holy Eucharist 454.

xxxv Pope John XXIII, Journal of a Soul, Dorothy White, trans. (New York: McGraw Hill, 1964) 17.

xxxvi Rev. Daniel M. Dougherty, Pearls of Prayer, (New York: Benziger, 1927) 31.

xxxvii Dom Lorenzo Scupoli, The Spiritual Combat and a Treatise on Peace of Soul, (Rockford, IL: TAN Books, 1990) 56-57.

xxxviii Sinner's Guide, 319.

xxxix From the "Prayer of Saint Ambrose before Mass for Saturday," traditional.

xl Fr. Stefano Manelli, O.F.M., Conv., S.T.D. Jesus, Our Eucharistic Love: Eucharistic Life According to the examples of the Saints, (Brookings, SD: Our Blessed Lady of Victory Mission, 1973) 59-60.

[xli] Jesus, Our Eucharistic Love 60.

[xlii] St. John Baptist Mary Vianney, The "Eucharistic Meditations of the Curé d'Ars," Carmelite Publications: 1961, 11 June 2004 <http://www.carmelites.ie/Archive/euchmed2.htm>.

[xliii] Holy Eucharist 349.

[xliv] "A Prayer for Purity," 7 March 2005 <http://www.columbia.edu/cu/augustine/arch/prayers/purity.html>

[xlv] "Homily XX on the Epistle to the Romans," 11 June 2004 <http://www.newadvent.org/fathers/210220.htm>.

[xlvi] Pius XII, encyclical, Mediator Dei 98-100, 11 June 2004 <http://www.ewtn.com/library/ENCYC/P12MEDIA.HTM>.

[xlvii] From the "Chaplet of the Holy Spirit," 11 June 2004 <http://www.miraclerosarymission.org/chs.htm>.

[xlviii] Footnote for Romans 12:2, Haydock's Douay-Rheims Catholic Bible, 1495.

[xlix] Sinner's Guide, 280.

[l] "Prayer Against Bad Thoughts," The Little Treasury of Leaflets, vol. II, 606. Author unknown.

[li] Prayer Against Evil Thoughts, traditional.

[lii] Triple Novena Manual 51.

[liii] Spiritual Combat 84-86.

[liv] The Spiritual Life 530.

[lv] From the "Chaplet of the Holy Spirit." 11 June 2004 <http://www.miraclerosarymission.org/chs.htm>.

[lvi] Vitae Patrum, Book V, Section 5, verse 13, 11 June 2004 <http://www.vitae-patrum.org.uk/page83.html>.

[lvii] CDF, The Message of Fatima, 11 June 2004 <http://www.cin.org/docs/message-fatima.html>.

[lviii] from an "Act of Consecration to The Immaculate Heart of Mary," traditional.

[lix] From the "Marylike Standards for Modesty in Dress" pamphlet.

[lx] From the "Divine Praises" and the "Prayer for the Virtue of Chastity," Holy Trinity Book of Prayers, 259.

[lxi] "Guardian Angel Prayer," 1 July 2004 <http://www.geocities.com/Heartland/Pointe/4772/religion.html>.

[lxii] Sinner's Guide, 280.

[lxiii] St. Michael and the Angels: A Month with St. Michael and the Holy Angels, (Rockford, IL: TAN, 1983) 33.

[lxiv] The Guardian Angels: Our Heavenly Companions, (Rockford, IL: TAN, 1996) 35-36.

[lxv] The Sayings of the Desert Fathers (3rd-5th centuries): The Alphabetical Collection, 11 June 2004 <http://www.pluscardenabbey.org/oblate-letter-august-2002.asp>.

[lxvi] From the "Prayer for the Virtue of Chastity," Holy Trinity Book of Prayers, 259.

[lxvii] Spiritual Combat 46-47.

[lxviii] Autobiography of Saint Anthony Mary Claret, 11 June 2004 <http://www.claret.org.uk/library/aut_clt/aut_012_msc.html>.

[lxix] St. Thomas Aquinas, Commentary on Saint Paul's Epistle to the Ephesians, trans. by Matthew L. Lamb, Albany: Magi Books, 1966: 280.

[lxx] Commentary on Ephesians, p. 281.

[lxxi] Commentary on Ephesians, p. 282.

[lxxii] Fr. Francis X. Lasance, My Prayer Book, (NY: Benziger, 1923) 476.

[lxxiii] "Prayer for the Third Station of the Cross," Way of the Cross at the Colosseum, Good Friday 2006, composed by Archbishop Angelo Comastri, 15 April 2006 <http://www.vatican.va/news_services/liturgy/2006/via_crucis/en/station_03.html>.

[lxxiv] Preparation for Death 135-136.

[lxxv] Preparation for Death 70.

[lxxvi] "Novena to the Holy Spirit for the Seven Gifts". The Catholic Family Book of Novenas, (New York: John J. Crawley & Co., 1956) 98.

[lxxvii] "Novena to the Holy Spirit for the Seven Gifts" The Catholic Family Book of Novenas, 98.

[lxxviii] "Prayer to be Freed of the Seven Deadly Sins," 11 June 2004 <http://www.catholic-forum.com/saints/pray0486.htm>.

[lxxix] Vitae Patrum, Book V, Section 5, verses 42, 46-47, 4 August 2004. <http://www.vitae-patrum.org.uk/page82.html>.

[lxxx] Imitation of Christ 1:XIX:4; 65.

[lxxxi] Dignity and Duties of The Priest, 260.

[lxxxii] Introduction to the Devout Life, IV:23, 11 June 2004 <http://www.ccel.org/d/desales/devout_life/htm/v.xxiii.htm#v.xxiii>.

[lxxxiii] Sinner's Guide, 328.

[lxxxiv] From the "Prayer of Saint Ambrose before Mass for Monday," Holy Trinity Book of Prayers, 43-44.

lxxxv Introduction to the Devout Life, IV:23, 11 June 2004
<http://www.ccel.org/d/desales/devout_life/htm/v.xxiii.htm#v.xxiii>.

lxxxvi Kontakion, Tone 4 for the Feast of St. Mary of Egypt.

lxxxvii Teresa of Avila, "A Prayer to Redeem Lost Time," Prayers and Heavenly Promises: Compiled from Approved Sources, by Joan Carrol Cruz, (Rockford IL: TAN, 1990) 105. Copyright © by Joan Carrol Cruz.

lxxxviii From The Precious Blood and Mother A Compilation of Prayers from Approved Sources by the Sister Adorers of the Precious Blood, Edmonton, Canada, (Manchester, NH: Monastery of the Precious Blood) 60.

lxxxix From the "Prayer for the Virtue of Chastity," Holy Trinity Book of Prayers, 258.

xc "A Prayer for Purity" 11 June 2004 <http://www.columbia.edu/cu/augustine/arch/prayers/purity.html>.

xci "Novena to St. Maria Goretti," The Catholic Family Book of Novenas, 142.

xcii "Alessandro Serenelli: A Miraculous Conversion" 23 March 2005
<http://www.mariagoretti.org/alessandrobio.htm>.

xciii "Prayer to be Freed of the Seven Deadly Sins," 11 June 2004 <http://www.catholic-forum.com/saints/pray0486.htm>.

xciv St. John Cassian, "Conferences" XII:10, from Cassian on Chastity, Terrence G. Kardong, trans. (Richardton, ND: Assumption Abbey Press, 1993) 42.

xcv Imitation of Christ, 4:XII:1; 379.

xcvi "Homily II on the Assumption of the Blessed Virgin Mary," St. John Damascene on Holy Images, Followed by Three Sermons on the Assumption, Mary H. Allies, trans. (London: Thomas Baker, 1898) 198-199. 5 March 2005
<http://www.balamand.edu.lb/theology/Jodorm2.htm>.

xcvii Dignity and Duties of The Priest, 243-4, 247.

xcviii Preparation for Death 32-33.

xcix Introduction to the Devout Life, I:13, 19 March 2005
<http://www.ccel.org/d/desales/devout_life/htm/iii.xiii.htm#iii.xiii >.

c Thomas à Kempis, The Following of Christ: A New Translation from the Original Latin to which Are Added Practical Reflections and a Prayer at the End of Each Chapter, (New York: Benziger Brothers, 1929), 104.

ci Sinner's Guide, 63.

cii Introduction to the Devout Life, I:14, 9 June 2005 <http://www.ccel.org/d/desales/devout_life.iii.xiv.html>

ciii Imitation of Christ, 1:XXIV:4-6; 88-90.

civ quoted by St. Alphonsus.

cv Sinner's Guide 80.

cvi Imitation of Christ, 1:XXIV:4-6; 90.

cvii Introduction to the Devout Life, I:16, 9 June 2005 <http://www.ccel.org/ccel/desales/devout_life.iii.xvi.html>.

cviii Preparation for Death 429.

cix "To Jesus Christ, King," Triple Novena Manual, 77.

cx "Renewal of Baptismal Promises," Enchiridion of Indulgences: Norms and Grants, William T. Barry, trans. (New York: Catholic Book Publishing Co., 1969) 131-132.

cxi A Book of Catholic Prayers, 15 June 2006 <http://www.bellarmine.150m.com/prayers.htm>.

cxii "Act of Contrition," The Little Treasury of Leaflets, vol. II (Dublin: Gill, 1914) 539 alt.

cxiii Our Lady's Book: prayers for numerous occasions seeking the intercession of the Mother of God. Ed. Rev. James Cashman, C.M.. (St. Louis, MO: Vincentian Foreign Mission Society, 1942) 23-24.

cxiv Lawrence G. Lovasik, Sex is Sacred: Youth at Prayer, (Tarentum, PA: Rev. Lawrence G. Lovasik, S.V.D.) 27-28.

cxv Lawrence G. Lovasik, Treasury of Prayer, (St Paul, MN: Catechetical Guild, 1954) 315.

AMDG et BVMH

Clean of Heart Order Form

Clean of Heart _____ copies at $17.99 each = _____

Shipping and Handling $3.00 per book U.S.
                                         $6.00 per book International

New Jersey residents add 7% sales tax   + _____

Total payment   _____

Paying by check: Send this order form with your check (in U.S. dollars drawn on a U.S. bank), to **R.A.G.E. Media PO Box 401 Mt. Laurel, NJ 08054**

Name: _____ Date:_____ Company: _____

Shipping Address: _____

City, State, Zip: _____

Country: _____

Day Phone: _____ Eve Phone: _____ Email: _____

How did you hear about **Clean of Heart**?

Comments:

For Credit Card order:

Credit Card: [ ] MasterCard [ ] VISA [ ] American Express [ ] Discover

Card Number: _____ Expiration Date: _____

3 or 4 digit CVV/Signature Code (on back of Visa/MC, on front of AMEX): _____

Name on Card: _____ _print exactly as it appears on credit card_

Billing Address: _____

_____

_____

Signature: _____

Or you can order online at http://www.DyingLight.com/store

9 780977 223459